The Social Nature of Psychological Research

The Social Nature o

BASIC BOOKS, IN

NEIL FRIEDMAN

Psychological Research

The Psychological Experiment as a Social Interaction

BLISHERS · NEW YORK · LONDON

© 1967 by Neil Friedman
Library of Congress Catalog Card Number: 67–16460
Manufactured in the United States of America
Designed by Jacqueline Schuman

To Joyce, Carole, Edward, and Frank Friedman

If you want to find out anything from the theoretical physicists about the methods they use, I advise you to stick closely to one principle: Don't listen to their words, fix your attention on their deeds.

Einstein

Where does our investigation get its importance from, since it seems only to destroy everything interesting, that is, all that is great and important. (As it were all the buildings, leaving behind only bits of stone and rubble.) What we are destroying is nothing but houses of cards and we are clearing up the ground . . . on which they stand.

Wittgenstein

Preface

Major features of contemporary psychology and the other social sciences have been exposed to considerable criticism recently. The complaints—as to the triviality of much of the research inspired by positivism, the disconnection of grand theory from minor studies, the withdrawal of social scientists from engagement with significant problems to an acceptance of statistical definitions of significance, the assumption of a "value-neutral" pose, methodolatry—all have played some part in changing the psychological climate in psychology and the other social sciences.

But the complaints have not gone far enough. They have not gone to the heart of the heart of the matter. A common answer to these criticisms has been, "Yes, but . . ." Following the "but" inevitably comes some statement to the effect that only by rigorous adherence to the accepted canons of scientific method will we accumulate valid, reliable, and precise knowledge. And that, after all, despite whatever personal interests we might have, is our professional job.

In other words, the criticisms have come from outside the frame of reference of the person to whom they are addressed. They do not, as a rule, get at what he sees as the central fact—the rendezvous with validity. The social scientist who recognizes himself or his work in these critiques retains an escape clause, for there is no critique from within his own value system. He has not been hoist with his own petard.

It is my aim to provide such a criticism. For the precise question is how precise and how valid the knowledge being accumulated by our rigorous methods really is. And the answer to that question depends upon how rigorous those methods really are.

I called an earlier draft of this book *Behavior in the Experiment*. A reader objected that such a title was indiscriminate. It could be applied, he claimed, to practically all psychological research, for practically all that is counted as valid psychological fact is the outcome of "behavior in the experiment." "That," I replied, "is precisely the point."

Let me elaborate.

My book has a thesis. It is that psychological experiments are quite other than what they are made out to be. Things do not proceed in them exactly according to Hoyle. But the characteristic source of firm psychological knowledge is the experiment. To an ever increasing degree, our understandings of human motivation, human personality, human learning, etc. are based upon experimental results. Thus, if much that is currently taken for granted in our thinking about the experiment is highly questionable, then the edifice of experimental psychology stands on shifting sands.

II

I can state my project in the vocabulary of Dewey and Bentley. Knowings are events in the social world as are the knowns which they name. The experimenter's own form of knowing behavior is the experiment. It is necessary then to inquire into the experiment in the same manner in which the experiment inquires into any other social event.

This research on research has proceeded in the operationist spirit, a spirit defined by a remark of Einstein's which can be paraphrased: an operational definition of a concept is one which relates it to observed operations. "Watch" is the watchword of the operationist.

And so we watched. In order to find out just what does happen in a psychological experiment we watched films taken of twenty-nine experimenters engaging eighty-six subjects in a person perception experiment. We saw that the experimental sessions were neither controlled nor standardized. Experimenters varied in their behavior. When we analyzed the results, we found that what the subjects did was influenced by what the experimenters did. And this, in turn, was influenced in part by the results which the experimenters had been led to expect.

These discoveries have been described by some people as depressing.

Actually, they are potentially quite liberating. Hyman, in his study of error in the interviewing procedure, makes this important point:

> . . . the demonstration of error marks an advanced stage of a science. All scientific inquiry is subject to error, and it is far better to be aware of this, to study the sources in an attempt to reduce it, and to estimate the magnitude of such errors in our findings, than to be ignorant of the errors concealed in the data. One must not equate ignorance of error with the lack of error. The lack of demonstration of error in certain fields of inquiry often derives from the nonexistence of methodological research into the problem and merely denotes a less advanced stage of that profession . . . (Hyman, 1954, p. 4.)

Note that Hyman here speaks entirely in the negative terms of "error." It may represent an even more advanced stage of the discipline when what to the methodologist is simply "error" has been converted into what to the theorist is a "principle." I will refer back to Riecken's insight on this point:

> Such variation [in experimenter behavior] is ordinarily regarded as "error," reflecting some mistake in procedure on the part of the investigator. . . . On the other hand, a broader perspective on the problem reveals it as a series of more fundamental questions about human interaction, interpersonal relations, or social behavior. The process of collecting data about human behavior is itself a social process and shares features in common with other situations and events of human interaction. Accordingly, the process of data collection can be studied as a particular type of interaction in a particular social situation . . . (Riecken, 1958, p. 1.)

Thus, on the positive side, this inquiry into the process by which psychological knowledge is obtained has as an avowed purpose the development of a full conception of the nature of the psychological experiment and the nature of psychology. It will be indicated that individualistic, intrapersonal, monadic, natural science perspectives on the psychological experiment and psychology need to be supplanted by interactional, interpersonal, dyadic, social science perspectives. One man's error variance is another man's social behavior.

III

Part I of this work is a historical introduction. It documents the development of the contemporary philosophy of psychological experimentation in terms of the emergence, submergence, and re-emergence of the study of the personal equation and experimenter bias. Part II presents a description of how the films were obtained and a discussion of what they showed. In

Part III, I argue that the generality of the findings related to experimenter effect, experimenter bias, and variability in experimental procedure cannot be restricted simply to this one case; in other words, the philosophy of experimentation outlined in Part I and thrown into question by the specific results presented in Part II is generally questionable. Part IV indicates some of the broader implications of the notion that the psychological experiment is a social interaction.

IV

I will say just a few words about the tone, the intended audience, the scope, and the future of this work.

Tone. I have been advised by some to sound less iconoclastic and audacious. In general, I have rejected this advice. I call them as I see them.

Audience. I address this book to, among others, members of the two families—the scientists and the humanists—who are currently competing for the favors of psychology. In this competition open and direct give and take is to be encouraged. The time for gentle interpretations is past; the time for confrontations has come. There is a chance that psychology is ready for a new philosophy of science and a new humanistic vision—and that the two will be compatible.

Scope. If this examination of the foundations of psychology uncovers some fundamental weaknesses, does it provide something new to build upon? Yes and no. Hopefully Part IV will suggest some blueprints which others more competent than I can act upon. This, however, is only an initial safari into a very tangled underbrush. I explicitly reject any notion that this book will of itself provide satisfactory solutions to the many problems raised. If successful, it will instead inspire others to think through and work out the fundamental consequences, implications, and reinterpretations which I try to identify.

Future. Perhaps some years hence I will return to this research on research, this business of observers watching observers watching observers, this methodical analysis of methodology. I am certain that by then others will have extended, modified, corrected, and improved upon these modest beginnings. But for now I have to take my own advice, leave the lab, and follow the substantive problems of our time, while trying to play a small part in the development of methods for studying them and the implementation of means for changing them.

NEIL FRIEDMAN

Miles College
Birmingham, Alabama
September 1966

Acknowledgments

An earlier version of this manuscript was submitted as a doctoral dissertation to the Department of Social Relations at Harvard University. The research was supported in part by research grant number GS-177 from the National Science Foundation. For their help in the thesis stage I want to thank the following people:

My former advisor and present colleague, Robert Rosenthal, for making available to me the films upon whose analysis all my work depended; for acting as a voice of reason and moderation, a veritable consultant scientific conscience during each phase of the project; and for engaging with me in a reciprocal learning process.

Daniel Kurland, for observing the films day after day, helping with statistical analyses and technological innovations, and contributing in innumerable ways with his various talents.

David Aldrich, Jack Fitzgerald, Gerald Solomon, Judith St. Lawrence, Noel Carota, and Pete Wagschal for observing the films.

Ray Birdwhistell, Anton Hardy, Maurice Stein, Richard Jones, David Bakan, Guy Swanson, Norman Storer, and especially Edward Friedman for reading and commenting upon specific chapters or the entire manuscript. And Kathy Silva for typing the dissertation.

The transition from thesis to book was lengthy. I have had the continued help of many of the people mentioned above—and some others.

I want to thank David McClelland, Arlene Daniels, Dorothy Miller, Harold Garfinkel, and especially Jay Haley for reading and commenting upon the manuscript while it was in revision. It should be said of all the readers that some agree with much of what I say, a few with most, and some with little. It is at least as true of this book as of most that the final responsibility for the acceptance and rejection of their suggestions rests with me.

Virginia Humphreys typed the final version of the manuscript.

Two special acknowledgments must be made. The first is to the writings of Edwin Boring, Martin Orne, Erving Goffman, and Sigmund Koch. I single these authors out from the many for the singular effect they have had on my thinking. The second is to my wife, Joyce Bengal Friedman, for proofreading, for listening patiently as I talked to myself about these ideas, while I was awake and asleep, and, most importantly, simply for being with me.

Contents

I Historical Introduction

*Those who do not understand their past
are doomed to repeat it.*

Santayana

1　From the Personal Equation to Experimenter Bias

"At Greenwich in 1796," writes Edwin Boring, "Maskeleyne, as every psychologist knows, dismissed Kinnebrook, his assistant, because Kinnebrook observed times of the stellar transits almost a second later than he did" (1957, p. 134). Boring goes on to trace the route by which this famous discovery of what was called "the personal equation" led directly to two of the initial experiments in psychology—the complication and reaction-time experiments. These eventually led, in turn, to the recognition that, in Boring's words, "perception depends upon predisposition—on attitude, as we should call it nowadays, when dynamic psychology emphasizes the fact" (p. 147). Boring's exposition shows that the initial impetus to work on both individual differences and the psychology of attitudes stemmed from observations of the attitudes and differences among astronomical experimenters themselves.

Appropriating this insight, psychology proceeded to forget the circumstances of its discovery. Experimental psychology studied the attitudes of—*subjects*. Correlational psychology studied the individual differences among —*subjects*. Both implicitly subscribed to the democratic notion that all *experimenters* are created equal; that they have been endowed by their graduate training with certain interchangeable properties; that among these properties are the anonymity and impersonality which allow them to elicit from the same subject identical data which they then identically observe and record. Just as inches were once supposed to inhere in tables regardless of the identity of the measuring instrument, so needs, motives, traits, IQs, anxieties, and attitudes were supposed to inhere in patients and subjects and to emerge uncontaminated by the identity and attitude of the examiner or experimenter. Individual behaviorism, the objective psychology, was to be a psychology of—the other one.

There were always dissenting voices. But, for a time, the major dissenting voice within positivistic methodology itself was that of Egon Brunswik (1956) bemoaning the psychologist's double standard by which the logic of statistical inference was applied to but the subject side of the experimenter-subject dyad.

More recently a number of investigators have taken up and expanded this self-conscious approach to the social psychology of the psychological experiment. They have rediscovered various neglected social aspects of psychological research. Henry Riecken has called for study of "those features of persons, situations, and events that are unintentionally . . . present or introduced into the process of data collection and that are responsible for unexpected . . . variation in the behavior of subjects" (Riecken, 1958, p. 1). Martin Orne has attracted psychologists' attention to the response-relevant consequences of the "demand characteristics" of the experimental environment (Orne, 1962). And, most relevantly for my immediate purposes, Robert Rosenthal has demonstrated anew the significance of both individual differences among experimenters—"experimenter effect"—and the attitudes of experimenters—"experimenter bias" (Rosenthal, summarized, 1963a).

These researchers have opened the door to an entirely new perspective on the psychological experiment. They have paved the way for supplementing and supplanting the study of statistical interaction in experimental results with the study of social interaction in the experimental situation. They have prepared us to look at the psychological experiment as a face-to-face interaction between experimenter and subject within a larger social structure.

By so doing these researchers have made it possible for our ideas about psychological experimentation to move in the same direction in which our ideas about psychological testing and psychotherapy have been moving for some time. Or, to put it historically, they have presented us with the opportunity for uncovering a remarkable basic similarity which has provided an insecure foundation for diverse and somewhat antagonistic portions of psychology. For, just as the majority of writings on experimentation still have very little to say about the experimenter, so most texts on testing have had little to say about the tester, and many reports of therapy have had nothing to say about the therapist. We shall speak more later about these surprising similarities. As Jay Haley has pointed out to me (in a personal communication), "including the experimenter is [just] part of a general trend." [1] For now we need only add that it was the supposedly "soft" areas of psychology which were first pushed in this general direction by the "hard" areas, while the "hard" areas are only just now themselves beginning to come up to date.

In other words, to make use of some convenient titles, the rediscovery of *Experimenter Effects in Behavioral Research* (Rosenthal, 1966) is a belated parallel to the rediscovery of *The Therapist's Contribution to the Treatment Process* (Mullan and Sangiuliano, 1964) and of "The influence of situational and interpersonal variables on projective testing" (Masling, 1960). Hence, I will try to set this rediscovery in its broadest context. However, there are some implications of this extension of "interpersonal thinking" to the experiment which are uniquely different from the implications of its extension into the other areas. To see this at a glance one need only consider that it was through psychological research that unintended social influence was discovered in testing and therapy—and now unintended social influence is being discovered in research itself! The epistemological dizziness caused by this turn of events will be a major topic of concern in this book and in the future.

Some of the other major issues upon which I will attempt to shed a bit of light are the following: the possibility of single-variable experiments; the concept of the stimulus; the criteria for adequate operational definitions; hidden sources of variance in research results; the feasibility of true experimental control as opposed to the amount of social control possessed by the experimenter; the role-distancing activities of the experimenter; the myth of the standardized experiment; and finally, the relation of individual to social psychology, of correlational to experimental psychology, and of experimental to general psychology.

These are some of the major issues upon which I will touch. Before

---

[1] In context, Haley is saying: "In a number of fields there is a re-looking at people in terms of the social structure, which was overlooked before. I see this most in psychiatry where I am working; the individual is being re-defined as his family is included in the description, and psychotherapy is appearing as a different process because both therapist and patient are included in the portrait. To me, including the experimenter is part of a general trend, and I think some statement of this would fit your work into a more general perspective." In another place (1964) he points out the "absolute primary assumption" underlying the groups "who express the most hostility toward one another, the Behavior Therapists and the Psychoanalysts," and in so doing convincingly demonstrates that "learning theory and clinical theory have essentially the same foundation"—they take *the individual* as the unit of analysis.

tackling them, I want to place their emergence in historical perspective. Therefore, I will now rewind the reel and slow up the camera so that we may all look more closely at some specific frames in the history of psychological methods. Our task is better to understand the cycle of appearance, disappearance, and reappearance of systematic study of the participation of the psychological researcher in his research.

II

The story has been repeated more often than its moral has been grasped. At Greenwich in 1795, Nicolay Maskeleyne, the royal astronomer, discovered that David Kinnebrook, one of his assistants, was observing the times of the stellar transits a half second later than he (Sanford, 1888–89; Woodworth, 1938; Duncombe, 1945; Boring, 1957; Polanyi, 1958). Kinnebrook's attention was called to the matter but, despite his undoubted effort to bring his observations into harmony with those of his superior, the discrepancy continued to increase until, in January 1796, it had become about eight tenths of a second. Maskeleyne then noted in the *Astronomical Observations at Greenwich* (1796) that Kinnebrook had fallen "into some irregular and confused method of his own" and would never return "to a right method of observing."

The "right method of observing" at that time was the "eye-and-ear" method of F. H. Bradley, which Boring describes in the following manner:

> The field of the telescope was divided by parallel crosswires in the recticle. The observational problem consisted of noting, to one-tenth of a second, the time at which a given star crossed a given wire. The observer looked at the clock, noted the time to a second, began counting seconds with the heard beats of the clock, watched the star cross the field of the telescope, noted and "fixed in mind" its position at the beat of the clock just before it came to the crucial wire, noted its position at the next beat after it had crossed the wire, estimated the place of the wire between the two positions in tenths of the total distance between the positions, and added these tenths of a second to the time in seconds that he had counted for the beat before the wire was reached. (Boring, 1957, p. 135.)

Boring remarks of this interpolation procedure, "It is obviously a complex judgment."

But the difference between Kinnebrook and Maskeleyne, though considerably smaller than differences in which F. W. Bessel would later participate, was deemed too large. Therefore, "though with great reluctance," Maskeleyne dismissed Kinnebrook. Thus, an obscure assistant at the

Greenwich Observatory was ushered out of a job and into a unique place in the history of experimental psychology.

This discovery of "the personal equation," as Bessel somewhat misleadingly called it,[2] exercised the astronomers from the time that Bessel resurrected the report of the Maskeleyne-Kinnebrook incident. A number of experiments by the astronomers upon the individual differences among astronomical observers themselves soon revealed the personal equation to be a very complex phenomenon. It depended on a variety of astronomical conditions. It varied according to the magnitude of the star, the direction of the star's motion, the rate of the star. It differed from the sun or moon to the stars and from occultations and emergences to transits. It depended likewise on several conditions of observation and recording: the position of the astronomer, the illumination of the reticle, individual preference for special tenths of the second. After the chronoscope was invented, the personal equation depended even upon the kind of key used; moreover, "a small but genuine difference of personal equation is introduced if observers hold the finger at different heights above the knob [of the chronoscope] when ready to make the record" (Sanford, 1888, p. 293).

As various as the conditions upon which the personal equation depended, so various were the explanations proposed of it. The complexity and importance of the phenomenon—the calibration of the clock depended on observations of the transits—made it ripe for becoming a battleground for the vying vocabularies of causation which were prominent in the period from 1830 to 1870.

The purely anatomical theories referred the personal error to astigmatism or other structural defects of the eye or to variations in the persistence of visual images upon the retina. The purely physiological explanations ascribed it to differences in times of conduction of the auditory and visual impressions. And, even before psychology had been formally established, there was Bessel's protopsychological explanation of personal errors occurring with the use of the eye-and-ear method:

[2] I say misleadingly because the word "equation" has for many people what in this case is a false connotation of stability. It lends itself to the optimistic notion that, if we could just calculate his personal equation, we could calibrate an observer just as we do any other measuring instrument. Actually, however, Bessel found that the personal equation between two observers might differ from one observation to the next. In fact, what seemed particularly vicious to the astronomers who were studying it was that not only did the personal error vary from observer to observer, but it was even variable for any individual observer. As we would say now, there was *within* as well as *between* observer variability. Moreover, adoption of the term "personal equation" instead of, say, "relative equation" has encouraged psychologists to think of it as a stable individual trait. This tendency militates against a situational or interpersonal analysis of observational differences.

"If it is assumed that impressions on the eye and the ear cannot be compared with each other in an instant, and that two observers use different times for carrying over the one impression upon the other, a difference originates; and *there is a still greater difference if one goes over from seeing to hearing, and the other from hearing to seeing*" (quoted by Boring, 1957, p. 142, my emphasis).

Though Bessel did not know it, the second part of his explanation implicates such factors as set, attention, and expectation. It indicates that an observer who sets his attention on the beat of the clock and another who sets his on the visual path of the star will come up with different calculations. Individual differences would then depend at least in part on attitude. The work in Wilhelm Wundt's laboratory bore out this theory.

III

The most active period of experimentation on the personal equation by the astronomers extended from 1860 to 1870, a period which coincided with the birth of Wundt's new psychology. During this time the astronomers' curiosity gradually gave way to more practical considerations. Faced with the perplexity of the phenomenon, the astronomers became mainly concerned with doing away with it. The eye-and-ear method of Bradley was replaced by the chronoscope. The personal error was thereby diminished but not eradicated. What remained was a nuisance and a blemish upon the record of nice accuracy upon which the astronomers prided themselves. Hence, with joy, the oldest science bequeathed the problem to the newest.

In 1861 Wundt spoke at Speyer on the psychophysiological explanation of the personal equation (Boring, 1957, pp. 152, 344). In his laboratory— the very first formal psychological laboratory—the eye-and-ear method begot the complication experiment. The measurement of the absolute personal equation by the chronoscope became the measurement of a reaction time.

In both cases the course of experimentation revealed the central place of attitudes. In 1885 W. von Tchisch conducted experiments using Wundt's complication clock. A pointer swept over a scale, and a bell sounded at a predetermined point. The observer's task was to note where on the scale the pointer appeared to be when he heard the bell. Some results showed an apparent negative displacement: "the bell appeared to sound when the pointer was at '4,' when actually it was known that the bell did not sound until the pointer had got to '5.' " Von Tchisch considered this observer effect to be either magical or miraculous, but it is neither. It is only an experimental demonstration of prior entry. What happens is that "attentive predisposition favors earlier clear perception. If you are listening for the bell, expecting it, then the sound comes into consciousness more quickly than does the visual appearance of the pointer." (Boring, 1957, p. 146.)

The reaction-time experiments similarly called attention to the factors of attitudinal predisposition. Ludwig Lange is the most important name here. He theorized that the observer's simple reaction time would vary depending on whether his attention was directed toward the stimulus to be received or the reaction to be made.

> His instructions for the *muscular reaction* were, "not to think at all of the coming sense impression, but to prepare as vividly as possible for the innervation of the movement to be made"; and for the *sensorial reaction,* "to avoid altogether all preparatory innervation of the movement, but to direct the whole preparatory tension towards the expected sense impression, with the intention however of letting the motor impulse follow immediately on the apprehension of the stimulus, without any unnecessary delay." (Woodworth, 1938, p. 306.)

The results can be predicted if we consider a common reaction-time experiment—that represented in track by the sequence ready, set, go. One runner "innervates" his muscles successively on ready and set; the other listens intently for the pistol shot and only upon hearing it "innervates the movement to be made." As one would expect, set made a difference. The muscular reaction time was about one-hundred milliseconds shorter than the sensorial.

Thus, via the astronomers' discovery of the personal equation, the new experimental psychology in Leipzig had inherited the problem of individual differences in observation and had confirmed the significance of the attitude of the observer. But a subtle shift in focus had occurred. These factors were no longer being considered from the standpoint of unintended experimenter variance. For the observer involved was no longer the experienced *experimenter* (astronomer), but the experienced *subject* (introspector). Observer and observed were now one and the same. To understand how this difference set psychology off on a long detour, we need to consider introspection.

IV

What is the difference between inspection and introspection, between the astronomer observing the star and the introspector observing his consciousness? Edward Titchener—and Wundt before him—did not consider the difference to be great. Near the outset of his discussion of the methods of psychology, Titchener states that "in principle . . . introspection is very like inspection," and at the conclusion he therefore affirms that "the method of psychology is much the same as the method of physics" (1926, pp. 23–24).

In between, he develops the notion that introspection is observation of a certain *class* of phenomena, namely that class which is dependent upon individual experience. The objects of inspection ("looking at") are independent of individual experience; they are "neither warm nor cold, neither dark nor light, neither silent nor noisy" (p. 8). The objects of introspection ("looking within") are "dependent upon some person"—in fact, since "it is only his own mind, the experience dependent upon his own nervous system, that each of us knows first hand"—they are dependent upon the person observing his own consciousness (p. 25).[3]

The third person reflexive pronoun introduces the first aspect of this difference which is of importance to us. Introspection fuses the observer and the observed. The astronomer's object of study is not himself but the distant star (not "his star"). In introspection, the observer is himself the object of his observation.

Another difference: introspection often introduces a second person into the experimental setting. As Titchener put it, "some experiments are best performed by oneself on oneself. Most, however, require two persons for their performance; the observer, O, who makes the introspection, and the experimenter, E, who handles the instruments and makes the records" (1901, p. xiii).

How did these modifications in the experimental situation affect the application of the astronomers' discovery to psychology? The fusion of observer and observed resulted in a profound deflection of the locus of interest. Bessel, the astronomer, was at once an *experimenter* and an observer. Wundt, the introspector, was at once an observer and a *subject*. Introspection became concerned with the issue of individual differences between subjects, not between experimenters.

In fact, it did not even study fallible observation on the subject side of the dyad. Bessel had handed psychology the problem of individual differ-

[3] For introspection the philosophical problem of "other minds" was the problem of generalizability of experimental results. Titchener was not nearly so tortured by this problem as are contemporary philosophers (Chappell, 1962). He wrote, "We have every reason to believe, not only in general that our neighbors have minds like our own, that is, are able like ourselves to view experience in its dependent aspect, but also in detail that human minds resemble one another precisely as human bodies do" (Titchener, 1926, p. 25). I would suggest that as immigrants with unlike bodies came together on the American shore, thus disrupting any semblance of an integral community, this argument from analogy became unconvincing. Thus, the behaviorists, who as David Bakan remarks, speak the language of strangers, developed a psychology which fit the new urban experience of the melting pot. Is it mere coincidence that Watson and Robert Park were both at the University of Chicago near the turn of the century?

ences. But Wundt was interested in mind, not minds. He employed an elite of practiced observers in order to diminish individual error. Of the experiment which was the direct descendant of the personal equation work, Boring writes that "it is said that no observer who had performed less than 10,000 of these introspectively controlled reactions was suitable to provide data for published research from Wundt's laboratory" (1953, p. 172).

Similarly introspection became systematically concerned with the attitude of the subject, which it did study.

> After Lange's work the task-attitude, or *aufgabe*, as it came to be called, was discovered to play a decisive part in nearly all psychological experiments. Not only in the reaction experiment, but in investigations of perception, recall, judgment, thought, and volition, the central importance of the *subjects'* preparedness became universally recognized. (Allport, 1935, p. 799, my emphasis.)

But introspection did not systematically and self-consciously study the effects of the attitude of the experimenter. Nor did it systematically or self-consciously study how the experimenter's attitude might affect the two-person interaction of experimenter and introspector. Social psychology, according to Wundt (1902, pp. 26–28), was a totally different subject matter from individual psychology.

However, it behooves us to note that Titchener was far from blind to the problems of unintentional variance introduced by the interaction of experimenter and introspector. In his laboratory manual he warns the student to be on guard against the possible contaminations involved in the dyadic interaction peculiar to psychological as opposed to physical experiments. Let us read both the lines and between the lines.

> All experiments of this kind [which require an experimenter and an introspector] must be done twice over, O and E changing places. Each student keeps the record of his partner's introspective results, not that of his own; so that it is his partner, and not he himself, who figures as O in his notebook. There should be no mutual discussion of results until the experiment is completed. Never, under any circumstances, must the idea of competition with one's partner be allowed to enter into the work . . . The idea of rivalry is fatal to introspection.

Is it unrealistic to suspect that his warning is itself evidence that such competition and co-operation were in fact contributing to some laboratory results? One does not legislate against the unthinkable. Titchener continues:

> The student who acts as E during the first part of a laboratory period has a certain advantage over his partner. When he comes to act as O,

> his introspection will, evidently, be guided to some extent by his
> knowledge of the instructions used and of the outcome of his partner's
> introspection. Hence it is advisable to alternate the functions of O and
> E. . . .

There follows some robust warning to the E not to play tricks on the O, for
"he will grow restless and unsteady and his introspection will be valueless.
. . . O is dependent upon E and E upon O. Each must do his very best
for the other." But neither should be overly helpful:

> Be very careful, however, not to suggest to him in any way that you
> wish to expect him to find this or that particular fact by introspection
> at this or that particular moment. Introspection is never easy; it be-
> comes doubly difficult when one knows the E desires one to reach a
> predetermined result. Many experimental series have been spoiled by
> some suggestion from E, and an answering complaisance on the part of
> O. (Titchener, 1901, pp. xiii-xviii.)

Were such efforts at attaining pure introspection untainted by the
nuances of social interaction successful? It seems not. Turning from the
students' lab to the "real" lab, Boring writes that the "laboratory atmosphere crept into the descriptions [of introspections], and it was not possible to verify, from one lab to another, the introspective accounts of the
consciousness of action, feeling, choice, and judgment" (Boring, 1953, p.
174).[4]

The contemporary relevance of all this can be anticipated from Boring's assertion that introspection is still with us, disguised, however, as verbal report (1953). But the niceties of the introspective vocabulary do seem
a bit archaic, for not long after Titchener wrote his manual, a fallible
introspector whose fallibility helped give psychology a new start entered the
picture.

V

From the very first the new psychology had been a hybrid. From the physi-
ologists Wundt had appropriated the problems of sensation and perception; from the astronomers had come the reaction-time experiments. The

---

[4] For "laboratory atmosphere" I would substitute some mixture of experimenter
effect and experimenter bias as the source of this failure to replicate introspective
results from laboratory to laboratory. It would seem that bias was especially encouraged by the customary use in the observer role of people who were themselves
working in the same laboratory in the experimenter role on similar psychological
topics and who, since the laboratories were forerunners of the schools of psychology,
were likely to share the outlook of the particular laboratory. Introspection overlooked the personal equation, but it did not escape it.

subject matter of the former was consciousness; of the latter, behavior. For a time the two lay side by side; then, what Wilhelm Wundt had wedded, John Watson cast asunder.

For the peaceful union of consciousness and behavior would endure only so long as behavior remained the silent partner. The reaction-time work was an unrecognized anomaly in a psychology which, at the turn of the century, was still being defined as the study of states of consciousness as such. This meant that psychologists studied neither writers writing nor readers reading—nor even readers temporarily not reading, although they were best equipped to deal with the latter, who might be imagining, thinking, or even introspecting.

Then along came Watson, who redefined psychology as the study of behavior. Watson could find "in the test tube of his science" no evidence for a stream of consciousness, "not even one so convincing as that described by William James" (Watson and McDougall, 1928, p. 27). Psychologists were now to study writers writing and readers reading—although, ironically, they would prove to have the greatest difficulty with readers who were temporarily not reading, because from their behavior one could not easily tell whether they were imagining, thinking, or introspecting, nor could Watson adequately explain the image, the idea, the thought.

Watson rebelled not only against the former definition of the proper subject matter of psychology but also against its accepted methodology. He saw that the two were intimately related:

> [Consciousness] has never been seen, touched, smelled, tasted, or moved. It is a plain assumption, just as unprovable as the old concept of the soul. . . . And how do we begin work on it? Not by analyzing it as we would a chemical compound, or the way a plant grows. No, those things are material things. This thing we call consciousness can be analyzed only by self-introspection, turning around, and looking at what goes on inside . . . instead of gazing at woods and trees and brooks and things, we must gaze at this undefined and undefinable something we call consciousness." (Watson and McDougall, 1928, p. 15.)

If, using modern terminology, we call the individual studied the "subject," then we may call his introspection "subjective observation." The correlative term, "objective observation," would refer—as it did originally in psychology—to observations made upon him by another person. In this original sense of the word, Watson replaced subjective observation with four kinds of objective observation: observation with and without instrumental control, conditioned-reflex methods, verbal-report methods, and the method of testing. Common to all these—and of paramount importance to us—is the splitting of that fusion of observer and observed which had obtained under the method of introspection.

The contrast between the real and the assumed implications of this development is crucial if we are to grasp the contemporary relevance of the personal-equation story. Fred Keller contrasts the old methodology with the new:

> A word about terminology . . . The "observer" of Titchener's experiments is the "subject" of Watson's. Introspective psychology called for an experimenter *and* an observer in laboratory studies. The experimenter set up the essential conditions and the observer reported upon his "experience," a report that was recorded, of course, by the experimenter. In behavioristic studies, *the true observer is the experimenter*, who observes, not his "experience," but the responses of the subject. (Keller, 1937, p. 63, my emphasis.)

The true observer is the experimenter. Thus behaviorism returns the experimenter to a position comparable to that of the astronomer. Immediately the ghosts of Maskeleyne and Kinnebrook return to view. But these were not the apparitions Watson saw. Bessel had demonstrated the existence of errors of observation in a physical science. But Watson seems to have modeled his psychology according to an image of science which granted to the experimenter that impersonality which Bessel had effectively challenged. For Watson, the sole moral of astronomy was that it had shed astrology long before, while psychology was still struggling with *its* prescientific heritage (1919, p. 3).

This is crucial. Strict application of the observer-star paradigm to the observer-subject situation would lead one to expect (1) the presence and study of individual differences among psychological observers (experimenters) and (2) the acknowledgment and scrutiny of the effects of their varying attitudes—their expectancies, hypotheses, and sets.[5]

But involved as they were in their attack on introspection and eager as they were to apply behaviorism to practical problems, the Watsonians did not systematically apply this paradigm. In a number of his own experiments Watson seems to have been the sole experimenter. He does not seem to have considered the possibility that the data obtained by one experimenter

[5] I make use here of the slippery meanings of the word "attitude." (See Allport, 1935; and Boring, 1957, pp. 715–16.) It is possible to say that the experimenter's hypothesis is his attitude, is part of his attitude, or influences his attitude. An important historical link was the description by G. H. Mead and John Dewey of the attitude as the internal stage of the act. Since Watson ignored this stage, attitude tended to become one of the behaviorists' bogy words and dropped out of their interpretation of the experiment altogether. Bakan (1953) has discussed how the subjects' attitudes influence their perception of the stimulus. I will be concerned with showing how the experimenters' attitudes can also influence the responses of their subjects.

might be peculiar to that experimenter. He was quick to identify the employment of objective methods with the attainment of objectivity.

E. W. Scripture saw that this assimilation of the difference between observation by oneself and observation by another to the difference between biased and unbiased observation was spurious. He noted that, "introspection does distort things and lead to erroneous conclusions [at times], but so does all observation. The objections to introspection apply just as completely to physical and botanical observations as to psychological ones." (Scripture, 1897, p. 11.)

But whereas Wundt and Titchener had been intent on stressing the similarities between inspection and introspection, the early behaviorists were at pains to render them as unlike as possible. Wundt's "new psychology" was now "the old psychology." As part of the clean break with introspection, the new psychologists considered the objective methods to be unsullied by the subjectivity of the subjective methods. Behaviorism, which sought to observe man as objectively as any physical phenomenon, forgot the lesson which had been imported into psychology from the study of physical phenomena.

And so behaviorism proceeded to develop a philosophy of experimentation in which the experimenter, his attitudes, the immediate social setting of his observations and the larger social structures within which they took place faded into the background. The experiment was conceptualized entirely in terms of the stimulus applied and the response recorded. All other conditions were considered to be held constant.

In adopting this philosophy, psychologists were apparently guided by Watson's belief that "Psychology . . . is a purely *objective* experimental branch of *natural* science" (1913, p. 158, my emphasis). That the experimenter became "a neglected stimulus object" (McQuigan, 1963) indicates the end point of the conceptual itinerary the term "objective" has taken. But Watson's statement also indicates another aspect of the incomplete conception of psychology which has in turn produced an inadequate conception of the psychological experiment. That is the notion that psychology is a purely *natural* science. An alternative perspective on experimentation is suggested by recognizing psychology's ties to *social* science.

VI

At the turn of the century, at about the time Watson entered the University of Chicago as a graduate student in the Department of Philosophy, George Herbert Mead, then an assistant professor of philosophy, offered courses in logic, movements of thought in the nineteenth century, Kant's cosmology, the philosophy of science, the philosophy of evolution, comparative psychology, and for the very first time in his very long career, contemporary social psychology.

Other courses would come and go in Mead's impressive teaching repertoire, but for the next thirty years, in courses entitled "Contemporary Social Psychology," "Social Psychology," and "Advanced Social Psychology," he proceeded to elaborate a systematic position which, in self-conscious contrast to Watson's *individual* behaviorism, he sometimes called *social* behaviorism.[6] The school of thought which he helped found—now variously referred to as Chicago, Meadian, sociological, or interactional social psychology, or symbolic interactionism—offers a new perspective on the psychological experiment, a perspective which can comprehend some of those features of it which elude the Watsonian point of view.

To see why this is so, we need to reconsider now the differences between the observer-star and observer-subject situations. The first difference is that in the latter case both parties are animate,[7] whereas in the former only one is. Unlike the observed star, the observed subject looks back. The second difference is the distance between observer and observed. The psychological experiment customarily brings the two parties into the same room, whereas the astronomer remains millions of miles removed from the star. The third difference is that the psychological experimenter both evokes and records the subject's response, while the astronomer only records the star's movement. The verbal structuring of the situation by the psychological experimenter for the human subject and the question-answer

[6] The historical relation between individual and social behaviorism is intimate. The careers of Watson, Dewey, Mead, and Thomas overlapped at Chicago. Watson has written personally of the others (1936). In philosophy he got, "strange to say, least of all out of John Dewey. I never knew what he was talking about then and, unfortunately for me, I still don't know." Of Mead he wrote, "I took courses and seminars with Mead. I didn't understand him in the classroom, but for years Mead took a great interest in my animal experimentation, and many a Sunday he and I spent in the lab watching my rats and monkeys. On these comradely exhibitions and at his home I understood him. A kinder, finer man I never met." Of William I. Thomas, with whom he lived the summer and fall after the scandal at Hopkins, Watson wrote, "What I should have done without his understanding counsel and his helpfulness on the economic side, I do not know." There is also evidence of contact on the theoretical level. Notice, for example, the ambivalent vocabulary of this statement: "In each adjustment there is always both a *response* or *act* and a *stimulus* or *situation* which calls [it] out . . ." (Watson, 1919, p. 9). Ultimately, of course, Watson stuck to the former concept of each pair and the social behaviorists stuck to the latter.

[7] From this point on I will refer mostly to experiments using human subjects. The reader should not assume, however, that what is said does not apply to animal experimentation as well. (See Rosenthal, 1963a and 1965.) It is probable that in the dyadic relation of man and beast tactual, auditory, and olfactory cues mediate the effect and bias phenomena, whereas with human subjects communication depends mainly upon gestures, words, and other symbolic kinds of impression management.

nature of the experimenter-subject interchange has no exact counterpart in the astronomer-star case.

Taken together these factors mean that the psychological experiment —unlike the physical experiment—often becomes a two-person interaction of a special kind. And the study of two-person interaction is one of the specialties of interaction social psychology.

In what ways, specifically, can the perspectives of social behaviorism comprehend the basic methodology of individual behaviorism more adequately than can individual behaviorism itself? How would adoption of the habits of mind of the symbolic interactionist improve upon what have become traditional ways of thinking about the experiment? How would they lead psychology to rediscover the moral of the personal-equation incident?

First, they would indicate the difficulties involved with habitual thinking in terms of the applied stimulus. The psychologist's problem is to identify the stimulus rather than to assume it.[8] The symbolic interactionist would warn that subjects may be responding to any number of things in the social environment of the experiment other than the intended stimulus. Therefore, it is better for the experimenter to start off thinking in terms of *the situation,* for then he will not be so easily deluded into thinking that the stimulus as constituted by himself is necessarily the stimulus as constituted by the subject.

Introduction of the concept of the situation—and recognition that the experiment is a social situation—also puts the problem of generalization from experimental results into a new light. The experimental psychologist is used to deriving from the data resulting from the interaction of one experimenter in one situation with a random sample of subjects principles, regularities, or laws of individual behavior. The social behaviorist would be inclined to view the responses given in a specific situation, initially at least, as situational. Only by systematically manipulating aspects of the total situation—experimenters, rooms, etc.—could he legitimately hope to abstract the data from the milieus and so be certain that his results were trans-situational.

Especially relevant in this connection is the standard use in psychological experiments of a *single* experimenter and a *sample* of subjects. Keeping

[8] S. S. Stevens: "In a sense there is only one problem of psychophysics, namely the definition of the stimulus. In this same sense there is only one problem in all of psychology, and it is the same problem. The definition of the stimulus is thus a bigger problem than it appears to be at first sight. The reason for equating psychology to the problem of defining the stimulus can be stated thus: the complete definition of the stimulus to a given response involves the specification of all the transformations of the environment, both internal and external, that leaves the response invariant. This specification of the conditions of invariance would entail of course a complete understanding of the factors that produce and alter responses." (Stevens, 1951.)

in mind the astronomers' discovery, this circumstance means that all the results are saturated with the specific experimenter's personal equation. The interaction social psychologist would add that the psychological experimenter is not just an observer; he actively elicits what he will observe. Hence, over and above the variance in results which might be introduced by differences in experimenters' observations, it is also possible that different experimenters would actually *get* different responses from their subjects. This factor, which involves what might be called *the interpersonal equation* (Joel, 1949), adds a potential source of variability to experimental results in psychology beyond that involved with the personal equation.[9] The point is that throughout contemporary psychological research much of this is ignored by the practice of using just one experimenter or not analyzing experiments for experimenter effects. It might turn out, though, if such analyses were carried out, that the results given by subjects depend, to some extent, on the specific experimenter and so cannot legitimately be chalked up in terms of principles, regularities, or laws of individual behavior.

The complexity of two-person interaction and the implications of this complexity for the ideal of experimental control tie all this together. The conception of an experiment as a *controlled* situation in which there are experimental and *control* groups which allow *controlled* observations to be made which will in turn lead to the prediction and *control* of human behavior—this whole conception stems from an individualistic frame of reference. Adoption of an interpersonal perspective changes the picture. Face-to-face interaction is very dense. A good deal of it goes on at a nonverbal level, the level of the "conversation of gestures" (Mead, 1934). It is difficult for a person to become aware of or to control his nonverbal behavior, especially in face-to-face encounters. Thus, the "unintentional expressions given off" (Goffman, 1959) by the experimenter—his winks and tics, smiles and grimaces, nods and glances—probably constitute a regular source of stimulation (which will vary from experimenter to experimenter) over and above that provided by the variables the experimenter intends to manipulate.[10]

---

[9] The term "interpersonal equation" can be misconstrued just as the term "personal equation" has been. But as Joel saw, "no research should be expected to yield an interpersonal equation in the sense of a constant correction to be used in the interpretation of tests administered by a given examiner" (Joel, 1949, p. 482). The fact that people behave differently depending upon with whom they are interacting should be sufficiently clear to provide a guard against the notion of a constant interpersonal equation.

[10] To anticipate: to the extent that experimenters vary in the expressions they give off and to the extent that these variations affect the specific response category under investigation, then there will be experimenter effects in the data. To the extent that the experimenter can wittingly or unwittingly control this behavior and manipulate it toward influencing subjects to give responses that validate his hypothesis, it will mediate experimenter biases.

And the experimenter may not be aware of this surplus stimulation. As Goffman puts it, under the conditions of face-to-face embodied communication, "any message that an individual sends is likely to be qualified and modified by much added information that others glean from him simultaneously, *often unbeknownst to him . . .*" (1963a, p. 15, my emphasis).[11]

I have begun to suggest here some aspects of the frame of reference to be developed in this book. The contemporaneity of Watson and Mead encouraged me to disregard chronology in this section in order to draw out the perspective on experimentation implicit in the work of the interaction social psychologists. It was some time, however, before social psychologists got around either to actually analyzing the psychological experiment as a social situation or to considering the implications of the fact that it is a social situation. In the meantime, social behaviorism and individual behaviorism continued to go their respective ways, drifting ever further apart with the increasing departmentalization of knowledge. Before they could be reunited, two methodological innovations characterized by their failure to appreciate the social psychological perspective intervened.

VII

For Watson "the rule or measuring rod" which the experimenter was to apply in his laboratory was, "Can I describe this bit of behavior I see in terms of 'stimulus and response'?" (Watson and McDougall, 1928, p. 20).

We have seen that the symbolic interactionist would reply in the negative—the experimenter would have to consider all the sources of information available to the subject in the experimental situation, especially those which become available to him in his interaction with the experimenter. And in fact a number of psychologists soon did answer this question with a resounding "No!" Different subjects did seem to react differently to what was intended to be the same stimulus. But the full insights of interaction social psychology were not immediately appreciated, for these differences were conceptualized as "individual differences" between *subjects* and were variously ascribed to the subjects' *past* social experiences (rather than to possible variations in their present social situation or their definition of that situation) or to the innate variability of human behavior.

In order to come to terms with the failure of Watson's measuring rod, the experimenters added organismic variables to the laboratory paradigm,

[11] Compare Estes: "By stimulating situation . . . I mean to indicate all sources of stimulation that are mentioned in the experimenter's description of the experimental situation." Such a definition gives the experimenter too much omniscience. Estes adds in a footnote that "this appeal to the experimenter's description may seem to make us unduly vulnerable to errors or omissions in conventional categorizations. I believe, however, that we are merely recognizing the existing state of affairs, not adding any new complications." (Estes, 1959, p. 455.)

while the correlationists, armed with the new statistical methods, made these individual differences the subject matter of their discipline. We will consider these contemporaneous developments in turn.

Early in their influential text Robert Woodworth and Harold Schlosberg institutionalize this unfortunate division of labor as "the two disciplines of scientific psychology":

> This book must leave aside the study of individual differences by test methods, inaugurated by experimentalists at about the turn of the century, with its modern statistical magic for correlation, analysis of variance, and factor analysis. The experimentalist needs some degree of competence in these methods, if only for checking on the reliability of his own results. The same psychologists, from the early days on, have contributed to both lines of study, and the contacts between them are close and should remain so. But the same book can scarcely do justice to both lines of attack.

Following this disclaimer, they introduce the notation for symbolizing an experiment:

> In a psychological experiment one obvious requirement is an organism to serve as subject by responding to stimuli. If we designate the stimulus . . . by the letter S, and the subject's response by the letter R, we can best designate the subject or organism by the letter O . . . the letter E stands for the experimenter. . . .

They then go on to apply this notation in what has become a standard schematization of the psychological experiment:

> A psychological experiment, then, can be symbolized by S-O-R, which means that E (*understood*) applies a certain stimulus (or *situation*) to O's receptors and *observes* O's response. (Woodworth and Schlosberg, 1954, p. 2, my emphasis.)

The authors then raise the question as to how the issue of experimental control is affected by the introduction of these organismic variables:

> At a certain moment the organism makes a response. The response depends on the stimuli acting at that moment and on factors present in the organism at that moment . . .
> $$R = f(S, O) \ldots$$
> As to the control of these variables, we readily admit that stimuli can be controlled so far as they come from the environment, for E can manage the immediate environment consisting of *the experimental room and the apparatus*. But how can he control the O variables? (Woodworth and Schlosberg, 1954, p. 3, my emphasis.)

Let us stop at this question—which for these authors defines the essential problem facing the experimenter—and look more closely at this standard formulation of the psychological experiment. Note first how the experimenter is relegated to a parenthetical position and then omitted from the S-O-R paradigm. Note also that the accepted notion of the stimulus still carries along with it, again in parentheses, the broader notion of the situation, the difference between the two remaining inexplicit. Note too that, even though they reserve the letter O for the subject, Woodworth and Schlosberg recognize that the experimenter is an observer but then do not consider the implications of the Maskeleyne-Kinnebrook affair. (If they did, would they consider the E "understood"?) And note finally that in concluding that the immediate environmental variables (room and apparatus) are easily controlled, Woodworth and Schlosberg lack a conception of the immediate social environment created by the interaction of O and E or the broader social environment in which the experiment takes place.

"But how can he control the O variables?" The foregoing considerations leave them with only this problem. Assuming easily controlled situational variables and an experimenter who is "understood," the subject is opened up as the sole source of uncontrolled—and in some versions uncontrollable—variance. The fact that experimenters are also organisms and so should be expected to display individual differences based on *their* past histories is omitted from consideration, as is the circumstance that the experiment is a social interaction. The problem is formulated as one of controlling the organismic variables of only one of the participating organisms, and the problem of controlling the variable career of the interaction does not appear in the text which played such a large part in shaping ways of thinking about the psychological experiment.

Individual differences among experimenters, the effect of the attitudes of the experimenter, and the ways in which both are mediated through differences in experimenter-subject interactions became "repressed" problems of experimental psychology. Furthermore, the correlational psychologist, who supposedly "is in love with just those variables the experimenter left home to forget" (Cronbach, 1957, p. 674), similarly ignored these considerations.[12]

To understand why, we have to consider the curious history of the controversy over the place of individual differences in psychology. We have seen that the personal equation represented the measurement of an individual difference between observers. But introspection set psychology off on

[12] Even the defenders of correlational techniques have discussed experimentation on its own grounds. Cf. Cronbach: "The well-known virtue of the experimental method is that it brings situational variables under tight control" (1957, p. 672). But is that well-known virtue actually a well-known assumed virtue? How "tight" is the control? This will become clear.

a quest for general laws of the human mind. In this search, individual differences among observers were as much of an annoyance as are individual differences among subjects to contemporary experimenters. Hence Wundt tried to eliminate rather than study them.

Thus it was that individual differences had to be *re*discovered by Francis Galton and Karl Pearson, who are usually given credit for their introduction into psychology, even though the Maskeleyne-Kinnebrook affair had occurred fifty years before.

Galton and Pearson represent a separate source of interest in individual differences and one which ironically would eventually have to assert itself against the disciples of Wundt. The meeting of the two schools took place in the controversy between James Mark Baldwin and Titchener over Baldwin's failure to replicate Lange's work on the sensorial and muscular reaction times. Using practiced observers, Lange, as we have noted, had found that the sensorial reaction time is longer than the muscular. Using unpracticed observers, Baldwin found an individual difference between "sensory" and "motoric" reactors. He argued that type of person rather than immediate set made the difference.

Titchener vigorously defended the practice of basing the laws of psychology upon the outcomes of practiced observers. Baldwin vigorously attacked it:

> The attempt of Wundt, Kulpe, and others to rule these results out, on the ground of incompetency of the reagents, is in my opinion a flagrant *argumentum in circulo*. Their contention is that a certain mental *anlage* or attitude is necessary in order to [be a subject in an] experiment on reaction times. And when we ask what the *anlage* is, we are told that the only indication of it is the ability of the reagent to turn out reactions which give the distinction between motor and sensory time which Wundt and his followers consider the proper one. In other words, only certain cases prove their result, and these cases are selected because they prove that result . . . to rule out all *anlagen* but one, is to get the psychology of some individuals and force it upon others, and thus to make the reaction-method of investigation simply the handmaid to dogma.

Baldwin went on to say:

> If one-third of mankind are to be taken to prove that a result is a universal principle, the rest being deliberately excluded because they cannot get the result that the one-third do, then what conclusions could not be proved in well-managed psychology labs? (Baldwin, 1895, p. 265.)

The argument, as Boring puts it, was between Germany and America. Eventually the *"ganz Amerikanisch"* position of Baldwin won out, and a psychology of individual differences built upon the correlation statistic and utilizing the method of testing was developed. But notice that Baldwin was talking about individual differences among *introspectors* (performers). The context of his remarks makes it clear that in his reference to "one-third of mankind" Baldwin did not include experimenters among mankind! The personal equation of *experimenters* had receded so far back into the prehistory of psychology that it was never part of the controversy. Thus, even though Pearson had written on the personal equation (1902), the intimate relation between the astronomers' errors of observation and the psychology of individual differences was not recognized. While experimental psychology was making the experimenter into a neglected stimulus object, so correlational psychology was treating the tester as a nonperson (Goffman, 1959). It proceeded to study the individual differences between subjects.[13]

These developments can be summarized schematically as follows:

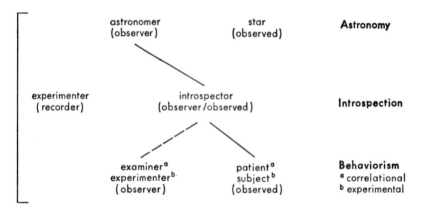

The study of individual differences and attitudes followed the solid line, whereas analogically it should have followed the dotted line.[14]

[13] "The production of projective material varies from one individual to another both in quantity and quality. Since the stimulus material is held constant, it has been assumed that such individual differences must be due to differences residing entirely in the personalities tested. This assumption, which is *basic* to the use of projective techniques for the study of personality, is faulty because it does not take into account the total testing situation, particularly the relationship between subject and examiner." (Joel, 1949, p. 479, my emphasis.)

[14] I do not mean to imply here that one should simply substitute the study of individual differences between experimenters for the study of individual differences between subjects. A full experimental psychology needs to consider both members of the dyad. Remember that the subject or patient is *also* an "observer" and the experimenter or examiner an "observed."

Again, however, the moral of the personal equation story was not grasped, and psychology proceeded to a different controversy.

VIII

Watson's coup had established the Stimulus on the throne of Psychology and had banished the former ruler, Mind, and his entire family—Consciousness, Feeling, Sensation, etc.—from the realm. But no sooner was the new monarch comfortably ensconced than the hue and cry went up once again. L. L. Thurstone suggested "that we dethrone the stimulus. He is only nominally the ruler of psychology. The real ruler of the domain . . . is the individual and his motives, desires, wants, ambitions, cravings, aspirations." (Thurstone, 1923, p. 364.)

Civil war broke out. The Correlationists attacked, and the Experimentalists retreated. Some newly popular members of the old royal family—Intelligence, Anxiety, Need, etc.—returned from exile. It looked as if the counterrevolution would reinstate the *status quo ante*.

But at this point the philosopher kings of a neighboring territory intervened. They offered to the strife-torn land of Psychology stability in the form of "the revolution that will put an end to the possibility of revolutions" (Stevens, 1935, p. 323). Both sides embraced their arbitration, and, in the spirit of *operationism*, set out to rehabilitate the family of the former king.

We can see why their aid was so necessary. Watson had complained that introspection allowed no element of control. The mind words, which were defined in terms of their properties or attributes, invited as many definitions as there were psychologists. Watson used the case of "sensation" to make this point:

> A sensation is defined in terms of its attributes. One psychologist will state with readiness that the attributes of a visual sensation are quality, extension, duration, and intensity. Another will add clearness. Still another order. I doubt if any one psychologist can draw up a set of statements describing what he *means* by sensation which will be agreed upon by three other psychologists of different training.

From this example Watson generalized to all mentalistic terms: "There is no longer any guarantee that we all *mean* the same thing when we use the terms now current in psychology." (Watson, 1913, pp. 164–65, my emphasis.)

Enter the operationalist. "In general we *mean* by any concept nothing more than a set of operations; the concept is synonymous with the corresponding set of operations" (Bridgman, 1927, p. 5, my emphasis). In a psychology which lived by this maxim, "sensations" could no longer be so promiscuously defined. They would be introduced into psychology not in terms of their imagined attributes but in terms of their methods of measurement. Since these methods would be public, the concepts of psychology would immediately become intersubjective. Psychologists of different training would all know what they meant by intelligence because they would all know the test by which intelligence was measured.

In this way, psychologists rehabilitated mentalistic concepts by referring them to a physicalistic meaning base. Organismic variables, which had been banished as hypothetical constructs, were welcomed back as intervening variables. Watson's metaphysical behaviorism gave way to methodological behaviorism, which became "a thoroughgoing operational analysis of traditional mentalistic concepts" (Skinner, 1945, p. 270).

From the standpoint of psychological language, operationalism introduced a principle for determining whether psychological concepts had meaning. From the standpoint of psychological methodology, it placed renewed emphasis on the need for standardizing experimental procedure.

It is in this latter function that operationism enters our story. Operationism deserves its place in a history of psychological methods because it gave to experimentation a place more crucial than it gave to theorizing. As part of the attack on mentalistic philosophy, "mental activity" (theorizing) took a back seat to "physical activity" (experimenting). And if concepts were now to be defined in terms of operations, then operations would have to be strictly and exhaustively described. Percy Bridgman's empiricism necessitated that no element of a laboratory situation, "no matter how apparently irrelevant or trivial, be dismissed as without effect on the final result until proved to be without effect by actual experiment" (1927, p. 3). Bridgman himself presented an admirable example to follow by meticulously describing the laboratory conditions under which his own concepts were defined. His "vicious particularism" demanded standardized laboratory procedures. As he put it, "we must demand that the set of operations equivalent to any concept be a unique set" (Bridgman, 1927, p. 6). Operationism as a methodological caveat was intended to require that the experimenter make explicit his every move.

The word "situation" reappears throughout Bridgman's work.[15] But operationism came into psychology via its interpretation by a psychophysicist, not by a Meadian social psychologist. Thus the potential resonance between the social behaviorists' position on interaction and the operationalists' position on experimentation passed unnoticed.

[15] For example, "One of the greatest advantages of an operational breakdown of a situation is that it reduces it to a description of an actual happening . . ." (Bridgman, 1945, p. 246). "So far as it is anything at all [operationalism] is a technique of analysis which endeavors to attain the greatest possible awareness of everything involved in a situation . . ." (quoted by Israel and Goldstein, 1944, p. 178).

Instead operationalism, which forced psychological language to adapt itself to a rigorous physicalism, was itself adapted in the laboratory to the prevailing mode of discourse. The passive-voice construction ("The Taylor Anxiety Scale was administered"), with its omission of the ablative agent, became accepted as adequate operational definition. The setting, the attitudes, and the *interpersonal operations* of the experimenter characteristically remained outside the formal operational description of the experiment. In this way operationalism was accommodated to psychology's individualistic orientation.

The experimenter himself was also ignored by operationism. Although it had been assumed rather than demonstrated that experimenter differences were without effect on experimental results, the experimenter was commonly omitted from the operational definition of the experimental situation. The personal equation remained unappreciated. And this despite the fact that operationism was the product of Bridgman's interpretation of relativity theory, and that relativity theory was responsible for explicitly recognizing what Bessel had implicitly demonstrated—the importance of the interaction of observer and observed. But the last words of one of S. S. Stevens' earliest articles interpreting operationism for the psychologist summed up the limits of its contribution to psychological methodology: "Science has a lot to say about the subject, but little about the experimenter. There is, in fact, little to say, for in all science the experimenter is assumed. . . ." (Stevens, 1935, p. 328.)

IX

We come now to the return of the repressed.

That which spilled over the formal textbook representation of psychological experimentation returned at first informally. The inadequate official symbolization of the psychological experiment bred a folklore of offhand remarks and offbeat articles which let out what had been left out.

For example, the fact that the interaction between experimenter and subject could produce effective stimuli other than the intended stimuli was pointed out by Woodworth who, in his review of Pavlov's work, warned that "there are pitfalls in such work; especially there is the chance that the animal is responding to the experimenter and his movements and unconscious expressions and not at all to the stimuli which the E is intentionally applying" (Woodworth, 1931, p. 64).

The ease with which experimenters might bias their subjects was indicated by A. H. Pierce, who wrote, "It is to the highest degree probable that the subject['s] general attitude of mind is that of ready complacency and cheerful willingness to assist the investigator in every possible way by reporting to him those very things which he is most eager to find, and that the very questions of the E . . . suggest the shade of reply expected" (Pierce, 1908, quoted by Orne, 1962).

This *entre-nous* knowledge was used at an early date to criticize experimental work which demonstrated results alien to the prevailing atmosphere of psychology. Thus, J. L. Kennedy, in his critical review of experimentation on ESP, delved into the various ways in which the influence exerted by the E in his dyadic interaction with the subject could lead to the latter's display of his "supernatural" powers (Kennedy, 1939).

The social psychologists who have got around to analyzing the psychological experiment also had prophetic ancestors within social psychology itself. In their review of social psychology of the 1930's, Leonard Cottrell and Ruth Gallagher predicted that in the future experimenters would be "more conscious of their own positions in the experimental situation and the inevitable interpenetration of experimenter and subject." They noted that "there is widespread evidence of attempts to make the complex situation explicit in experimental analyses" but were sorry that "this has not yet reached the point where experimenters are fully aware of the necessity of making explicit . . . the laboratory context." (Cottrell and Gallagher, 1941, p. 310.)

While the "New Look" people were rediscovering and refining the concept of attitudes, M. Preston explicitly formulated the impact of the experimenter's attitude upon experimental results:

> The extent to which a subject develops a conditioned response is a function of the attitude of the experimenter. This attitude acts to produce constant errors in the records of the conditioning. The attitude of the E undergoes subtle changes as he progresses in skill. The change in the attitude acts to produce changes in the record of the conditioning process. Hence it becomes difficult to conclude whether differences in rate of conditioning are due to differences in the E's skill or to the differences in the independent variable of the experiment. (Preston, 1951, p. 34.)

Like salmon, these commentators were swimming against the stream of objective psychology. Their forthright statements—and the multitude of anecdotes about experimenter X whose data were contaminated by this or that personal motive or interpersonal event—passed relatively unremarked. Looking backward, one can find these scattered testimonials to the inadequacy of the accepted frame of reference. But they did not give rise to a fundamental revision of the conceptions of psychological experimentation. In the experimental textbooks the idealized experimenter remained a nonperson, the idealized experiment a nonsituation, and the idealized experimenter-subject encounter a noninteraction. Systematic study of the personal equation—which was the birthright of experimental psychology—proceeded elsewhere.

Survey researchers and census takers were among the first social scientists systematically to study the personal equation (Rosenthal, 1963b). Their interviews were carried out on a large scale. Hence, especially where there was interpenetration of samples, differences in response associated with differences in interviewers became highly visible. This work can be organized in accordance with the personal-equation paradigm. Some investigators began to study individual differences between interviewers—that is, interviewer effect (e.g., Hyman, 1954); some began to study the impact of the interviewer's attitude—that is, interviewer bias (e.g., Rice, 1929). Moreover, to extend a psychoanalytic metaphor, the knowledge of the interviewer's contribution to the outcome of the interview could pass the censor. Since the interviewers were usually nonprofessionals, it could be admitted that they influenced their interviewees' responses without the admission's obviously implicating the work of more experienced, rigorous, and professional behavioral scientists.

Another early break came from the clinical psychologists, who began to study examiner effects (e.g., Baughmann, 1951) and examiner bias (e.g., Lord, 1950) at a relatively early date. This work will be reviewed in detail in Chapter 6. Again we have the widespread use of psychological testing in the clinic to thank for calling attention to examiner differences. And again the distance which allowed this knowledge to come into consciousness also served to preclude insight on the part of researchers. Since they were engaged in a virtual civil war with the clinicians, for them to demonstrate experimentally or correlationally that clinical results could be contaminated by the personal equations of clinicians seemed to be a feather in the cap of the researchers, who could still imagine their own results to be free from such interpersonal taint.

Thus it is evident that some resistance to the systematic study of what has been unsystematically known in experimental psychology since its very beginnings still exists. For a while Brunswik was almost alone in his criticism of classical experimental design—to which he opposed representative design.

Representative design approached the problem of the personal equation obliquely from the perspectives of statistical inference and ecological validity. Brunswik believed that for the responses *of* a sample of subjects to be generalizable to nonexperimental situations, they had to be responses *to* a sample from the relevant population of stimuli or situations. Of the testing situation, Brunswik acknowledged that, "since in any testing procedure the examiner constitutes part of the external stimulus situation, representative design demands that examiners should also be sampled" (1956, p. 131).

But even Brunswik stopped short of challenging the acceptance of the experimenter as a nonstimulus, for he never applied this insight concerning the situation of the examiner to the situation of the experimenter. Therapists, counselors, testers, examiners, interviewers—all were regaining person status, whereas the status of experimentation remained based upon the concept of the experimenter as a nonperson. Moreover, Brunswik's reforms were based solely on statistical rather than social-psychological reasoning. In contrast, the developing self-consciousness with regard to psychological experimentation touches the experiment directly and supplements considerations of statistical interaction with considerations of social interaction.

In 1958, in a paper which is on its way to becoming a classic, Riecken "legitimated" study of the social psychology of the psychological experiment. He described his paper as "a first attempt to outline a problem in empirical social psychology and to suggest some ways of attacking it." The problem was "the identification and analysis of some sources of unintended variance in data collection." Riecken recognized that "such variation is ordinarily regarded as 'error,' reflecting some mistake in procedure on the part of the investigator," but he also saw the fundamental importance of the fact that

> on the other hand, a broader perspective on the problem reveals it as a series of more fundamental questions about human interaction, interpersonal relations, or social behavior. The process of collecting data about human behavior is itself a social process and shares features in common with other situations and events of human interaction. Accordingly, the process of data collection can be studied as *a particular type of interaction in a particular social situation* (Riecken, 1958, p. 1, my emphasis).

A particular type of interaction in a particular social situation—with these words Riecken explicitly formulated the perspective on psychological experimentation which we earlier drew out of interaction social psychology. The rest of his paper was devoted to an exploratory analysis of features of this particular social situation and the provision of imaginative suggestions of techniques to study it.

Work in the new field spread rapidly. The titles of some of the relevant papers reflect the renewed newness of the concern. F. J. McQuigan rediscovers "The Experimenter: A Neglected Stimulus Object" (1963); Joan Criswell discusses "The Psychologist as Perceiver" (1958); Irwin Sarason, "The Human Reinforcer in Verbal Behavior Research" (1964); Donald Campbell, "Systematic Errors to Be Expected of the Social Scientist on the Basis of a General Psychology of Cognitive Bias" (1959); Paul Ekman and Wallace Friesen, "Status and Personality of the Experimenter as a Determinant of Verbal Conditioning" (1960); and Walter Reitman, "Experimenter Bias as an Interaction Phenomenon" (1959).

Two major research programs are currently focusing on the psychological experiment. Each is basically concerned with a particular aspect of the social psychology of the psychological experiment. One of these programs is being conducted by Martin Orne and his associates. Through his research on hypnosis,[16] Orne came to the conclusion that it was difficult to find out how much control the hypnotist actually has over his subject because the experimenter himself has so much control (1959). This discovery led to a general interest in the factors which are apt to affect the subject's reaction to the stimuli in the experiment. Orne became concerned with "isolating the effects of the experimental setting from the effects of the experimental variables" (1962). His major conceptual contribution has been his christening of one set of contextual variables in the experimental setting as "the demand characteristics of the experimental situation." The experimenter may or may not be aware of some or all of these demand characteristics, characteristics which cause the subject to redefine the intended stimulus in various unintended ways. Orne has demonstrated that the demand characteristics, rather than the intended stimuli, have been significant determinants of subjects' behvaior in experiments on hypnosis and sensory deprivation (Orne and Evans, 1965; Orne and Scheibe, 1964). He suggests that the degree of control inherent in the "quasi-magical phrase . . . this is a psychological experiment" makes the psychological experiment an unfit vehicle for the study of the effects of dangerous, illegitimate, or meaningless stimuli, for by definition the situation of being in an experiment makes the subject respond to almost anything as if it were safe, legitimate, and meaningful. This, of course, seriously restricts the range of activities open to experimental inquiry. Orne's work, while not explicitly addressed to the question of the feasibility of experimental control, has shed light on the phenomenal amount of what he calls the "fate control" held by the experimenter. Orne has also made some comments in passing upon the effect of the larger social structure and, as Boring would say, the Zeitgeist, which grant such control and power to the experimenter. For example, in an at-

[16] It is historically apt that the rediscovery of the unintended stimuli sent by experimenters should include a goodly number of studies in hypnosis besides the major work of Orne (for example, Rosenhan, 1964; Tart, 1965; Troffer and Tart, 1964). For the hypnotist Mesmer was one of the first investigators to mistake the true independent variable in his experimental procedure. As Boring wrote, "undoubtedly Mesmer's personality and his growing confidence in his power were the reasons for his power, but Mesmer did not know this" (1929, p. 101). He thought it was his apparatus. One wonders how many subsequent subjects in experiments have been "mesmerized."

tempted replication in 1960 of a study done originally in 1939, members of a nonhypnotized informal control group more readily picked up a venomous snake than did the members of the informal control group in the first study; Orne speculates that perhaps "the psychological experiment is more institutionalized for University of Sydney students in 1960 than it was for University of Tulsa students in 1939." (Orne and Evans, p. 197.)

The second major research program is that of Robert Rosenthal and his associates. It is fitting to end this historical introduction with a brief summary of Rosenthal's work, for it represents most clearly empirical psychology's belated rediscovery of the personal-equation incident.

Much of Rosenthal's work can be organized around the two factors, attitudes and individual differences, which we have seen to operate in the personal-equation incident. He has shown in experimentation on rats (Rosenthal and Fode, 1960; Rosenthal and Lawson, 1961), planaria (Rosenthal and Halas, 1962), and humans (Rosenthal, 1963a) that the experimenter's expectancy can be a significant partial determinant of the results he obtains ("experimenter bias") and that psychological experimenters can obtain significantly different data from comparable subjects ("experimenter effect"). In the paradigmatic study of experimenter bias, rats are randomly assigned to cages labeled "maze-bright" and "maze-dull" respectively. Analysis of the results of maze-learning experiments run by naïve experimenters shows that those rats labeled "maze-bright" have done significantly better than those labeled "maze-dull." In the paradigmatic study of experimenter effect, a number of experimenters carry out the same experiment, seeing subjects in two treatment groups. Then the data are analyzed by any one of a variety of possible methods to see whether experimenters get significantly different results. The effect and bias phenomena have been studied by Rosenthal's group in verbal conditioning (Rosenthal et al., 1963d), person perception (Rosenthal and Fode, 1960), maze learning, discrimination, and Skinner box problems; in individual and group situations; at various levels of experimenters' motivation; in both grief and longitudinal studies; at different universities; and by correlational as well as experimental techniques. Rosenthal has also reviewed with bibliophilic integrity the literature on observer error and observer bias in the physical and natural sciences, in interviewing, medical and psychological diagnosis, and in psychotherapy. In the light of this accumulation of evidence demonstrating the existence of effect and bias, he has proposed major reforms in the design and analysis of experiments. Of his book (Rosenthal, 1966), which pulls together this decade of activity, it may be said, as Charles Tart has noted in a more restricted context, it "should be mandatory reading for all those carrying out research . . ." (Tart, 1965, p. 88).

X

We have come full circle. After a long eclipse, studies of individual differences among experimenters and of the attitudes of experimenters have once more appeared upon the horizon of experimental psychology. The possibility rises that, just as the 1860's and 1870's saw widespread interest in and investigation of the personal equation, the 1960's and 1970's will see a similarly widespread interest in and investigation of the interpersonal equation.

In this possibility lies much hope. For, as pointed out earlier, psychologists increasingly tend to base their theories of personality, motivation, learning, memory, etc., upon the results of experimentation. But, so long as the theory and the practice of experimentation remain at odds—well, the upper stories of skyscrapers do depend for their support upon the firmness of their foundations.

However, the mediation of experimenter effect and experimenter bias through social interaction has yet to be intensively studied. And their far-flung implications for both methodology and social psychology—as well as the more general implications of looking at the psychological experiment as a social interaction—have been only dimly appreciated.

It is to such topics as these that we now turn.

II

An Experimental Study: The Mediation of Experimenter Effect and Experimenter Bias

We can study the phenomena that go on between the observer and the observed in the situation created by the observer participating with the observed.

Sullivan

We turn now from the theory of psychological experimentation to an analysis of a single psychological experiment.

At the end of the historical review I noted that, though their *occurrence* has been experimentally established, little work has yet been done on the *mediation* of experimenter effect and experimenter bias. In the absence of such research, the question which is often raised—how do they work?—often receives rather fanciful replies. Some wonder whether it is magic. Some wonder whether it is ESP.

Such appeals to the supernatural are readily understandable. They reveal that the traditional philosophy of experimentation outlined in Part I exerts a tremendous power even over those minds which are willing to accept the existence of experimenter effect and experimenter bias. For within the traditional philosophy there is no room for a mediation process. The experimenter is "understood"; experimental conditions are controlled; experimenters behave standardly. It must be magic.

However, as will become clear, when we reconceptualize the psychological experiment as a particular type of interaction in a particular social situation, the mysteriousness of the mediation process disappears. At the same time, we make a great rediscovery. The experimenter has been, if anything, "*mis*understood"; experimental conditions are not controlled; experimenters do not behave standardly.

This rediscovery could not have been made through a reading of journal reports of completed experiments. These are usually written up as if the experiments were the controlled and standardized events the philosophy of experimentation says they are. In fact, from many reports in psychological journals one cannot even be sure who interacted with the subject; methods sections do not commonly include a subheading "Experimenter(s)" to go with the common subheading "Subjects." What was needed, therefore, was an independent method of finding out what went on in a psychological experiment, a method which would incidentally throw light on the exhaustiveness or lack of exhaustiveness of journal write-ups of experiments.

Films filled the bill. In order to look at the psychological experiment in a new way (that is, from a new point of view), we literally looked at it. And when we looked we saw that experimenters differed from one another in their verbal and nonverbal behavior. And it looked as if these differences were a function of both their learned styles of dyadic interaction and their immediate expectancies.

The question at hand in this specific experiment is, then: which behaviors mediate the experimenter-effect phenomenon and which the experimenter-bias phenomenon?

2 The Person-Perception Experiment and the Filming Procedure

Nineteen experimenters engaged 107 subjects in a person-perception task.[1] The task called for each subject to rate the amount of success or failure experienced by the person pictured in each of ten photographs. In an effort to standardize the manner in which the task would be presented, the experimenters were carefully instructed as to procedure. In the "face-sheet period" of the experiment, the experimenter was to ask the subject's name, age, marital status, field of concentration, and year in school. Having recorded these preliminaries on a prepared form, the experimenter was to read to the subject from a mimeographed sheet the following instructions:

> I am going to read you some instructions. I am not permitted to say anything which is not in the instructions, nor can I answer any questions about this experiment. OK?

[1] Chapters 2 and 3 present a radically condensed version of the methods by which the films were gathered and analyzed. The more detailed and technical versions are found in the dissertation from which this is adapted (Friedman, 1965) and in a journal article based on the film analysis (Friedman et al., 1965). These lengthier expositions should be consulted by those interested in the numerous methodological subtleties which are necessarily omitted in the following chapters.

We are in the process of developing a test of empathy. This test is designed to show how well a person is able to put himself into someone else's place. I will show you a series of photographs. For each one I want you to judge whether the person pictured has been experiencing success or failure. To help you make more exact judgments you are to use this rating scale. As you can see the scale runs from − 10 to + 10. A rating of − 10 means that you judge the person to have experienced extreme failure. A rating of + 10 means that you judge the person to have experienced extreme success. A rating of − 1 means that you judge the person to have experienced mild failure, while a rating of + 1 means that you judge the person to have experienced mild success. You are to rate each photo as accurately as you can. Just tell me the rating you assign to each photo. All ready? This is photo number one.

At the moment the first photo is raised, the "instructions period" ends, and the "rating period" begins. The subject is to rate each of the ten photos. The experimenter has been instructed to allow the subject a maximum of five seconds in which to make each rating. The experimenter has been further instructed to say to the subject only what is on the instructions sheet, plus hello and good-bye at the proper times.

All the experimenters were male graduate students enrolled in a course in advanced educational psychology at the University of North Dakota. The subjects, 75 per cent of whom were females, were enrolled in beginning undergraduate courses at North Dakota.

The filming was done as part of a larger research project on experimenter bias. In accordance with the usual procedure of such experiments (Rosenthal, 1963a), experimenters' expectancies concerning the photo ratings their subjects would give them were systematically manipulated by having an assistant read the following to the experimenters just before they met each subject:

> According to several personality tests we have given the subjects, we are able to predict how they will rate the photos. Some of these subjects tend to rate the photos on the average extremely high; and some tend to rate them on the average extremely low. The next subject that you will run should average a + 5 (− 5) which is a pretty high (low) average.

Each experimenter met from three to eight subjects. For some he was given no expectancy, for some a + 5 expectancy, for some a − 5 expectancy. The order of expectancy was counter-balanced.

Actually, of course, subjects were assigned to experimenters at random. Moreover, the mean rating of the photos in the standardization group was zero (Rosenthal and Fode, 1963). Hence, the experimenters' induced expectancies were the main systematic input to the experimental sessions.[2]

The experimenters met their subjects in a room measuring about forty feet by twenty feet. Experimenters and subjects sat at a trapezoidal table expressly placed near the entrance of the room. The experimenter sat at the shorter length of the table; the subject sat at his side to the left.

A soundproof room containing a camera and cameraman had been constructed behind the wall opposite the experimenter. Unknown to either experimenters or their subjects, Robert Rosenthal filmed fifty-three of the interactions during the person-perception task.

To test the success of the various devices by which the window through which the films were made was camouflaged, a number of graduate students and faculty members were asked to sit in the chairs intended for experimenters and subjects and were invited to locate the camera and microphone. None was able to do so. When permitted to approach within a few feet of the window, however, they were able to see the camera when the shutter was fully open. Consequently a number of tables were placed between the table and the observation window to discourage exploratory behavior. From the extensive evidence of apathy displayed by both experimenters and subjects concerning the far side of the room, it seems safe to conclude that the filming proceeded undetected.

With the following limitations, the films provide a complete record of the interactions of experimenter and subject.

1. The experimenter is always on camera; the subject is sometimes not. An "average" filming pans the entire room as the subject enters, focuses on both the subject and experimenter for the greater part of the face-sheet period, zeroes in on the experimenter for part of the instructions period, draws back to include both members of the dyad as the experimenter reads, "All ready," remains with both in the picture for the early ratings, zeroes in on the experimenter again near the middle of the rating period, slowly moves back to include both parties as the rating period draws to a close, and ends with the subject rising to leave.

2. The filming of the dyad is sometimes incomplete. Often the subject has already been seated before the film begins; this eliminates observations of the greeting period. Sometimes the filming of the dyad was interrupted before the task was completed. This happened if the twelve-minute reel ended in the middle of the experimenter's third or fourth subject, or if the experimenter was exceptionally slow, in which case the filming of a dyad was occasionally purposely stopped so as to obtain on film at least a portion

---

[2] There were other systematic inputs whose effects are not considered here. Some experimenters were made more conscious of their procedure by the addition of the clause "if you follow instructions and the proper experimental procedure" to the last sentence read by the assistant. Some saw male and some female subjects. For a data analysis in terms of these inputs, see Rosenthal et al. (1963b).

of the experimenter's later encounter with a subject for whom he had the opposite expectancy.

These two limitations resulted in missing observations in the data and complicated the computer program needed for the data analysis.

A third "limitation" is of such a different order that it should scarcely be mentioned in context with the above; it is the limitation of our level of technology, a limitation to which Robert Pittenger, Charles Hockett, and John Danehy refer:

> The fullest sort of observational procedure would make use of some sort of freely repeatable record of the interview that could be examined over and over again by various specialists; say a film with not only a sound track but also an olfactory tract, a taste track, and a touch track. Such a complete record is at present technologically impossible. If it were possible its analysis would require the participation of anthropologists with specialties that do not yet exist. . . . The fullest record that at present is technologically possible is the sound film. (Pittenger, et al., 1960, p. 6.)

Thus, a final caveat before we proceed to analyze the data: our technology limits the extent of the observers' hidden presence in the experimental situation. We are there with only our eyes and our ears. But dyadic interaction can be influenced, as the halitosis commercials remind us, in other modalities too. Perhaps experimenters differ in their odors; perhaps, if we had been able to measure smells, we would have found that experimenter odor correlates more highly with subject behavior than does any of our measures. It is a possibility to keep in mind; but, in this case, of that which we did not observe, of that we shall not speak.

3

Methods: Analysis
of the Films

The films were processed. Then, to make a
pilot study, I watched them, keeping an incomplete running transcription
of what went on during each encounter. Enlightened by this experience, I
decided to put blinders on for a while and systematically study the following: experimenter glances, smiles, clothing, accuracy of instructions reading; exchange of glances between experimenter and subject; the duration of
each interaction.[1] I wanted to find out whether there was significant exper-

[1] A few words about the selection of these variables. Most are linked by varying
degrees of directness to the theory of social interaction I introduced in Part I and
which I will call for now "symbolic interactionism." However, I did not deduce
from symbolic-interaction theory that such-and-such variables should be selected for
observation and that they should have so-and-so effects. The interplay of observation
and theory was very complex, and I cannot honestly say whether my interpretation
of the results in terms of symbolic-interaction theory is *either* prediction or post-
diction. Observation and hypothesis evolved together, as did results and interpretation at a later date. My work did not conform to a hypothetico-deductive model of
scientific procedure; nor will I reconstruct it as if it did. I find Skinner's words on
this subject somewhat reassuring: ". . . it is a mistake to identify scientific practice
with the formalized constructions of . . . scientific method . . . We shall not do

imenter variation in any of these areas and, if so, whether it could mediate experimenter effects and/or biases.

The experiment was divided into the face-sheet, instructions, and photo-rating phases. Observers were equipped with materials[2] for recording, for each of these phases, how many times each experimenter glanced at each subject, how many times he smiled at each subject, how many times each experimenter and subject exchanged glances, and how long each phase lasted for each dyad. Observers also checked lists describing each experimenter's clothing, and listeners compared the instructions as heard on the sound film with the instructions as mimeographed.

Scales were then constructed from these observations. Along with appropriate dependent variables the numerical data were fed to an IBM 7090 computer programmed for a missing-observation matrix. Minutes later 2,888 correlation coefficients appeared.

A few selected aspects of this year-long process will be described in greater detail.

The observers sat in the orchestra pit of a small theater and watched the films in shifts. These shifts were arranged so that, while one person was listening to the instructions, another was watching the same film segment for exchanged glances. Actually no single verb would do justice to the position of all the observers at any one time. Now one is sitting stage left, straining to find the best angle to catch that perhaps glance of the experimenter with horned-rim glasses. Now one is prone on a table, huddled near the movie projector, ear cupped to the speaker box, trying once again to tell whether that "were" is a "was." Now one is sprawled out on a bench at the rear, resting and reading *Life against Death* while two others watch a sequence frame by frame for the nth time over, trying to decide whether that snicker was a sneer or a smile. Now one is reclining in a wooden chair to the right of the projector, munching a pastrami sandwich, kibitzing, and arbitrating a lunch-time disagreement as to how to define the three periods of the experiment when the experimenter does not do any of the things by which the periods were so meticulously defined for the observers. In this manner—and it is often done in this manner—the business of science went on.

The observers were nonplussed and elated to learn that, despite feelings of uneasiness which I experienced during the observation procedure, the reliabilities obtained are adequate (Table 1).

The reliability figures were computed by Pearson r. Fluctuations in the number of dyads observed by both raters is due both to the absence from

the young psychologist any favor if we agree to reconstruct our practices to fit the pattern demanded by current scientific methodology." (Skinner, 1959.)

[2] See the Appendix for copies of materials provided the observers.

some films of later periods of the experiment and to scheduling difficulties of the observation team.

A minimum of manipulation was needed to construct, from these observations, scales for glances, exchanges of glances, smiles, and time. For the three periods of the experiment, the scales were simply the frequency counts of one of the observers dyad by dyad. For the entire pre-rating period, the scales were constructed by adding the frequency counts for the face-sheet and the instructions period. Finally, scales for total experimenter glances, smiles, and time were made by adding the frequency counts for all three periods for the respective variables.[3] (See Table 1.) These manipulations produced eighteen scales.

Two more scales emerged from the observations of the experimenters' clothing. The first was a presence-absence scale: did the experimenter wear glasses or didn't he? The second was a three-point scale of experimenter's dress, the points labeled "formal," "informal," "casual," and the definitions being:

Formal: tie and jacket
Informal: sport shirt, collar buttoned
Casual: sport shirt, collar unbuttoned

Constructing a scale of reading accuracy proved to be more troublesome. Should grammatical errors, minute prepositional changes, paraphrasing half the instructions, and reading $+ 1$ where one was supposed to read $+ 10$ be weighted equally in deciding how accurately the instructions had been read? Obviously not. But how to decide which errors were most important, which errors could be lumped together to form a class, and which class represented a more important kind of reading error than another class?

Two categories were finally decided upon. Readings of the instructions were categorized as "accurate" or "inaccurate." Accurate readings were either perfectly faithful in content to the mimeographed sheet provided the experimenters or deviated from it only by the addition or omission of at most two sentences. Thirty-three of the dyadic interactions fell in this category. Inaccurate readings were those in which the experimenter deviated from his script in one or more serious ways: reading the instructions before gathering the face-sheet data; changing the anchoring of the scale ("Plus 10 means mild success"); paraphrasing two or more sentences; adding or omitting interpersonal references in the instructions ("I am going to read you some instructions, dear"); omitting "OK?" or "All ready?" while committing at least one other minor or major deviation from the printed instructions. Twenty of the interactions fell in this category. Only six of nineteen

[3] There is no scale for exchanged glances in the rating period and hence no scale for total exchanged glances. This is because in the rating period the experimenter holds the photo between himself and the subject. This precludes exchanged glances except in about five exceptional cases.

Table 1. Reliability Coefficients

Variable	Period	Number of Dyads Observed by Two Raters	r
Exchanged glances	Face-sheet	81*	0.7340
	Instructions	86	0.8233
	Pre-rating period	81	0.7248
E glances at S	Face-sheet	28	0.9650
	Instructions	31	0.9722
	Photo-rating period	18	0.9762
	Total experiment	18	0.9825
E smiles at S	Face-sheet	27	0.9289
	Instructions	—	——†
	Photo-rating period	18	0.8537
	Total experiment	18	0.8861
Time	Face-sheet	53	0.9947
	Instructions	53	0.9711
	Photo-rating period	49	0.9979
	Total experiment	48	0.9968

* All in all twenty-eight films were observed. The statistical part of this study is based on films 11–28, in which, as previously mentioned, nineteen experimenters interact with fifty-three subjects. On films 1–10, ten experimenters interact with thirty-three subjects. On these films, both experimenters and subjects have previously performed the person-perception task (Rosenthal *et al.*, 1963a). However, as part of the purposeful ignorance in which *all* observers were kept, I was not told that the early films featured experienced subjects. After learning this, I reasoned that, if there is any test-retest reliability to the person-perception task, this would decrease any effect the experimenter might have. Therefore, for the statistical analysis I decided to use only the data produced by inexperienced subjects. (A later check showed a test-retest correlation of .60 for subjects' mean photo ratings.) But I was informed of the difference between films 1–10 and 11–28 only after the observations had been made and reliabilities computed; hence the Ns of 81 and 86 here.

† Data were taken from the two observers whose data are used throughout, but who, in this instance, watched different dyads. Their reliability with a third observer, none of whose data were used, was 0.6731 (N = 53) and 0.7617 (N = 31).

experimenters had no readings which fell in the category labeled "inaccurate." [4]

As a kind of shorthand I have thought of these two categories as representing "journal" and "nonjournal" readings of the instructions. By this I

[4] The division of the readings into the inaccurate-accurate dichotomy correlates approximately .75 with a scale of "total reading errors" in which every word added to or omitted from the printed instructions is weighted equally. For more on variations in the instructions period see Chapter 5, sections V to X.

mean that for the "accurate" readings the customary procedure of saying in journal articles that the experimenters read the content of the instructions as printed is substantially though not exactly correct, whereas for the "inaccurate" readings it is neither substantially nor exactly correct.

Each category was operationally defined for the listeners much more explicitly than is done here. The interjudge reliability of sorting readings into these two categories was 1.

The manipulations discussed so far produced twenty-one scales which measured variations in behavior in the experimental situation. These became the independent variables. To these were then added two dependent variables: (1) the mean of the photo ratings given by each subject; (2) the experimenter's "bias score." The latter was defined in various ways; the most conceptually satisfying was as follows: the bias score was defined as the mean of the ratings an experimenter obtained from the filmed subjects for whom he had $+5$ expectancies *minus* the mean of the ratings he obtained from filmed subjects for whom he had -5 expectancies. Thus, a higher bias score would indicate a better biaser.

The question was whether the subject's response or the extent to which it was biased could be predicted from knowing, say, how many glances he or she exchanged with the experimenter or how many seconds the instructions period lasted or how many times in the face-sheet period the experimenter smiled, etc.[5]

II

Before we can fairly evaluate the answers to these questions, we must consider another one.

Doing research on the behavior of experimenters makes one self-conscious as to his own behavior as a researcher of research. The question is sometimes asked: Are you the only one who is biased? I will discuss the

[5] The correlations of the twenty-one situational variables with the two dependent variables are central to this work. I should mention, however, that other variables, which will be referred to here only subordinately, were also included in the matrix that went to the computer. Some were antecedent measures of "stable" experimenter and subject attributes (e.g., anxiety, social desirability). Some were ratings of the filmed experimenters upon global dimensions (e.g., dominance, professionalism, friendliness, activity, likability). These global ratings were made by Rosenthal, Persinger, Mulry, Vikan-Kline, and Grothe while all were still at North Dakota. There is an outside possibility that these ratings are contaminated. (See Rosenthal, 1964, p. 37.) Some were behavioral measures of the experimenter at specific points in the experiment (e.g., E smiles at S at "Name"; E looks at S at "OK"). Some were observations of various kinds of experimenters' nonverbal behavior (e.g., body slant, head activity). These observations were made under the supervision of Richard Katz who kindly made them available to me. Some were alternative measures of experimenter bias (e.g., an S bias score).

implications of this question more fully when I discuss the problem of the generalizability of these results. Now, before turning to the results, I want to review some of the precautions which were taken so as to insure finding, if any, their fingerprints and not our own.[6]

It is important to recognize at the outset that the observers could not have perpetrated the same kind of experimenter effect or bias that is being studied here. That is the beauty of working with films rather than with live subjects. That is, the kind of bias and effect being studied here occurs when the subject *actually* gives either the desired response or a response he would not give to another experimenter. Since experiments in progress are seldom observed, this is a less public type of error than is one of observation or interpretation (Rosenthal, 1963e). However, films remain the same, though observers may vary.

The only way that bias similar to the one being studied could have occurred would have been if the filmer, who knew what expectancy the experimenter had, had filmed experimenters with different expectancies in different manners. For example, if the experimenter had a $+5$ expectancy, the filmer might have focused the camera on him when he smiled whereas, if the experimenter had a -5 expectancy, the filmer might have turned the camera away from him just before he seemed ready to smile. This would represent a recording bias which to someone working solely from the films would seem to be an actual difference.

However, we are well protected against this rather far-fetched possibility by the circumstances that the filmer (RR) had a theoretical orientation in mind when he made the films which is quite different from my orientation. His hypothesis was, to put it metaphorically, that something "in" the experimenter (e.g., anxiety, dominance) would correlate with experimenter bias. That is why the camera sometimes zooms in on the experimenter and leaves the subject off screen. But since the mediating variables I have used are *behaviors* in the experiment rather than experimenter *attributes*, it seems that whatever possibility of bias there might have been in the filming procedure could not have been systematic, or rather could only have been according to a different system.

The real problem was to guard against observer error or observer bias. Accordingly the following precautions were taken: at no time before or during the observation procedure did any of the observers (including myself) have access to information concerning either the expectancy of any experimenter or his bias score. The observers were able to see the assistant give the expectancy to the experimenter about four times, but each time the sequence had been cut from the film just before the magic number ($+5$ or -5) was uttered. As noted above (footnote to Table 1), the observers did not even know that the experimenters in the earlier films were

[6] Donald Cohen suggested this suggestive metaphor to me.

experienced while those in the later films were naïve. Nor did we know that in some of the early films the experimenters had the same expectancy for all their subjects.

Finally, at no time during the subsequent handling of the data—computing reliabilities, making up scales, selecting which observers' data to enter into the matrix—did the persons involved know either the expectancies of the experimenter or the ratings of the subject.[7]

To the best of my knowledge, the observation and analysis of the films was carried out "blind." However, one need not simply take my word for this. Again, that is one of the scientific advantages of working with films. They can be viewed over and over again, and in this way independent checks upon any team of observers can and should be made.

---

[7] A single exception: observations of the photo-rating period were sometimes made with the sound on. In such cases the observers could hear some of the subject's photo ratings. However, the poor quality of the sound track plus the sheer difficulty of adding up and taking the mean of ten (at best) faintly heard photo ratings while busily counting glances or smiles makes this seem unlikely as a source of bias.

Hypotheses, Results, Discussion of Results

My guiding notion was that in many ways experimenters behave differently from one another, even though they are not supposed to do so. Scales were developed for some of the variables on which I thought they might behave differently, variables which have been pointed to by the symbolic interactionists as affecting the course of interaction. My *general* notions were that in the interaction of experimenter and subject (1) some of these variations mediate the "experimenter effect" phenomenon and (2) some mediate the "experimenter bias" phenomenon.

Since the correlation statistic is based upon variance, if the behaviors of the experimenters correlate significantly with the *photo ratings* given by the subjects, my guiding notion and my first general notion are supported. If the behaviors correlate with the experimenter's *bias score*, my second general notion is supported. Since the experimenter-bias scores and the subjects' ratings can be related in many ways, it is possible to get some behaviors mediating the effect phenomenon and some the bias phenomenon.[1]

Bringing together the twenty-one scales of behavior in the experiment

---

[1] It turns out that for this sample effect and bias are correlated only .005. Hence, they will be treated independently.

and the two dependent variables—the subjects' ratings and the experimenters' bias scores—I have altogether forty-two *specific* hypotheses, each to be tested by Pearson r, all significance tests to be two-tailed (see Table 2).

Table 3 summarizes the main results concerning the mediation of experimenter effects. Only p levels of .05 or less will be considered. Inspection of the table shows that six of the hypotheses are confirmed at the .05 level and that three of these are confirmed beyond the .01 level. Statistical analyses indicate that these results could occur by chance alone very seldom.[2]

All the significant correlations are in the positive direction. They should be read as follows:

1. The more glances exchanged between experimenter and subject in the instructions period, the more likely the subject is to perceive success in neutral photos ($r = .41, df = 51, p < .01$).

2. The greater the number of times the experimenter glances at the subject in the instructions period, the more likely the subject is to perceive success in neutral photos ($r = .27, df = 51, p = .05$).

3. The longer the duration of the instructions period, the more likely the subject is to perceive success in neutral photos ($r = .43, df = 51, p = .005$).

4. The longer the duration of the pre-rating period, the more likely the subject is to perceive success in neutral photos ($r = .36, df = 33, p = .04$).

5. The longer the duration of the rating period, the more likely the subject is to perceive success in neutral photos ($r = .36, df = 46, p < .02$).

6. The longer the duration of the total experiment, the more likely the subject is to perceive success in neutral photos ($r = .46, df = 33, p = .007$).

One might ask whether variations in experimenter behavior in the face-sheet, instructions, pre-rating period, or the entire experiment make the most difference. Alternatively, one might ask whether variations in experimenter glances, exchanged glances, experimenter smiles, or time make the most difference. Table 4 combines these questions.

[2] It should be mentioned that the entire correlation matrix was tested for possible randomness and this possibility could safely be rejected. Various kinds of statistical tests other than those reported here were applied to the data resulting from different definitions of "effect" and "bias." I am reporting those results which hold up regardless of the particular test employed. I have placed numerical probability values only where they seem to be reached by various statistical methods. In other places I have used terms like "very seldom" since there is general controversy about certain statistical manipulations and hence citing an exact numerical probability value would be impressive but also misleading. Someone might some day consider in greater detail the amount of "effect" and "bias" which can come about through the many degrees of freedom the researcher has in choosing his favorite statistic! I have tried to be conservative and, if anything, err in the direction of minimizing the number of correlations considered significant.

Table 2. Forty-two Hypotheses

Hypotheses

1–6   The number of glances exchanged in the instructions period will correlate with the Ss' photo ratings, Es' bias score.

     face-sheet
     pre-rating

7–16   The number of experimenter glances at the subject in the pre-rating period will correlate with the Ss' photo ratings, Es' bias score.

     face-sheet period
     instructions period
     rating period
     total experiment

17–26   The number of experimenter smiles in the pre-rating period will correlate with the Ss' photo ratings, Es' bias score.

     face-sheet period
     instructions period
     rating period
     total experiment

27–36   The duration of the pre-rating period will correlate with the Ss' photo ratings, Es' bias score.

     face-sheet period
     instructions period
     rating period
     total experiment

37–38   Whether or not the experimenter wears glasses will correlate with the Ss' photo ratings, Es' bias score.

39–40   The experimenters' score on a formal/casual dress scale will correlate with the Ss' photo ratings, Es' bias score.

41–42   The accuracy of the experimenters' reading of the instructions will correlate with the Ss' photo ratings, Es' bias score.

Table 3. *Correlations of Behaviors in the Experiment and Subjects' Photo Ratings*

	N	r	p
The number of glances exchanged in the instructions period will correlate with the Ss' photo ratings.			
face-sheet	48	.10	
instructions period	53	.41	<.01
pre-rating	48	.27	(.07)
The number of experimenter glances at the subject in the pre-rating period will correlate with Ss' photo ratings.			
face-sheet period	48	−.12	
instructions period	53	.27	.05
pre-rating period	35	.00	
rating period	48	.05	
total experiment	35	.05	
The number of experimenter smiles in the pre-rating period will correlate with the Ss' photo ratings.			
face-sheet period	48	.05	
instructions period	53	.13	
pre-rating period	35	.08	
rating period	48	.09	
total experiment	35	.14	
The duration of the pre-rating period will correlate with the Ss' photo ratings.			
face-sheet period	48	.13	
instructions period	53	.43	.005
pre-rating period	35	.36	.04
rating period	48	.36	<.02
total experiment	35	.46	.007
Whether or not the experimenter wears glasses will correlate with the Ss' photo ratings.	53	.27	(.06)
The experimenters' score on a formal/casual dress scale will correlate with the Ss' photo ratings.	53	.13	
The accuracy of the experimenters' reading of the instructions will correlate with the Ss' photo ratings.	53	−.08	

Table 4.   *Correlations of Behavior in the Experiment with Subjects' Photo Ratings by Variable and Period*

	E glances	Exchanged Glances	E Smiles	Time	Mean Correlation
Face-sheet	−.12	.10	.05	.13	.04
Instructions	.27	.41	.13	.43	.31
Pre-rating	.05	.27	.09	.36	.19
Rating	.00		.08	.36	.15
Total	.05		.14	.46	.18
Mean correlation	.05	.26	.10	.35	

It shows that, of the variables, time and exchange of glances correlate most highly on the average with subjects' ratings and that, of the periods, the instructions period seems to be the one that makes the most difference.

This evidence suggests that it is the variables time and exchange of glances, and the instructions period, to which we should devote our discussion of the mediation of experimenter effect.

Table 5 summarizes the main results concerning the mediation of experimenter biases. Only p levels of .05 or less will be considered. Inspection of the table shows that two of the hypotheses are confirmed at the .02 level and that one of these is confirmed beyond the .01 level. Again, statistical analyses indicate these results could occur by chance alone very seldom.

One of the correlations is significant in the negative direction and one in the positive direction. They should be read as follows:

1. The fewer the number of glances exchanged between experimenter and subject in the instructions period, the better biaser the experimenter is likely to be ($r = -.31, df = 51, p < .02$).

2. The more accurately the experimenter reads the instructions, the better biaser the experimenter is likely to be ($r = .52, df = 51, p < .001$).

* There is a possible objection to the interpretation of Pearson r with the experimenter bias score. The bias score is a repeated entry, and each experimenter ($N = 19$) reads to and exchanges glances with two or three subjects. Hence it is possible that the assumptions for Pearson r are violated; they are not violated in other cases since the *dyad* and not the experimenter is taken as the unit. However, employing an S *bias score* which is not a repeated number does not essentially change the picture. The correlation between the number of exchanged glances in the instructions period and the S bias score is $-.34$ ($df = 34, p < .02$). The correlation between the accuracy with which the experimenter reads the instructions and the S bias score is .42 ($df = 34, p < .01$). The definition of the S bias score is that when the experimenter has a $+5$ expectancy the subject's bias score is his mean rating of the photos minus the mean photo rating of the subjects for whom that experimenter had a -5 expectancy. When the experimenter has a -5 expectancy, the subject's bias score is the mean photo rating of the subjects for whom that experimenter had a $+5$ expectancy minus the subject's mean rating of the photos.

Table 5. *Correlations of Behaviors in the Experiment and Experimenter Bias Score*

	N	r	p
The number of glances exchanged in the instructions period will correlate with the Es' bias score.			
face-sheet	48	.04	
instructions period	53	−.31	<.02
pre-rating	48	−.07	
The number of experimenter glances at the subject in the pre-rating period will correlate with Es' bias score.			
face-sheet period	48	.13	
instructions period	53	−.06	
pre-rating period	35	.20	
rating period	48	.22	
total experiment	35	.22	
The number of experimenter smiles in the pre-rating period will correlate with the Es' bias score.			
face-sheet period	48	.07	
instructions period	53	−.07	
pre-rating period	35	−.03	
rating period	48	.05	
total experiment	35	−.05	
The duration of the pre-rating period will correlate with the Es' bias score.			
face-sheet period	48	−.04	
instructions period	53	−.14	
pre-rating period	35	.04	
rating period	48	−.01	
total experiment	35	.05	
Whether or not the experimenter wears glasses will correlate with the Es' bias score.	19	.20	
The experimenters' score on a formal/casual dress scale will correlate with the Es' bias score.	19	−.15	
The accuracy of the experimenters' reading of the instructions will correlate with the Es' bias score.	53	.52	<.001*

II

Let me drop, for the moment, the vocabulary of effect and bias and try to say over again in ordinary English what these results show. They show that these experimenters behaved differently from one another in conducting this experiment. If they hadn't, there would be no variance in one of the things to be correlated and all correlations would be zero. The results also show that these differences made a difference; that is, what the experimenter did in the experiment was a partial determinant of what the subject did.

That these results have broad implications for the philosophy of psychological experimentation and the philosophy of psychology will be clear to anyone who has kept in mind the popularly held philosophy of psychological experimentation and the philosophy of psychology outlined in Part I. Experimenters are not supposed to vary or be variable in their behavior. Like psychoanalysts, they are supposed to be blank screens. They are supposed all to be cut from the same pattern. If they were, then the experimental manipulation (the independent variable) could be isolated as the determinant of the subjects' responses. Or, in a correlational as opposed to an experimental study (Cronbach, 1957), antecedent intrapsychic variables associated with individual differences among subjects could be used by themselves to predict the subjects' responses.

The only problem is that, just as analysts are not blank screens, so experimenters are neither homogeneous nor anonymous. And because of this, those aspects of contemporary methodological and philosophical thinking in the social sciences which depend upon the experimenter's being conceptualized as a nonperson will have to be reconsidered. Just how much of contemporary social scientific thinking does depend upon this illusion is a complicated and controversial issue which will be taken up in later chapters. There I will sketch in some of the implications of the confirmation of the *general* notions that experimenters behave variably in their interactions with subjects and that these variations can mediate experimenter effects and experimenter biases. The present discussion, in contrast, will be limited primarily to a discussion of why, in this experiment, of the *specific* hypotheses, the ones dealing with exchange of glances, time, reading accuracy, and the instructions period were supported.

The psychological experiment is often discussed as if it were an experiment in the natural sciences. This analogy has produced a formal psychological vocabulary which speaks the language of stimuli, responses, apparatus, operational definitions, statistical manipulations, and laboratory procedures. But the analogy tends to obscure consideration of the fact that the psychological experiment often consists of two people exchanging some time together in a closed room ("laboratory") in some building, in some area of the country, at a certain period in history.[3] In other words, like all analogies, the assimilation of the psychological experiment to the vocabulary of experiments in the natural, physical, and physiological realms conceals as much as it reveals. And, though it is true that every way of seeing is also a way of not seeing, some ways are less helpful than others.

In order to comprehend the results reported here, we have to begin to think of the person-perception experiment—and the psychological experiment in general—as a social occasion. Goffman defines a social occasion as existing "when persons come into each other's immediate presence" (1963a, p. 18). One special form of the social occasion is the face-to-face focused interaction which Goffman calls a "face engagement":

> Face engagements comprise all those instances of two or more participants in a situation joining each other openly in maintaining a single focus of cognitive and visual attention—what is sensed as a single mutual activity, entailing preferential communication rights . . . Mutual activities and the face engagements in which they are embedded comprise instances of small talk, commensalism, love-making, gaming, formal discussion, and personal servicing (treating, selling, waitressing, and so forth). (Goffman, 1963a, p. 89.)

The person-perception task can be considered a face engagement with an instrumental rationale and a preordained division of labor, including a predetermined division of definitional labor which cedes to the experimenter the right to define the situation for the subject. This means that

> Characteristically, the experimenter gives the instructions, decides when the action starts and stops, and hands out the measuring instruments. The experimenter does the talking while the subject listens. The latter is a status subordinate who presumably listens in order to

[3] For the effects of different rooms on experimental results see Rosenthal and Haley (1964). For the effect of the area of the country see Griffith (1961): "As the situation now rests alcoholics perceive more water [in Rorschach blots] in Kentucky; in Massachusetts and Washington they do not" (p. 311). Griffith goes on to relate this discrepancy to the fact that unlike the other two states, Kentucky has no coastline. For the possible misinterpretations that can arise when experimental and control groups are seen in different locations see Haley (1964, p. 7): "The naïveté evident in the past . . . is illustrated by the tests given to schizophrenics in hospitals to measure their anxiety levels (or any other supposed characteristic of schizophrenics) with control groups composed of college students. Schizophrenics are found to be more anxious, and this is said to be a different something *within* them. If the hospital is a savage place where the patient is caught up in a network of relationships where anything might be done to him, it would seem reasonable to assume that a difference in test results is a product of a difference in the context unless one can assume that the college environment is equally savage." For the possible effect of the period in history see Orne and Evans (1965, p. 197), and the discussion later in this chapter.

find his place in the situation—a situation that is oriented around the experimenter's purposes. (Riecken, 1958, p. 11.)

Goffman points out two crucial characteristics of encounters of copresence:

> When one speaks of experiencing someone else with one's naked senses, one usually implies the reception of embodied messages. This linkage of naked senses on one side and embodied transmission on the other provides one of the crucial communication conditions of face-to-face interaction. Under this condition any message that an individual sends is likely to be *qualified and modified by much additional information that others glean from him simultaneously, often unbeknownst to him* . . .
>
> Ordinarily . . . in using the naked senses to receive embodied messages from others, the individual also makes himself available as a source of embodied information for them. . . . Here then is a second crucial communication condition of face-to-face interaction: not only are the receiving and conveying of the naked and embodied kind, but each giver is himself a receiver, and each receiver a giver.

In a magnificent paragraph, Goffman draws out the conclusion of these communication characteristics:

> . . . sight begins to take on an added and special role . . . Each individual can see that he is being experienced in some way. . . . Further, he can be seen to be seeing this, and can see that he has been seen seeing this. Ordinarily, then, to use our naked senses is to use them nakedly and to be made naked by their use. (Goffman, 1963a, pp. 14–16.)

What is the relevance of the framework of face-to-face interaction to the interpretation of these results? I want to explain why mutual glances between experimenter and subject are associated with the subject's perception of success in neutral photos. Georg Simmel wrote:

> Of the special sense-organs, the eye has a uniquely sociological function. The union and interaction of individuals is based upon mutual glances. This is perhaps the most direct and purest reciprocity which exists anywhere. This highest psychic reaction, however, in which the glances of eye to eye unite men, crystallizes into no objective structure; the unity which momentarily arises between two persons is present in the occasion and dissolved in the function. So tenacious and subtle is this union that it can only be maintained by the shortest and straightest line between the eyes, and the smallest deviation from it, the slightest glance aside, completely destroys the unique character of this

union. No objective trace of this relationship is left behind, as is universally found in, directly or indirectly, all other types of associations between men, as, for example, in interchange of words. The interaction of eye and eye dies in the moment in which the directness of the function is lost. But the totality of social relations of human beings, their self-assertion and self-abnegation, their intimacies and estrangements, would be changed in unpredictable ways if there occurred no glance of eye to eye. This mutual glance between persons, in distinction from the simple sight or observation of the other, signifies a wholly new and unique union between them. (Simmel, 1921, p. 358.)

And Goffman adds:

Eye-to-eye looks . . . play a special role in the communication life of the community . . . mutual glances ordinarily must be withheld if an encounter is to be avoided, for eye contact opens one up for face engagement . . . an eye-to-eye ecological huddle [tends to produce] a shared definition of the situation . . . a "working consensus," involving a degree of mutual considerateness, sympathy, and a meeting of opinion differences. Often a group atmosphere develops—what Bateson has called "ethos" . . . A "we-rationale" develops. (Goffman, 1963a, pp. 92–98.)

A prosaic deduction from these paeans to the mutual glance would be that in exchanging glances with the experimenter, the subject is given a "good" experience; he feels accepted; he feels that their interaction has been "warm." He has no context in the picture from which to judge whether the person pictured has been experiencing success or failure. Might it not be that he uses the feeling-tone of his interaction with the experimenter in making his judgment? Having felt success, does he perceive success?

What about time? Why should the duration of all periods of the experiment except the face-sheet period correlate with the subject's ratings? Why should the dyad's being in existence for a longer time be associated with the subject's perceiving success?

When we think about time, our thoughts often run in metaphors. Frequently we speak of "the river of time." Then the temptation arises to drop the variable and conclude that time is merely the medium in which whatever is correlating with the subject's photo ratings goes on. Such an approach would treat the duration of interaction as a vehicle rather than as a means in itself of nonverbal communication.

It is probably better to think of time as a relevant variable in this experiment than as an artifact. In general, if two strangers come together for a brief face engagement, the longer they stay together the more likely they are to have a good feeling about their interaction. This conclusion is suggested by the complicated etiquette of interaction which Goffman has so vividly described (1955). To the extent that both parties comply with the social norms of "face-work" and, to vary the anatomical metaphor, keep from stepping on each other's toes, to that extent the more time they are together, the warmer the interaction.

It may also be true that in an experiment in a college setting as distinguished from certain other focused or unfocused dyadic interactions, special factors may make the duration of the experiment important. I will suggest just two of these. As will be described in greater detail in Chapter 5, the experiment can proceed with bureaucratic curtness. In such a case, the subject may feel as though he is being treated like an object, a means to an end, an uninteresting appendage to an interesting numerical score. To the extent that the greater length of time spent in the interaction indicates to the subject that he is being treated as a human being of some intrinsic interest or worth, to that extent he may have a better feeling about it. College students who are intensely concerned about issues such as whether the college is simply a factory performing mechanical functions with impersonal efficiency do not enter the experiment having forgotten totally such broader concerns. It is also most likely to be college-age people who are concerned with seeing either experimenters or therapists "face to face," both literally and metaphorically (Erikson, 1958, p. 17). In any case, the film analysis shows that although the duration of the entire experiment varies only from two and a half to five minutes, the longer the experiment takes—regardless of any one specific activity which takes place in that time —the more likely it will be that the subject leaves with a smile rather than a shrug.

Thus, for both general and specific reasons, except in the case of those experiments in which the independent variables are shocks or the like, the longer (within limits) the experimenter and subject interact, the more likely it will be that the subject feels the experimenter is interested in him, cares about him as a person, accepts him, etc. And so, by the same reasoning that was applied to the mutual glance, the longer the interaction, the more likely the subject will perceive success in the neutral photos.

Taken together, these two interpretations amount to a projection hypothesis—a projection hypothesis which I put forward very tentatively: the subject sees in the photos what his interaction with the experimenter leads him to feel himself. Support for such a hypothesis can be found in some of Rosenthal's earlier studies using the same task.

In one study (Rosenthal et al., 1960) all experimenters were given an expectancy of getting on the average ratings of $+7$ from their subjects. After the experiment was concluded, each subject filled out a questionnaire dealing with his perception of his experimenter. The study was designed to discover whether experimenters who are better biasers are seen differently by their subjects than are experimenters who are worse biasers; but since, in the study, bias and perception of success in the photos are practically co-varied, it is possible to look at the results as indicating the association between the subject's perception of the experimenter and the experimenter's obtaining plus data.

Four of the reported correlations are relevant. All four fit the interpretation being presented here. Experimenters who obtain perceptions of success are liked ($r = .56$, $p = .10$), are rated as "personal" ($r = .53$, $p = .10$), "interested" ($r = .71$, $p = .01$), and "slow-speaking" ($r = .64$, $p = .05$). I understand the latter correlation in connection with the finding that the longer the experiment takes, the more perception of success there is.

Another source of support is a study which was designed to find out whether elimination of verbal or visual cues makes more of a difference in reducing experimenter bias (Rosenthal and Fode, 1963). In the nonverbal group (i.e., the experimenters did not speak to their subjects), all experimenters expected to get photo ratings averaging $+ 5$; that is, expectancy and perception of success were covaried. Hence, the results can be interpreted as referring to plus-getting.

The nonverbal group failed to obtain data in the expected ($+ 5$) direction. In fact, the nonverbal group mean was nearly identical with the mean of a control group which was led to expect $- 5$ data. Thus, "an . . . interpretation of the performance of the nonverbal group's Ss might be that rather than not having biased into the ($+ 5$) direction as predicted, they were actively biased into the ($- 5$) direction" (Rosenthal and Fode, 1963, p. 499).

It is highly likely that these silent experimenters were perceived by their subjects as cold, nonaccepting, unfriendly, etc. If so, then these data support the interpretation that subjects who experience interpersonal failure in their relation with the experimenter are likely to perceive failure in the photos. As Rosenthal and Fode put it, "Possibly the climate created by a silent E led to Ss' seeing the people on the photos as less successful" (1963, p. 499).

A study of the effect of early data returns on data subsequently obtained by biased experimenters can likewise be interpreted in such a way as to provide support for a projection hypothesis (Rosenthal et al., 1963c). In this study all experimenters were led to expect on the average photo ratings of $+ 5$ from their subjects. One group of experimenters obtained $+ 5$ data from their first two subjects, who were accomplices; another group obtained $- 5$ data from their first two subjects, who were also accomplices. Experimenters in each group then met four naïve subjects. Results indicated that experimenters who obtained from the accomplices data in line with their expectancies also obtained the expected data from their naïve subjects, while experimenters who obtained from the accomplices data contrary to their expectancies continued to obtain contrary data from their naïve subjects.

Now since expectancy and plus-getting are covaried in the study, the results also indicate that those experimenters who obtained + 5 ratings from the accomplices continued to obtain + 5 ratings from their naïve subjects, whereas those experimenters who obtained − 5 ratings from the accomplices continued to obtain − 5 ratings from their naïve subjects.

One of Rosenthal's interpretations of the results of the study is that if the experimenter has received from the accomplices + 5 ("good") data his "mood may . . . be considerably brightened, and this might lead him to be a more 'likeable,' 'personable,' and 'interested' person in his interaction with subsequent subjects," in which case he continues to get plus data. But if the experimenter has received − 5 ("bad") data "he may experience a mood change making him less 'likeable,' 'personable,' and 'interested,' " whereupon he continues to get minus data (Rosenthal et al., 1963c, p. 497).

One final source of support may be mentioned. It comes from an examination of some of the correlations between the global ratings referred to in Chapter 3 (footnote 7), the subjects' photo ratings, and the observations of exchanged glances in and the duration of the instructions period.

There is a significant negative correlation between ratings of experimenters' professionalism and subjects' photo ratings ($r = -.33$, $df = 51$, $p < .02$). And there is a significant negative correlation between ratings of experimenters' friendliness and ratings of experimenters' professionalism ($r = -.30$, $df = 51$, $p = .02$). That is, experimenters who are rated as more professional are also rated as less friendly. And what do experimenters who are rated as more professional (i.e., less friendly) do? They exchange few glances with their subjects in the instructions period ($r = -.40$, $df = 51$, $p < .01$) and go through the instructions period quickly ($r = -.31$, $df = 51$, $p = .02$).

So it seems that experimenters who exchange few glances with the subject in the instructions period and go through the instructions period quickly are rated by observers as less friendly and obtain perception of failure in the photos. If the subjects experience the experimenters in the same way as the experimenters are rated by the observers, these results are consistent with a projection hypothesis.

Having felt success, does the subject perceive success? Despite the supporting evidence discussed above, I continue to put the interpretation in its weak rhetorical form both because without my adding a great deal of excess philosophical verbiage it smacks of an explanation according to the myth of "the ghost in the machine" model (Ryle, 1949) and because I am aware that simple theories of projection have not stood like powerful oaks before the storm of empirical inquiry. However, there are a few factors which raise this interpretation above the level of the simple projection hypotheses usually studied. For one thing, the inference that the subject experiences "success" is based upon observation of what went on in the experiment, rather than on what experience the experimental design was *intended* to create for the subject. Moreover, I know of no projection study in which the manipulated variables were mutual glancing or duration of the experimental interaction. And finally I must emphasize the fact that it was not just the exchange of glances in any phase of the experiment or the experiment as a whole, which is the usual unit of study, but exchange of glances in the *instructions period* that made a difference.

This leads me to the last of the findings whose discussion with reference to the mediation of experimenter effect was promised. Why should the instructions period prove to be so crucial?

It is difficult to say. A number of factors might account for this result. Riecken (1958) suggests that of all the phases of the experiment it is in the instructions phase that the subject is most alert, for he is trying his hardest at this point to see through the instructions in order to read the latent purpose of the experiment. It may be that in the instructions period the subject who is hoping that the experimenter will give himself away is most alive to the cues and clues which the experimenter intentionally or unintentionally gives off.

An alternative (or supplementary) explanation would turn from a consideration of the subject's situation to that of the experimenter. The instructions period presents the experimenter with a problem. He has to read the instructions, and he has to read them to someone sitting at the table with him. Faced with this potential dichotomy, the experimenters split into those who are task-oriented and those who are interpersonally oriented. On a viewing of the films this division is quite striking. Some experimenters cut off all interaction with the subject and bury their heads in the instructions sheet. Others look up at the subject from time to time (or even from sentence to sentence) in order to check to see that the subject is getting the message. It seems that this looking up—especially when it is reciprocated—itself becomes a message which influences the subject to give positive data.

These explanations are put forth very tentatively. Indeed, psychologists know woefully little about what goes on "in the head" of the subject as he sits outwardly docile and is read to. But, whatever the interpretation, the finding that it is the instructions period which makes such a difference in the subjects' responses, and not the experimenters' behavior in the rating period itself, argues against an interpretation of the mediation process along the lines of simple conditioning theory, for in the instructions period the subject makes no rating of the photo to be conditioned.

III

In this correlation matrix there is more experimenter effect than experimenter bias. A reciprocal relation between the two makes sense. For, as I have defined them, experimenter effect represents a kind of within-treatment variance. Therefore, the larger it is, the less chance that the result of the treatment condition will be able to transcend this variance.

On the whole, then, this group of experimenters did not display experimenter bias. Why? Well, for one thing, though the group was a "group" in the sense that all the experimenters were males who were naïve to the task, it did consist of three subgroups: more procedure-conscious experimenters meeting female subjects, less procedure-conscious experimenters meeting female subjects, and more procedure-conscious experimenters meeting male subjects. Elsewhere evidence has been presented that under some of these conditions bias is likely to occur, while under others "reverse bias" is found (Rosenthal *et al.*, 1963b). It could be that these cancel each other out when the subgroups are combined.

However, there is a theoretically more interesting possibility. That is that under certain social-psychological conditions of induced expectancy and incentive for fulfilling the expectancy, bias is less likely to occur than under other conditions.[4]

For example, in one of the studies which most clearly demonstrated the occurrence of experimenter bias (Rosenthal and Fode, 1963), the experimenters were undergraduates in a course in experimental psychology. The rationale for the induced expectancy fit the students' situation. It was that they were replicating "well-established experimental findings as students in physics labs are expected to do" (p. 494). The appeal to tradition ("well-established") is thus beautifully combined with the appeal to the prestigious discipline ("as students in physics labs"). Moreover, the study was structured as a lab exercise, and experimenters were offered a dollar an hour for their participation and two dollars an hour if they did a good job.

I consider the monetary payment in the study to be icing on the cake. The important thing seems to me to be that the payment would not have been seen as bribery because the rationale for fulfilling the induced expectancy had been meaningfully related to the beliefs (replication), role situation (a lab exercise), and internalized status symbols (physics) of the

---

[4] I think it is worthwhile to make this rather obvious point because, in a reaction against the belief that in psychological experiments bias is impossible, some people, despite Rosenthal's protestations to the contrary, have come to feel that bias (getting the results you believe in or want) is inevitable. But the world is not all that co-operative. It should be pointed out that the inevitability theory of bias presents an empirical quandary: if experimenter bias were inevitable, it could never be experimentally demonstrated, for all experimental demonstrations of bias would themselves inevitably be biased.

experimenters. The expectancy had been legitimated in terms which the experimenters were likely to accept.

In the present study, however, the expectancy was induced on the basis of the results of unnamed personality tests. (And it is at least conceivable that experimenters at North Dakota knew something about the predictive validity of personality tests.) Moreover, the experimenters were volunteers and were in no other subordinate-superordinate (e.g., student-teacher) role relation to the investigators. And they had no personal stake in the results (e.g., they were not fulfilling a lab exercise).

It is probable that when expectancies are induced in these different ways, and when the incentives for fulfilling the expectancies are different, the treatment conditions will be differentially effective. Relative to each other, the manipulation used in the first study decreases experimenter effect and increases experimenter bias; the manipulation used in this study increases experimenter effect and decreases experimenter bias.

But this study was not designed to see if experimenter bias exists. The important point is that within the overall picture, there are individual differences. Some experimenters proved to be better biasers than others. These gradations are reflected in the experimenter bias scores. The higher the bias score, the better the biaser. Hence, it is possible to say something about the mediation of experimenter bias by seeing what experimenter behaviors correlate with the bias score.

As we have seen, these behaviors are correctness of instruction reading, which correlates positively with bias, and exchanged glances in the instructions period, which correlates negatively with bias.

These two behavioral variables, which correlate $-.38$ with each other, can best be subsumed for purposes of interpretation through the global construct of *professionalism*. There is a significant positive correlation between correctness of instruction reading and global ratings of how professional the experimenter is $(r = .54)$. And there is a significant negative correlation between the number of glances exchanged in the instructions period and ratings of how professional the experimenter is $(r = -.40)$.

Now, of all the global ratings (dominance, activity, likability, friendliness, professionalism), it is the professional dimension that correlates most highly with the experimenter bias score. In this sample, the more professional the experimenter is rated to be, the significantly more likely he is to be a good biaser $(r = .60, df = 51, p < .0001)$. This finding fits in with Rosenthal's general conclusion that the experimenter with the more professional manner is more likely to bias his subjects (Rosenthal, 1964). One contribution of this study has been to specify two of the components that go into the make-up of the global rating of experimenter professionalism, each of which by itself correlates with experimenter bias.

In other words, generally speaking, there are experimenters who read the instructions correctly and do not exchange glances with their subjects during the instructions period. They are rated as "professional"; they are good biasers. And there are experimenters who do not read the instructions correctly and do exchange glances with their subjects during the instructions period. They are rated as "nonprofessional"; they are not good biasers.[5]

A question remains: why should experimenters who are rated as more professional be more likely to obtain the results they expect than experimenters who are rated as less professional? To end these explanations on the note that it is some experimenter attribute ("professionalism") that accounts for experimenter bias would be to perpetuate in reverse the individualistic framework in which some *subject attribute* was called upon to account for experimental results. Instead of simply replacing "subject explanations" by "experimenter explanations" we have to develop an "experimenter and subject" explanation.

Interesting answers of this kind to the question of why the experimenter's professionalism is a factor in obtaining the results he expects can be pulled out of Orne's and Rosenberg's analyses of the attitudes of the experimental subject (Orne, 1959 and 1962; Rosenberg, 1965).

Orne calls attention to the subject's "frequent questions at the conclusion of an experiment, to the effect of, 'Did I ruin the experiment?' " Orne sees in this question the subject's desire to be "a good subject." According to him, "Did I ruin the experiment?" means both "Did I perform well in my role as experimental subject?" and "Did my behavior demonstrate that which the experiment is designed to show?"

But why should the subject's desire to be a "good subject" lead him to be ready and willing to help the experimenter validate his hypotheses? Orne answers that

The participation of the college student volunteer in psychological studies is usually due, not to the relatively low remuneration, but, rather, to his interest in taking part in scientific research, which in turn is likely to be based, at least in part, on a desire to further "progress in science" by his participation. *Since the experimenter is perceived as knowing what he is doing,* furthering "progress in science" may well be equated with "making the experiment work" or, in more sophisticated

---

[5] Note that it is neither the sloppy experimenter nor the inexperienced beginner who breaks the rules, nor the "nonjournal" reader who gets the data he expects to get. It is the professional. This is an important point which relates to the generality of these results. It should be mentioned that in a later study experimenters who read the instructions *less accurately* were more likely to bias the results (Rosenthal *et al., J. exp. Res. Pers.,* 1966). I believe that the weight of the evidence indicates that this is a deviant result which should not change the general conclusion, so long as that conclusion is stated in probability terms.

terms, having his individual performance support the hypothesis of the experiment. (Orne, 1959, p. 281, my emphasis.)

The experimenter's attitude and the subject's attitude fit very well. Both parties have a stake in fulfilling the experimenter's expectancy. All that has to be done is for the experimenter to convey that expectancy to the subject via "the demand characteristics of the experimental situation."

But at least one assumption has been smuggled into the conclusion that the subject's stake in the experiment will be to give the experimenter the results he expects. That assumption is contained in the italicized clause. *Will* the experimenter be perceived as knowing what he is doing? Does this not depend, in part, upon how professionally he goes about his business? The answer to this question seems to be yes. And so it would appear that the finding that more professional experimenters are better biasers can be partially understood according to my amendment of Orne's analysis.

Of course there is something slightly provincial about Orne's notion of the typical subject's attitudes. Perhaps he has overextended it. For there still do exist pockets of non- or anti-scientifically oriented subjects. As those experimenters who have encountered some art and music majors, some working-class people, or some aborigines can testify, not all subjects are motivated by a desire to further science. There is, however, another attitude some subjects display which may also help explain why the more professional experimenters were more likely to get the data they expected.

Riecken (1958) has spoken of the experimental subject's need to "put his best foot forward" and Rosenberg (1965) has called attention to subjects' "evaluation apprehension." Although people generally want to be evaluated favorably there are special pressures for such favorable evaluation in the experimental situation. The experimenter may be a scientist, a professor, and a psychologist who is credited with knowing more than the subject likes to believe possible about people in general and the subject in particular (Riecken, 1958). The experimenter's favorable evaluation of the subject is therefore the more important to the subject as the experimenter shows himself by his experimental behavior to be more like any of these high status persons. To the extent that the experimenter shows himself to be fully professional, the subject is likely to care whether he is favorably evaluated . . . and be sensitive to covert . . . communication. If aware of a less professional experimenter's expectancy the subject may give the experimenter data opposite to that expected, for the experimenter who is less professional can not, after all, exercise the same degree of "fate control" that a more fully professional experimenter could exercise. (Friedman *et al.*, 1965).

"Evaluation apprehension" and "furthering progress in science" are thus two subjects' attitudes which, alone or together, may make subjects amenable to helping the experimenters confirm their hypotheses. It would seem reasonable to expect that in research in differently labeled social settings—"The Center for Research" versus "The Psychological Counseling Center"—these attitudes would be activated in different proportions. In any case, by his no-nonsense manner, the "professional" experimenter impresses upon his subjects both the scientific seriousness of the experiment and his high status position. His subjects will therefore be sensitive to covert communication of his hypothesis. They will be inclined to give him the responses he expects both because they will perceive validating his hypothesis to be furthering scientific progress—an aim which they too have internalized—and because they will be concerned about how he will evaluate their performance. It takes two to bias.

This social-psychological analysis of the meshing of the attitudes of experimenter and subject begins to free us from the false dichotomy of either "subject explanations" or "experimenter explanations" of the results of psychological experiments. The explanation indicates how the bias-ability of the professional experimenter is related to the bias-ability of the undergraduate subject. And so it reminds us once again of the circumstance formulated so long ago by Titchener in a statement cited earlier: "E is dependent upon O and O upon E."

IV

There is yet another cluster of factors to take into consideration. Orne sometimes seems to be saying that by definition the experimenter has fate control over the subject, and that demand characteristics inhere in the experimental setting. But we must take one step back. How has the experimenter come to exercise such fate control? Whence do the demand characteristics obtain their demanding nature? To suggest the contours of answers to such questions we have to move from the perspective of dyadic interaction to a more socio-historical perspective.

One of the very first irreverent thoughts I ever had about psychological experimentation is that it is necessarily to a certain degree a-historical. Let me explain what this means. Psychological researchers seek regularities in human behavior. They regularly issue announcements in journal articles that *people* who are high on this or that test will probably do well at this or that task or that when *people* are exposed to this or that treatment they will probably respond in this or that way. However, since they cannot draw samples from the population of the dead, the regularities they find are at least restricted to the people in the historical present upon whom they experiment. Usually, of course, they are actually considerably more restricted than that—either to a college population or a city population or, at best, a national population. Cross-cultural psychological experimentation which also cuts across class and educational lines is still too rare.[6] But it could be done. The limitations are technical rather than necessary. However, the limitations I am concerned with are incorrigible. So long as one remains with an experimental methodology alone, one can never hope to say anything about how the galvanic skin responses of eighteenth-century Italians would be affected by a stressful situation—not even Galvani's! Hence, in historical perspective, the use of the term "people" in the conclusions of psychological research is a case of overgeneralization of experimental results which further experimentation can correct only up to a certain point.

So what? Is there any reason to believe that people in the thirteenth century might have given different kinds of responses to the MMPI from people in the twentieth century after having been shocked or bribed or given some other experimental treatment? Are there any grounds for suspecting that all our successful replications still lack what Brunswik called "ecological validity" (1956) so long as we write as if they were generalizable to the population of all people who ever lived?

There are a number of sociological grounds for believing the answers to these questions to be yes. Analyses of the attitudes of the experimental subject may indicate yet another one. For we live and experiment in the Age of Science and what Philip Rieff (1959), among others, has called the Age of Psychological Man. Science and the scientist have an aura about them which they did not enjoy in the twelfth century. And the psychological professionals likewise enjoy a wary prestige which in other periods of history was reserved for folk healers. Thus, whether our subjects come in to the experimental situation with evaluation apprehension or the desire to further progress in science, they would have had neither before the scientific and psychological revolutions had occurred.

[6] Availability sampling procedures often covary sociological and psychological variables. Psychologists often write such studies up as if sociological variables did not exist. I am thinking in particular of a study of the attitudes of Negroes in which the population sampled was a class at Howard University, and conclusions of the sort "Negroes do not dislike whites" were drawn from the data. Obviously socio-economic, educational, and age (among others) variables intervene here. Psychologists often see this when social issues are being studied but less frequently when working in areas such as psychophysics, verbal conditioning, and other "pure" research. However, although I do not like his use of the word "law," I agree with Thomas Szasz's notion that "the laws of psychology cannot be formulated independently of the laws of sociology" (1961, p. 7). Cross-cultural research which is in actuality cross-university research does not quite satisfy, since all it will produce is a science of the behavior of students in college settings in many lands. One context is changed (the country), but another remains the same (college). And as we shall see, this means that those members of the other country who are most likely to share a scientific and, to a lesser extent, psychological world view, and so are most likely to share the attitudes Orne and Rosenberg have identified, become the subjects.

I am suggesting that, at the highest level of abstraction, the demand characteristics of the experimental situation obtain their demanding nature from, to use a convenient shorthand, "the spirit of the times." The fate control enjoyed by the experimenter is a function of distinctive socio-historical circumstances in which we live. Psychologists inspire evaluation apprehension nowadays because, to name but one reason, "in some sense we are all Freudians" (Skinner, 1963, p. 323). Thus, there may be a powerful and powerfully hidden biasing variable in all psychological experimentation which is not replicated on populations in which the experimenter, the experiment, the psychologist, and psychology do not have the same prestige they have in our society at the present time. We really do not know whether the aborigines, the older Navajo, the Bambara, the Malagasi, the Nyakusa, or other peoples living within a nonscientific world view would do the same as do biasable American college sophomores in various kinds of psychological experiments.

What I am doing here is extending onto a socio-historical scale Orne's admonition that the demand characteristics of the experimental environment be manipulated so that we can isolate the true effect of the experimental manipulation from the effect of confounding situational variables (Orne and Schiebe, 1964). I am suggesting that we take as one overwhelming demand characteristic to be varied the subjects' belief in the scientific world view and its resultant situational concomitants such as docility in the face of the awesome scientist. Of course the sad fact is that, as Quinn McNemar once wrote, "The existing science of human behavior is largely the science of the behavior of sophomores" (1964, p. 333).[7] We can now see one of the saddest implications of this fact; for it is the college sophomore (or any other college student) whose attitudes make him among the most likely to be influenced by the demand characteristics of a scientific experiment.

This too brief consideration of the socio-historical perspective will not be our last. The perspective of social interaction must be supplemented some day with adequate social structural and socio-historical analyses of research in the social sciences. For now we must simply ponder the possibility that just as the profession of psychological experimentation was an outcome of the scientific revolution, so the outcomes of an unknown proportion of contemporary experiments would not be the same if replicated on nonbelievers in that revolution.

[7] Of course this is not quite so true as it was in 1946. Even then, McNemar was doing an injustice to the white rat. Nowadays, of course, mental patients, persons in industry, and other inhabitants of total institutions other than colleges are increasingly becoming subject to becoming subjects. However, as new groups have been added, the scientific world view has also expanded to reach these new groups.

III

The Generality of Experimenter Effect, Experimenter Bias, and Variability in Experimental Procedure

Our present guess is that, in pseudo-statistics, probably no more than 30 to 35 per cent of the social meaning of a conversation or an interaction is carried by the words.

Birdwhistell

The ideal of experimentation and testing in psychology has been a false objectivity, defined implicitly as the observation of behavior without an observer. This is, of course, epistemological nonsense. . . .

Wohl

Early in the preceding chapter I made a distinction between what I called specific hypotheses and general notions. I then proceeded to present interpretations as to why the specific hypotheses pertaining to time, exchange of glances, reading accuracy, and the instructions period were supported in this particular experiment.

From here on we turn from interpretations to implications and from specific hypotheses to general notions. The discussion will now begin to focus on the implications for the philosophy of experimentation and the philosophy of psychology of the general notions that (a) a psychological experiment is a social interaction; (b) experimenters behave variably in their interactions with subjects; (c) these variations can mediate experimenter effects and experimenter biases.

But questions immediately arise concerning how far one can properly generalize from the confirmation in this specific experiment of the general notions (b) and (c). Do they hold, perhaps, only for this sample? Is there any reason to believe that any other experimenters behave variably? Is it possible that experimenter effects and biases are indigenous to this particular task or set of experimenters? In other words, to what extent are these results unique and to what extent are they representative?

These are weighty issues. In Part II a single piece of psychological research was discussed. In Part IV psychological research will be discussed. That is a big jump. The question is whether it is a legitimate one.

The gap can be bridged in two ways: by demonstrating that it would in fact be legitimate to generalize from this single test of the general notions to the universe of psychological research and/or by reviewing relevant studies which provide supporting evidence, thus reducing the burden placed upon this study alone. The former is a theoretical, the latter an empirical, approach to the establishment of the generality of these results.

The following two chapters are devoted to the problem of generalization. Both theoretical and empirical evidence is accumulated. The generality of the notion (b) that experimenters behave variably in their interactions with subjects is *primarily* established by theoretical reasoning based upon observations of just these films. In Chapter 5, the general existence of experimenter variability is deduced from the contrast between the traditional philosophy of psychological experimentation and the social nature of psychological experimentation. The generality of the notion (c) that these variations can mediate experimenter effects and experimenter biases is *primarily* established by citing relevant studies. In Chapter 6, a body of literature in which the influence of the E (examiner or experimenter) has been amply demonstrated is reviewed.

Of course it would be nice to be able to survey all the many areas of empirical social science, citing research studies of research which would indicate in what areas experimenter variability is particularly general, in what areas experimenter effect is particularly general, and in what areas experimenter bias is particularly general. It would also be nice to be able for each problem or task area to estimate how much of the research in the area has been contaminated by undesired variations in procedure, which setting, social interaction, experimenter, and contextual variables are the key ones in each subtype of research, which areas are more immune than others to each of these phenomena, etc. Such a survey would establish a very sophisticated index of the generalizability of these results to specific areas of research. Unfortunately we would have been able to make such a survey only if more experimenters had built such questions into their own research designs. Actually, if we had the data to answer such specific questions, we would not need to bother establishing generalizability in the less sophisticated manner done here. But, in the absence of such information, our aims must be to make simply a modest beginning.[1]

The two chapters are multipurpose. Besides dealing with the generalization issue, each also indicates some of the broader implications of the existence of experimenter effect, experimenter bias, and variability in experimental procedure.

[1] I want to thank David McClelland for drawing my attention to this point.

5 What Happens in a Psychological Experiment: The Standardization Myth

One of the key issues of experimental psychology—the issue on which this entire book bears—is stated in the first half of the title of this chapter. What does happen in a psychological experiment? We have seen in Part I the view of what should happen. An experiment should be a controlled situation in which there are experimental and control groups which allow controlled observations to be made which will lead in turn to the prediction and control of human behavior.

We have reviewed in Part II a filmed experiment which when reviewed over and over again disclosed results which cannot be circumscribed within the traditional point of view. Those who wish to cling to that point of view have to dismiss this experiment as a fluke, a mutation, an exception. But how exceptional is it?

Much of what follows could be labeled "Results, Continued." The bulk of the chapter is a case study in which, step by step, what the films of this psychological experiment revealed is described. The format of the chapter allows me to introduce results which are empirical though not always statistical.

However, though the chapter relies heavily on empirical detail, it is basically theoretical in its approach to the topic of the generality of the findings. It does begin to show the sheer range of differences—above and beyond those reported in Part II—in ways in which the experimental sessions are conducted. But more importantly, it relates these differences to periods that most psychological experiments have in common (e.g., a greeting period, an interview period) and types of behaviors in which all psychological experimenters must indulge (e.g., nonverbal behavior). The crucial point is that the rules by which experimenters are to behave in a standard manner do not include rules of greeting behavior, interviewing behavior, or nonverbal behavior. Hence, it is concluded, in the absence of regulation there will be irregularity. In other words, the occurrence of between-experimenter variability—variability which stems from the social nature of the experiment and which helps create the possibility of experimenter effect and experimenter bias—can be logically deduced from a consideration of the inadequacy of the traditional philosophy of the experiment.

II

Let me try to say some of this over again in another way. At the beginning of my research I asked myself two questions: What is the nature of a psychological experiment supposed to be? What are psychological experimenters supposed to do? To find answers to these related questions I skimmed through the following texts: Woodworth and Schlosberg, *Experimental Psychology* (1954); Postman and Egan, *Experimental Psychology—An Introduction* (1949); Edwards, *Experimental Design in Psychological Research* (1950); Fisher, *The Design of Experiments* (1942); and Guilford, *Fundamental Statistics in Psychology and Education* (1942).

These books are both prescriptive and practical. They are designed to tell the experimenter what to do and how to do it. They tell him how to perform a number of the necessary steps preparatory to the proper conduct of an experiment: how to set up factorial designs, how to randomly sample subjects, how to adjust apparatus, etc. They tell him how to analyze the results of an experiment: how to calculate means and standard deviations, how to set confidence limits, how to do analyses of variance, etc.

But compared to the enormous amount of care paid to these *practical* matters in the discussion of the preparation of the experiment and the analysis of the resulting data, those far briefer portions of the texts which are concerned with the conduct of the experimental session itself are practically entirely *normative*. They tell the experimenter that he should vary the stimuli he wants to vary and hold constant those he wants to hold constant; that is, he ought to create conditions which will allow controlled observations to be made.

However, the "how-to-do-it" exercises are missing. The experimental texts are silent when it comes to the matter of techniques of carrying out the rather high-level role prescription: behave standardly. The experiment is not conceptualized within the frame of reference of social interaction. One seeks in vain for answers to such questions pertaining to social interaction and nonverbal communication as: How should the subject be greeted? How far apart should the experimenter and the subject be seated? Should the experimenter ever look or smile at the subject? How long should the experimenter take in reading the instructions? In what tone of voice should different parts of the instructions be read? At the conclusion of the experiment, how should the subject be dismissed?

We have already seen some of the reasons for the omission of such considerations from the texts. They stem in part from a failure to appreciate the fact that a psychological experiment is a social interaction. Experimental psychology speaks the language of stimulus, response, laboratory, and apparatus. Moreover, social psychology has been identified by too many with the study of crowds, mobs, panics, and riots. Hence, those peaceful everyday events of interaction between experimenter and subject, existing as it were in the interstices between the two disciplines, have passed relatively unnoticed.[1]

I have no desire to become the Emily Post of experimental psychology. But, given the sedentary nature of the experiment described in this chapter —and of many other experiments—one could say that it is the table manners of experimentation that have been neglected. The textbooks simply do not concern themselves with the simple niceties of social interaction. And so I deduce that these simple niceties are carried out in different ways by different experimenters.

I am now going to describe the natural history of this experiment and contrast it with the textbook idealization of an experiment. I will be concerned with reporting what, after their subjects have entered the sessions, these experimenters do. The "Methods" sections of papers in psychological journals are crammed with reports of what experimenters say they do. But discrepancies between what people say they do and what they are observed

[1] This slighting of the experimental session may also be the result of the relative amount of time spent in the conduct of it. Bugelski's experience may be accepted as fairly representative: "The average psychological experiment takes relatively little time in doing. Much of the work comes in preparation, building and testing apparatus or materials, working out procedures, and finally in analyzing the results. One experiment of a simple sort performed by the author took twenty hours to prepare, one hour to do, and one hundred forty hours to compute data, analyze, and organize into a form from which conclusions could be drawn." (Bugelski, 1951, p. 88.) However, even if, as in the case of this person-perception experiment, the actual conduct of a single session should take no more than five minutes, it is obvious that these five minutes have an irreversibility and importance disproportionate to their brevity. And anyone who has read *The First Five Minutes* (Pittenger *et al.*, 1960) is aware how much can go on in just five minutes of face-to-face interaction.

to do are encountered in all walks of life, including science. Einstein called attention to such a divergence in the area of physics when he wrote:

> If you want to find out anything from the theoretical physicists about the methods they use, I advise you to stick closely to one principle: Don't listen to their words, fix your attention on their deeds. (Einstein, 1933, p. 30.)

As the reader peruses those pages he might ask himself whether the same caveat may be profitably directed at students of experimental psychology. Are our methods as reported congruent with our methods as observed? Are our observed operations and our published operations the same operations? Does our abstract vocabulary for formal discussion of psychological experimentation encompass without remainder the significant happenings observed in sound films of psychological experiments? Are our experimental situations really standardized? Do we do what we say we do?

III

Interactions commonly begin with a greeting of some kind. This opening gambit acknowledges the fact that the participants have crossed some visible or invisible boundary and entered each other's ecological space. When the parties to the interaction are *strangers*, the greeting phase takes on a special importance, for in these initial seconds the newcomers quickly size each other up. The whole folklore surrounding the importance of first impressions—don't lead with your chin, put your best foot forward, love at first sight—attests to the fact that a good deal of information is transmitted and received in these opening stances. And first impressions, like first moves in board games, have subtle persuasiveness—especially in fleeting interactions[2]—which is reinforced by their usually remaining unverbalized. They affect the way we are set to act and the way we continue to act during the encounter.

As we have seen, psychological experiments involve interaction between experimenter and subject. What is more, the experimenter and subject are sometimes relative or total strangers. Therefore, the greeting period of the experiment is especially important.

But there is no standard etiquette of the experimental greeting. It is bound by no hard-and-fast rules. Hence, it is probable that experimenters

---

[2] Concerning the interviewing of job applicants Oldfield warns: "It is characteristic of the first impression that it may be stable and persistent in a degree which often appears to be out of keeping with the length and nature of that part of the encounter which gave rise to it. It may remain sometimes in a recognizably compulsive form, when further evidence regarding the candidate thoroughly belies it. . . ." (Oldfield, 1943, p. 103.)

vary in the manner in which they greet their subjects. And it is possible that these variations contribute to unintended variance in subjects' responses.

For example, utilizing all the films, we can observe in the experiment under consideration the interactions of twenty-nine experimenters with eighty-six subjects.[3] In most cases the experimenter and subject are meeting for the first time. The experimenter sits at a trapezoidal table just inside a large room. There is a knock at the door; the subject enters and closes the door behind him. The experiment begins.

As befits their status as subordinates, most of the subjects wait for the experimenter to make the first move. However, beyond this degree of uniformity—which some subjects violate by entering talking—the sheer variety in the pre-face-sheet exchanges is impressive. The extremes are represented by the experimenter who, introducing himself by name, rises and shakes hands with each of his subjects and the seated experimenter with the sour expression whose very first line is, "I am going to read you some instructions."

Between these extremes there are various typical greetings.

E (S walks in and sits down.): How are you this evening?
S: Fine. What's going on?
E (Laughs.): I can't tell you.

E (There is a knock at the door.): Come in. (S walks toward the chair. E looks up and smiles.) Hi. Sit down, please.

E (S walks in. E is busy putting away rating sheets from previous Ss. He has them spread over the table. Looking down and continuing his work.): Hi.
S: Excuse me.

S (As she walks in.): What's all this mystery about?
E: (Smiles and immediately begins to read the instructions.)

E (S is sixteen. E is forty.): Have a seat, young lady.

S (Walks beyond the table. E has to gesture to her to come back to the chair. S sits down.): Do we work together or something?
E (Gesticulates with a sweep of his hand.): I'll show you as we go along.

[3] In order to increase the generality of the results I have drawn examples in this chapter from the interactions of both experienced and inexperienced experimenters. See note to Table 5, p. 50.

E   (Extends his arm toward the chair.):   Have a chair.

S: Thank you.

E: How are you?

S: Fine, thank you.

E   (As S walks in.):   The next subject! (He bangs the back of pho-
      tos on the table and looks down into his data sheets.) Hello.

Obviously these openings start the experimental sessions off in very
different directions. Even when the experimenters stick to a single-word
greeting, the difference between a chummy "Hi" and a formal "Hello" is
liable to be enough to create for the subjects quite different first impressions of the new situation. And different *definitions of the situation*
(Thomas, 1951; Goffman, 1959) are certainly being projected when one
experimenter opens with an interpersonally oriented "Warm evening, isn't
it, young lady?" and another begins with a task-oriented "I am going to
read you some instructions."

IV

But the subject's first impression does not depend solely upon the experimenter's opening move. It is based on many other factors as well. Two
related factors are the experimental setting and the subject's expectations.
Although it will cause us to digress for a moment from the films themselves, let us consider briefly how these two factors contributing to the first
impression can influence in usually unintended ways research results.

The importance of the setting from the point of view of what Goffman calls "the art of impression management" is well known to psychologists who have read Jerome Frank's book *Persuasion and Healing* (1961).
Frank shows how the aura created when the appropriate statues, photographs, diplomas, and other paraphernalia are liberally displayed in eye-
catching places can influence the outcome of psychotherapy. It is surprising
that so little attention has been paid to the effect of such scenic persuasion
in research. The influence of elements of the experimental setting—as opposed to the influence of the experimental manipulations—has been nicely
demonstrated by Orne and Scheibe (1964), who in their experiment on
nondeprivation factors in sensory deprivation research varied the presence
of a panic button, a release form, and other usual accouterments of sensory
deprivation settings and obtained starkly different results from subjects for
whom these elements were or were not present.

It is possible that one reason that the setting has not received the
attention it deserves in research is that sometimes an entire study is carried
out in a single setting. In such a case, it is usually only when there is a

failure to replicate the results in another setting that special features of the setting come under consideration (Sidman, 1962, pp. 343ff). However, in some research, groups are met in different settings. For example, in some studies different rooms in the same building are consistently used for different treatment conditions. Unless the rooms have been equated on what are still usually unknown dimensions, such studies confound scene and treatment. Of greater concern are those studies in which the responses of, say, mental patients and college students to the "same" test are compared, the two groups being tested in their natural habitats—mental hospitals and colleges. In such cases, differences between kinds of persons and kinds of contexts are confounded and, although the stimulus as defined by the researcher may be "the same," the setting may lead to its being differently redefined by the different subject groups (Haley, 1964, p. 7).

This leads us to the interrelatedness of the setting and the subjects' expectations. The initial expectations of the subject are influenced in subtle ways by gross and subtle aspects of the setting of the research. We can delve into this fertile area for study only superficially. For example, the psychology majors in a college in which dissonance studies have been carried out and publicized are likely for some time afterward to enter any research conducted on that campus with expectations radically different from those of psychology majors in a college in which psychological research using deception has never been done. Experiments which take place in a building labeled "Center for Research" are more likely to evoke in the subjects initial expectations of furthering scientific knowledge, whereas experiments which take place in a building labeled "Center for Counseling" are more likely to arouse the initial expectation called by Rosenberg "evaluation apprehension."

Haley considers another problem created by the different expectations of different groups of subjects. Discussing research comparing schizophrenic and nonschizophrenic families he makes the point:

> It would be naïve to assume that if two families are given the same verbal instructions for an experiment, they will be in the same experimental context. If a schizophrenic family is brought in feeling accused because something has gone wrong with their child and defensive about what will be shown wrong in their family, they are hardly in the same experimental context as a family coming in with no accusation of anything wrong in the family but merely to be cooperative with some research. Inevitably in a schizophrenic family any request that the parents be brought together with the patient is a suggestion that they have something to do with the patient's illness. A contrast family without a patient cannot approach the experimentation with the same frame of reference. Even if the "non-schizophrenic" family is told that

the research centers on family organization and mental health, this is doubtfully accusation enough for the family to be as defensive in proving their mental health as is the schizophrenic family where the patient has been diagnosed and hospitalized. (This problem is quite separate from the question of whether a major characteristic of the schizophrenic family is some form of defensiveness, and therefore something to be measured with experimentation.) It is not possible to separate the performance in any experiment from the context in which the experimentation takes place, nor is it a simple problem to find a way to provide a "schizophrenic" and a "non-schizophrenic" family with the same context. If the context is not the same, performance differences are doubtfully valid. (Haley, 1962, p. 275.)

The initial expectations, then, of the two groups being compared may differ, especially if the research is carried out with each group seen in a different setting.

One further note on the initial expectations of subjects before we return to the films. Thus far I have been considering the problem of *differing* initial expectations. There is also a problem of *similar* initial expectations which subjects in any one setting or sharing any one world view (for example, the scientific one) may have. Evidence that subjects do have similar initial sets can be found in studies of subjects' perception of imaginary and biased experimenters (Rosenthal *et al.*, 1960; Rosenthal and Persinger, 1962). These studies indicate a stereotype effect—the subjects come ready to see the experiment in a certain way. For example, all experimenters are rated as quite honest. Orne has found the common initial expectation of the subject to be that what will go on in an experiment will be legitimate, safe, and meaningful. Thus, although we have to know more about local contingencies[4] which modify these similarities, it is probably true that subjects on the whole come to psychological experiments quite ready to do what is asked of them and do it well. Thus, their initial willingness to assist the investigator in every possible way needs only to be capitalized upon through a proper self-presentation by the researcher in order for him to get what he wants.

V

Even before he does anything, the experimenter's appearance helps to set the tone of the encounter. His clothing is an important component of his appearance. Emily Post overstates the matter:

[4] An example of a "local contingency" would be the well-publicized dissonance study. There is some discrepancy between Orne's experiences with subjects and those of investigators who have found subjects to be, at times, either supersuspicious or apathetic.

Clothes are to us what fur and feathers are to beasts and birds; they not only add to our appearance, but they ARE our appearance. The first impression that we make upon others entirely depends upon what we wear and how we wear it. Manners and speech are noted afterward, and character is discerned last of all. (Post, 1940, p. 698.)

Mrs. Post is being too democratic in this statement. Certain things that we change less easily than we do our clothes—such as our physical attractiveness, sex, age, color, height, weight, etc.—certainly contribute to our appearance.[5] But let us—with Mrs. Post—take for granted the countless variations among our experimenters along these dimensions and consider for a moment the consequences of their variations in dress—variations to be expected of experimenters in general since just as there is no uniform experimenter, so there is no experimenter uniform.

The attire of the male experimenters ranges from casual sport shirts with sleeves rolled up and collars unbuttoned to suits, sport jackets, and ties. The female experimenters wear dressy suits or informal skirts and blouses. Although this variety is not so great as that presented by the subjects—who add pedal pushers, shorts, slacks, sweatshirts, and tee shirts to the clothing spectrum—it is great enough to raise the following considerations.

The experiment is supposed to present a standardized situation in which variables other than the experimental ones are held constant. However, at least two vastly different definitions of the situation—casual and formal—can be projected by the gestalt of the appearance and opening gestures of the experimenters. Moreover, the components of these first impressions may contradict, modify, or reinforce one another. A casually dressed experimenter may act very formally or very informally. All in all, the possible permutations of appearance and greeting variables guarantee that even be-

[5] The effect of certain of these stable experimenter attributes on some response classes has been demonstrated. (See Rosenthal, 1963c). In retrospect, given the distribution of heights, weights, ages, sexes, and races among psychological experimenters, it is difficult to see how experimental texts could define experiments as presenting "standardized" situations. Of course this was accomplished by defining the experimenter out of the experiment.

In his paper, Rosenthal discusses the following experimenter attributes: sex, religion, race, status, warmth, likeability, acquaintanceship (surely not an attribute but a relational variable), personality. Obviously to call all these "attributes" is to mix sheep and goats. The experimenter's sex and his warmth, his race and his personality, are not constructs on the same "level" of reality. I have tried to do without inferred constructs in this part and to stick to behaviors that can be observed. (See the last lines of Rosenthal's paper: "experimenters will obtain different data from their Ss as a function of how the E is regarded [!] by his Ss on the attributes of (1) likeability, (2) prestige, (3) professional skill, (4) trust, and (5) sex." If this list were to appear in a multiple-choice item, it would be fair to say that (5) is out of place.

fore the "standardized" sessions are fifteen seconds old, they will be quite heterogeneous.

VI

In this experiment, in all but nine of the dyads, a truncated interview follows the greeting. I have dubbed this the fact-sheet period. Most experiments contain such a period. It consists of a brief give and take of information, with the subject giving and the experimenter taking. The information in this one-way flow is of the classificatory variety. It resembles what might be required for a census, an application for a license, or a job interview.

There is an entire literature on interviewer effect and interviewer bias (see Hyman, 1954). The recognition that many experiments on human subjects do contain this radically brief interview should suggest that the same phenomena have a chance to operate.[6] Yet, as has the greeting period, this period has generally been omitted from journal write-ups of the "official" experiment. The omission conceals another potential source of variability in experimenter behavior and subject responses.

As it happens, the interview can approximate bureaucratic curtness or friendly chit-chat. The extremes are well represented by the following two interactions:

E   (never looking at the subject):   Last name?

S: Ashton.

E: First name?

S: Carol.

E: K or C?

S   (spelling it out):   C-a-r-o-l.

E: Age?

S: Twenty.

E: Married?

S: No.

E: Major field?

S: English.

[6] I use "interview" here in a very restricted sense. In a sense more in keeping with Hyman's loose definition of the term (Hyman, 1954, Ch. 1), the entire experiment is an interview. Hyman says that "Interviewing as a method of inquiry is universal in the social sciences" (p. 1). But the notion that psychology is a completely natural science has acted as an occupational illusion which has contributed to the disinclination of experimenters to apply the results of studies of interview effect and bias to the experimental interview.

E: Class?
S: Junior.

Compare:

E: Have a chair.
S: Thank you.
E: How are you?
S: Fine, thank you.
E: Your name?
S: Joyce Dicholson
E: Joyce, spell the last, please.
S: D-i-c-h-o-l-s-o-n. It's a Scotch spelling.
E (looking up at her): Dicholson?
S: Yes, Dicholson.
E: Oh! Dicholson! Uh-huh.
S: Hm-hm.
E: Age?
S (pause, then coyly): Ah-ah . . . (E looks up.) Thirty-four. (E and S laugh.)
E: Marital status?
S: Single.
E (who is single too): Single, huh. Major field?
S: Speech therapy.
E: I see.
S (leaning over to see what he is writing): Junior year.
E: You're a junior, huh? (Pause.) Where are you from, Joyce?

Do we detect in this latter interview a hint of interest in a single female on the part of a single male? Is the experimenter exhibiting *role distance* (Goffman, 1961), behaving for a moment in the bachelor role rather than the experimenter role? I will discuss such matters more fully later on. At this point it will perhaps be easier to illustrate the great diversity injected into the face-sheet period in this experiment by going through it step by step. The italicized words at the start of each segment represent the standard form which the experimenters were to follow.

Name. Name? Your name? Your name, please. What is your name? Name, please. Can I have your name? May I have your name, please? I want to get some information about you. First, your name. What's your name? Can I have your name, please? First name? Last name; first name.

Let's have your name, please. Your name, miss? Now, I'd better get your name.

Omitting completely consideration of variations in loudness, pitch (Name! Name?), and distribution of stress, these examples define the range of manners of name-asking employed by these experimenters. They differ on a number of dimensions—the number of words used; the use of a personal pronoun ("your") or personal reference ("Miss"); the use of contractions; the use of the last-name, first-name paradigm; the use of a question, request, or command form. Probably most importantly they differ in the extent to which the experimenter *personalizes* his bookkeeping function.

The experimenter's asking for the subject's name does not end the name sequence. The subject has to give it, and the experimenter has to catch it. This apparently automatic event sometimes hits a snag. A subject who has an unfamiliar name or an experimenter who has a limited spelling ability can produce a new exchange.

A new exchange means a new nonconformity with the standard operating procedure.

The first variation occurs between those instances in which the subject has to repeat his or her name and those in which the experimenter gets it on the first try. Within the repeaters group there are variations in how the repetition is "requested" (Spell your last name . . . How do you spell your last name? . . . Please spell your last name), and how many times it has to be requested.

The name sequence also gives rise to what may be called, following Goffman (1961) and ordinary language, incidents. These are unanticipated events which suddenly change the character of the supposedly standardized interaction. Two examples follow.

E: May I have your name, please?

S: Laurel Harkness.

E: How do you spell that?

S   (Suddenly laughs.):   I can't spell my own last name because I just got it. (E and S laugh together.)

Watch another experimenter being drawn almost against his will into the interaction.

E   (Formally.):   Name.

S: Noel Hanzegagen.

E   (Not looking up from the paper on which he is writing.):   How do you spell that?

S: N-o-e-l.

E   (Repeating.):   N-o-e-l.

S: Two dots above the . . .

E   (Cutting her short.):   OK. And last name?

S: H-a-n-z-e-g-a-g-e-n.

E   (Cutting her short.):   OK. And last name?
     written. Then he smiles quizzically.) What kind of name is that?

S   (Also smiling now.):   Norwegian.

Age. Amy Vanderbilt cautions:

You might ask a man's age—though many men are less than anxious to
divulge that information if they are past forty—but you never ask that
of a woman over 21, except for official reasons. Even then, the courtesy
of letting her say "over 21" usually is accorded a woman—except by
the U.S. State Department, the various Motor Vehicles offices, and
other sternly realistic representatives that must know all. (Vanderbilt,
1952, p. 214.)

Psychologists are often bracketed in the latter category. Hence, these
experimenters demand as often as they ask for the subject's age (Age! Age?).
And no subject refuses to give his or her age—or for that matter to hand
over any of the required information. But just because age can be a touchy
topic (or a pseudo-touchy topic) this question is liable to affect the set of
the subject and the course of the interview, as we have seen in an earlier
example:

E: Age?

S   (Pause, then, coyly.):   Ah-ah . . . (E looks up.) Thirty-four.
     (E and S laugh.)[7]

Marital Status. This question is probably as close as the interview
comes to getting personal. And the behavior of both parties shows this.
There is more hemming, hawing, and giggling at this point than at any
other in the experiment. When a male experimenter is interviewing a female subject, the cross-sex situation seems to interfere here with the conduct of the textbook experiment. Different experimenters handle this part
of the interview differently, and different subjects respond differently to the
way the question is raised.

---

[7] This is a nervous or awkward laugh rather than a hearty ho-ho-ho. Compare the
laugh here:

    E: What's your age?

    S: Eighteen and a half.

    E: Eighteen and a half. (Nods his head from side to side as if to say, "Well,
    well, well.") Well, I think I'll just put eighteen. OK?

    S: OK. (They both laugh, and the S moves her chair closer to the table.)

E: Marital status?

S   (Pauses. E looks up. S laughs.):   Well, the boys are pretty tame. (E laughs too.)

E: Marital status.

S   (Hesitates, lifts arm to gesture.):   Divorced . . . single. (Turns her head away.)

E: Married? (S nods her head "no" wistfully.)

E: Single? Married?

S: Single. (E grins slightly.)

E   (S has said she is sixteen.):   Marital status? (E looks up knowingly.) Single, I suppose. (Smiles.)

S   (Giggling.):   Single.

E: Marital status, none?

S: Right. (She crosses her legs.)

Major Field. Class. In most cases the experimenter and subject return in these last two questions to a fairly standard interchange. This is accomplished by the experimenters' sticking to the bare "major field . . . class" in the majority of the dyads, whereas in the previous questions the experimenters characteristically embellished the impersonal form (name . . . age) in some way.

However, even here, in a composite picture the experimental sessions would display only a family likeness. And there are mutations. The two questions show that eventualities often beyond the prescience of the chief investigator arise which render impossible the goal of maintaining literally exact conditions for all subjects. Variations are introduced when the subjects have no major field or are not yet in college and so have no class. These developments often draw the experimenters into overtime interactions in which they are forced to ad lib.

E: And, uh, you're a freshman?

S   (Explains that she is a high-school junior.)

E   (Listens with thumb to lips.):   Oh, I see. I'll put down high-school junior.

E: And you are a freshman, sophomore, junior, senior?

S   (Shakes head from side to side and rolls eyes.):   I don't know.

E   (Looking at her.):   You don't know?

S: Probably I have senior rating. I had my R.N. and came back for the summer to get credits in education.

E: OK. I guess I'll put down . . .

S: Let 'em figure it out. (Smile.)

E (Laughing.): OK.

VII

It could be objected at this point that the foregoing treatment of the face-sheet period capitalized on bad experimentation that might be unique to this particular case. That is, many of the examples show that these experimenters did not follow orders; they broke the rules of experimental procedure. Granted that neither consumers of research nor, at times, chief investigators know once that door closes how many experimenters say exactly what they intended to say and chief investigators will report they said. But one might argue that there is no compelling a priori reason to believe that such malfeasance is widespread. Therefore, I need to make the case for the *generality* of experimenter variability in the face-sheet period more airtight. And I might as well make such a case for the instructions period too. That is the dual aim of this section.

Up to now I have been considering the experiment chronologically and limiting my description primarily to the content of the verbal interplay and byplay. Research reports usually limit themselves even further—to a description of what was to be the standardized verbal input of the experimenter. However, even though it improves and throws light upon standard practice, my description thus far still leaves out too much. For, experimenters behave nonverbally as well as verbally. To take two examples, at various points in the experiment they either do or do not look at their subjects and either do or do not smile at their subjects. Let us see how well the procedure in this experiment is standardized along these dimensions. Then we will see how the case for generality is affected by this inquiry.

In Table 6 we see, broken down for the face-sheet and instructions periods of the experiment, the number of times the experimenters look at their subjects. We see that in the face-sheet period one subject may be looked at anywhere from zero to twelve times, and in the instructions period anywhere from zero to fifteen times. We see that over all three subjects the total number of experimenter glances in the face-sheet period ranges from four to twenty-two, and in the instructions period from zero to thirty-one. The analyses of variance show that not only are there differences between experimenters in the number of times that they look at their subjects during these periods but that these differences are statistically significant.

In Table 7 we see, broken down for the face-sheet and instructions

Table 6. Experimenter Glances at Subject

E	10	11	12	13	14	15	16	17	18	19	20	21	22	23	24	24a	25	26	27	28
FACE-SHEET																				
S_1	1	3	3	0	1	4		2		3	12	2	3	4			2		5	2
S_2	3	1	1	1	5	1		3		4	4	3	3	4			3		3	2
S_3	2	2	1	3	3	5		3		2	6	3	4	6			2		6	4
Σ				4							22									
INSTRUCTIONS																				
S_1	0	7	2	1		0		2	0	0	6	2	1	6			3	4	3	1
S_2	1	9	6	1		0		2	1	1	11	2	1	6			1	12	4	1
S_3	1	15	3	1		0		2	1	1	10	3	1	10			4	10	6	3
Σ		31				0														

ANALYSES OF VARIANCE

FACE-SHEET

	df	SS	ms	F	p
Experimenters	13	91.2	7	2.91	<.02
Position	2	3.6	1.8		
Error	26	61.7	2.4		
Total	41	156.5			

INSTRUCTIONS

	df	SS	ms	F	p
Experimenters	15	572.8	38.2	16.6	<.001
Position	2	38.8	19.4		
Error	30	69.9	2.3		
Total	47	681.5			

Table 7. Experimenter Smiles at Subject

FACE-SHEET

E	11	12	13	14	15	16	17	18	19	20	21	22	23	24	24a	25	26	27	28
S_1		0	0		1		0	0	0	8	1	0	3					0	1
S_2		1	4		1		0	0		5	1	0	3					1	1
S_3		0	1		1		1	0		6	1	0	3					2	1
Σ								0		19									

ANALYSES OF VARIANCE

	df	SS	ms	F	p
Experimenters	10	101.4	10.1	12.6	<.01
Position	2	.4	.2		
Error	20	17.3	.8		
Total	32	118.1			

INSTRUCTIONS

E	11	12	13	14	15	16	17	18	19	20	21	22	23	24	24a	25	26	27	28
S_1	3	0	3		0		0	1	0	3	2	0	2			0	2	0	0
S_2		2	3		1		2	1	1	3	1	1	2			0	3	1	0
S_3	1	0	1		0		2	2	0	6	2	0	3			0	2	0	0
Σ										12						0			

ANALYSES OF VARIANCE

	df	SS	ms	F	p
Experimenters	14	54.3	3.87	4.66	<.02
Position	2	.8	.4		
Error	28	23.2	.83		
Total	44	78.3			

periods of the experiment, the number of times the experimenters smile at their subjects. We see that in the face-sheet period one subject may be smiled at anywhere from zero to eight times. We see that over all three subjects experimenters smile from zero to nineteen times in the face-sheet period and from zero to twelve times in the instructions period. The analyses of variance show that not only are there differences between experimenters in the number of times they smile at their subjects in these periods but that these differences are statistically significant.

From the point of view of the possibility of attaining experimental control, a particularly interesting set of variables are the relational or transpersonal ones. Even though only one person does it, a smile or a glance can be studied as an interpersonal variable; for the smile may be elicited by the antics of the other, and the glance may be pulled by the looks of the other. However, with respect to experimental control, it is possible for the experimenter not to react to such diversions and so keep the experimental conditions standard on variables such as "experimenter glances" or "experimenter smiles" even though a subject may be dancing on the ceiling.

But with the relational or transpersonal variables such is not the case. I am thinking here of variables such as the distance between experimenter and subject and the duration of the experimental session. With regard to these variables, although the experimenter may behave standardly, this does not necessarily mean that the sessions will be standardized before each subject makes his response. The experimenter may not move an inch, but each subject may move his chair either closer or farther away (thus perhaps indicating his social distance from the experimenter). The experimenter may clock his reading of the instructions by a stopwatch, but one subject may ask (as one does on the films), "What is empathy?" and so succeed in destandardizing the time of the sessions. Thus, although the experimenter does have a great deal of "fate control" over the subject, experimental control does not reside solely in his hands.

A variable somewhere in between the smile variety and the distance variety is the exchanged glance. It takes two to exchange a glance, but the experimenter can keep the sessions standardized on this variable by never looking up (or down). Does he?

In Table 8 we see, broken down for the face-sheet and instructions periods of the experiment, the number of glances the experimenters exchange with their subjects. We see that in the face-sheet period a single experimenter and subject may exchange from zero to five glances, and in the instructions period from zero to three glances. We see that over all three subjects the total number of exchanged glances in the face-sheet period ranges from zero to eleven, and in the instructions period from zero to seven. The analyses of variance show that not only are there differences between experimenters in the number of glances they exchange with their

Table 8. Exchanged Glances

FACE-SHEET

E	10	11	12	13	14	15	16	17	18	19	20	21	22	23	24	24a	25	26	27	28
S_1	1		0	0		0		0		1	5	0	1	0					4	0
S_2	1		0	0		1		1		0	3	0	1	0					2	0
S_3	0		0	1		2		1		0	3	0	4	4					2	1
Σ		7									11									

INSTRUCTIONS

E	10	11	12	13	14	15	16	17	18	19	20	21	22	23	24	24a	25	26	27	28
S_1	2		1	0		0		0	0	0	0	0	1	0			2	3	1	0
S_2	1		3	0		0		1	1	0	1	0	1	0			0	2	0	0
S_3	0		1	0		0		0	0	1	0	0	0	0			0	2	1	0
Σ		7		0																

ANALYSES OF VARIANCE

FACE-SHEET

	df	SS	ms	F	p
Experimenters	11	43.4	3.9	3.54	<.005
Position	2	3.5	1.75		
Error	22	23.8	1.1		
Total	35	70.7			

INSTRUCTIONS

	df	SS	ms	F	p
Experimenters	15	28	1.87	4.68	<.001
Position	2	.7	.35		
Error	30	12	.4		
Total	47	40.7			

subjects in these periods but that these differences are statistically significant.

It would be needlessly repetitive to present the analyses of variance for each variable in the experimental sessions that I have thus far studied. To do so would be to produce a list of tables for glances, smiles, time, nods, uhs, eyebrow raisings, etc., for each phase of the experiment. Out of twenty-five such analyses that I have carried out, fifteen showed significant between-experimenter variability.

Before passing on to a systematic study of the instructions period of this experiment, let me make two points about these variations in experimenters' nonverbal behavior.

The first point refers to the generalization issue. It is important to recognize that the variability between these experimenters in their nonverbal behavior does not represent deviation from the instructions given to them or so far as I know experimenters in general. It does not represent—as do some of the verbal improvisations discussed before—any petty truancy on the part of an experimenter if he glances, smiles, or exchanges glances with his subjects. Hence, telling the experimenter to stick to the letters of the script will not in principle eliminate this variability. The experimenter is not changing the standard script provided him. Rather, he is behaving in areas in which no standards have been set either for this specific experiment or so far as I know for psychological experimentation in general. It is not a case of bad experimentation but an inadequate philosophy of experimentation. The experimenters' nonverbal behavior is not against—but beyond—current experimental philosophy. The inexperience of some of these experimenters cannot be held against generalizing from *their* nonverbal behavior, for there are no rules for them not yet to have learned. Unmade rules cannot be broken.

The second point refers to an inadequacy of this chapter. Notice that I have discussed in turn specific verbal improvisations and, in gross numbers, variations in three specific areas of nonverbal behavior. The truly difficult thing both for me to depict and for researchers to *control* is the parallel occurrence of verbal and all kinds of nonverbal behavior. For example, the same total number of glances for two experimenters can be the result of glances at different sentences in the interview, and during any one sentence an experimenter may look at the subject before, while, or after he speaks. Moreover, different experimenters regulate (usually unwittingly) their nonverbal behavior to coordinate with their verbal behavior in different ways. In other words, the specific message that is modified by the glance can be different even though the total number of glances is the same. Similarly, each exchanged glance can be further broken down into consideration of which party initiated it, the duration of the latency period before it was "mutualized," the duration of eye contact, which party broke it off, and the length of time before the other turned his gaze away. A typology of mutual glances could be developed which would show still more of the variability in the experimental interactions and further vitalize this description of them. Some of the drama-like dialogue employed in this chapter (with its parenthetical stage directions) begins very inadequately to suggest the different ways in which these experimenters interweave the verbal and the nonverbal. However, it fails to capture either the full spectrum of gradations or the specific seconds of simultaneity and so underestimates the true range of differences to be expected in the "standardized" sessions of experimental psychology.

VIII

We come now to the instructions period of the experiment. The give and take is over. The experimenter is supposed to read, and the subject is supposed to listen. The experimenter has been provided with a mimeographed sheet which contains the instructions to be read to the subject. The rating scale referred to in the instructions has been taped to the table right in front of the subject.

The instructions period has received more attention in the journal literature than have the greeting and face-sheet periods. The notion stressed in the literature is that the instructions have been standardized so as to insure that every subject in a treatment group will receive the same set. As Festinger puts it, the use of verbal instructions is "the most obvious technique for controlling or manipulating variables" (1953, p. 157). As Riecken puts it, "the experimenter has a script that provides lines and business" (1958, p. 12).

The typical criterion of standardization is some form of "stencilization." The typical research report will say something like "All Es read identical instructions to the Ss (see Appendix)." In the methods section or the appendix will be reproduced the mimeographed instructions (see, for example, Rosenthal, 1963a, pp. 279, 283). And that will be that.

However, such a procedure fails to consider at least two contingencies. One is the possibility that the experimenters did not read the exact instructions mimeographed for them but added, omitted, or changed words. The other is the more pervasive probability that the identical instructions were not identically read. In other words, an experimenter may not say just what he is to say, or in saying just what he is to say he may say it in his own way. In either case, unanticipated (and usually unreported) variation will be introduced into the instructions period.

In regard to the issue of the generality of these results, the two possibilities roughly parallel the distinction made previously between verbal improvisations and nonverbal behavior. The first possibility—changes in verbal content—is a case of sloppy experimentation. There is no way unless experiments are monitored to judge how peculiar to this experiment such sloppiness is.[8] But the second possibility—vocal and gestural accompaniments to the content—represents an area in which no standards have been made public. Hence, I think that, in the absence of standardized rules, nonstandardization is the rule.

We need, then, in going bit by bit through the instructions actually read in this experiment, to be on the lookout for gross verbal deviations from the printed instructions and subtle vocal and gestural idiosyncrasies.

IX

I am going to read you some instructions. I am not permitted to say anything which is not in the instructions, nor can I answer any questions about this experiment. OK?

The experimenter is to introduce the instructions period with these words. Note their professional tone—eschewing contractions, calling for a "which" rather than a "that," a double negative, and an official-sounding "am not permitted." The paragraph has obviously been designed to inform the subject that it is time to get down to business. The cold declarative sentences which build a wall of negation between experimenter and subject finally give way to the experimenter's somewhat disingenuous "request" at the end of the paragraph for the subject's permission to continue. No subject refuses.

The major deviant pattern here requires no changes in the words the experimenter reads. Instead, there is a change in the order in which the experiment is done. In nine cases the experimenter reads either just this first paragraph or the entire instructions *before* getting the face-sheet data, which he then picks up either immediately afterward or at the end of the experiment.

In other words, nine subjects are met with these rather forbidding negations, instead of with the interview, with results which at least one subject verbalizes:

> E   (S is in the process of sitting down.):   Hello. I am going to read you some instructions. (E waves his pencil in the air to further emphasize capitalized words.) I am NOT permitted to say any-

[8] After having completed the statistical part of this study, I utilized a participant-observation strategy to monitor experiments. That is, I became a subject and had accomplices do likewise. In many cases I was able to obtain access to what the experimenter was supposed to say, what he did say, as well as what the journal article reported he said. Based on this experience, which I hope to replicate and report in the future, I would say that such sloppiness in instructions reading is far from unusual.

thing which is NOT in the instructions, nor can I answer any questions about this experiment. OK?

S (With a bewildered look on her face, hands outstretched, palms up.): Before . . . Can I ask questions before you start? (E shakes his head and the extended index finger of his left hand from side to side.) No? No questions at all? (E continues to shake his head. S drops hands into her lap dramatically and heaves a sigh.) All right.

E: So listen carefully.

In a second deviant pattern, the experimenters tend to informalize the rather formal beginning called for. One experimenter adds the personal touch: "I am going to read you some instructions, Diane." A number of experimenters say in an offhand manner, "*I'm* going to read you some instructions" (and then some of them pick up the mimeographed sheet and read, "*I am* going to read you some instructions"). A few experimenters change "anything which" to a less literary "anything that," and a few likewise change the artificial "nor can I" to a more conversational "and I can't" (or "I cannot").

But these changes could be peculiar to this experiment. A more general matter which becomes apparent at the very outset is the difference in the ways in which the experimenters read. I will postpone detailed consideration of this matter until later (see below, "crucial sentences," section XI). Right now I want to discuss just one aspect of reading styles—the variations in the way in which the experimenters distribute their attention between the instructions sheet and the subject.

Reference was made to this point in the discussion section of Part II. What is the experimenter's task? He has to read the instructions, and he has to read them to someone who is sitting at the table with him. He is not reading in a vacuum but in the context of a social interaction. His preparations characteristically do not prepare him for the social side of the coin. He has to decide (or not decide) on his own how to regulate his focus between the reading task and the interpersonal relationship.

The way in which the experimenter handles the prop, the instructions sheet, is related to how he apportions his attention. Some experimenters leave the sheet on the table directly in front of them and glance alternately down to it and up at the subject. Some hold it up in the air so that it acts as a barrier between themselves and the subject. Some leave it on the table but slant it toward the subject, who usually gets the message and reads along with the experimenter, their heads nearing each other at complementary angles.

These three basic positions introduce all kinds of variance in the *kinesic* (Birdwhistell, 1952) behavior of the experimenters during the instructions period. And we have seen that for this specific experiment kinesic variance in the instructions period is related to variance in the subjects' photo ratings.

Again I must take up one vocal matter here, while deferring a more general consideration of paralinguistics (Birdwhistell, 1959) to a later place (see Section XI). Goffman writes that "the most fortunate of normals is likely to have his half-hidden failing, and for every little failing there is a social occasion when it will loom large . . ." (1963b, p. 127). For one of our experimenters the experiment becomes such a social occasion, for he is a stutterer and his subjects hear as the first sentence of the instructions, "I am going to read you some ins-ins-ins-ins-ins-ins-structions." From this point forth his subjects become focused on *him*, rather than on what he is saying, an alienation from interaction which Goffman calls "other-consciousness" (1957). They do recover after a while (and so does he), but the instructions they hear are not the standard instructions.

We come finally to the end of the first paragraph of the instructions with its "OK?" which should change the subject from a listener to a participator. But in twelve of the dyads the "OK?" is omitted and the experimenter goes right on to the second paragraph.

Even when the "OK?" is said, it is said in a variety of ways. By varying pitch, stress, the position and number of pauses, and accompanying nonverbal behavior, the experimenters imply sometimes, "Is it OK with you?" sometimes "OK, here we go," and sometimes, "OK, that's that."

X

We are in the process of developing a test of empathy. This test is designed to show how well a person is able to put himself into someone else's place. I will show you a series of photographs. For each one I want you to judge whether the person pictured has been experiencing success or failure. To help you make more exact judgments you are to use this rating scale.

This opening segment of the second paragraph of the instructions carries us from the introduction of the task to the introduction of the rating scale. The experimenter provides a rationale, an explanation of the task, which seems to satisfy the subjects, only one of whom even bothers to ask, "What is empathy?" The paragraph allows the experimenter to identify with some unnamed larger group ("we") and again calls upon him to use formalisms rather than informalisms—"we are" and not "we're," "into" and not "in," "photographs" and not "photos," "person pictured" and not "person in the picture." Finally it calls on him to bring the subject's attention—which often begins to wander at this point—back to the task by referring to the rating scale in front of him.

Again, any original intention to impress upon the subject the official-

ness of his task by means of the formality of the instructions is partly sabo-
taged by those experimenters who slip back into the more conversational
tones eschewed in the mimeographed instructions which usually appear in
their staid form at the back of a research report. Thus, some experimenters read "we're" and not "we are," "in" and not "into," "photos" and not
"photographs," "in the picture" and not "pictured."

The generally pedantic tone of the instructions also elicits from the
experimenters a goodly number of what are called speech disturbances or
nonfluencies (Mahl and Schulze, 1962)—slips of the tongue, repetitions
("You, uh, make more exact . . . exact judgments"), false starts ("exper-
experiencing"), intrusions ("all right now . . ."), mispronunciations,
breaks, and grammatical errors ("this here rating scale"). It is difficult to
assess the effects of these (plus the usual quota of ahs, ums, coughs, and
silent pauses) upon the subjects, most of whom monitor any overt reaction
except a furtive glance or a half smile. Suffice it to say that when all these
sounds are taken into consideration, no two readings of the instructions,
like no two fingerprints, are exactly alike.

Out of context, "You are to use this rating scale," is likely to evoke the
question, "What rating scale?" Some experimenters do, and some experimenters do not, foresee the naughtiness of a "this" with no antecedent.
And so here too we get a patterned deviation from the standardized instructions, which then is elaborated upon in different ways by different experimenters. The experimenters split into those who do and those who do
not embellish the "this" with a gesture and/or verbal addition, and in the
second category there are different ways of sending the message:

E_1: You are to use this rating scale. (Without looking up he points
to the scale with the index finger of his left hand. S immediately
looks down to it intently.)

E_2: You are to use this rating scale. (E_2 looks up and points with his
pencil.) This one here, Phyllis.

Finally, even in this segment of the instructions, though much less so
than in the one to come, a few experimenters subtly change the task con-
fronting their subjects. Three examples follow.

1. Instead of "To help you make more exact judgments . . ." one experimenter reads "To help you make exact judgments . . ." This version of
the sentence changes the person-perception task into one which requires
incredible skill. Psychologists are well aware of the problems involved in the
way in which subjects variously interpret phrases like "more exact"; here is a
case in which a very scrupulous interpretation would not be the result of
the subject's invention.

2. Instead of "This test is designed to show how well a person is able

to put himself into someone else's place," one experimenter reads, "This test is designed to show YOU how well a person . . .[9] The added and emphasized reference to the subject reinforces any tendency he might already have to see himself rather than empathy as the topic of the experiment. Riecken divides experiments into what he calls "task-ability" and "self-quality" tasks (1958, p. 15), and Rosenberg (1965) contends that even in clearly labeled task-ability tasks, some subjects will be wary as to the "real" self-quality evaluation going on in the experiment. By putting "you" into the sentence, this experimenter invites the subject to construe the experiment as a self-quality task, thus arousing latent evaluation apprehension which may affect the spontaneity of this subject's responses.

3. Though they will become much more salient in the "crucial sentences" (see below, section XI), the words "success" and "failure" are introduced for the first time in this segment of the instructions. One extremely vigorous reader reads the sentence in which they occur, "for each one I want you to judge whether the person pictured has been experiencing EXTREME success or failure." He thus inserts and emphasizes a word which can for this subject alter the meaning of the end points of the rating scale. But that is our very next topic.

XI

As you can see the scale runs from − 10 to + 10. A rating of − 10 means that you judge the person to have experienced extreme failure. A rating of + 10 means that you judge the person to have experienced extreme success. A rating of − 1 means that you judge the person to have experienced mild failure, while a rating of + 1 means that you judge the person to have experienced mild success.

I call these the "crucial sentences" of the instructions. In them the experimenter explains to the subject how to use the scale upon which he

---

[9] In two other dyads the "you" is inserted in this sentence but without emphasis. It is worthwhile to look at the preceding lines in the interaction which led to this howler. Omitting the face-sheet period completely, the experimenter begins the experiment with the instructions.

    E: I am going to read you some [etc.] OK?
    S: Is this blind man's bluff or something?
    E   (Smiles.): We are in the process of developing a test on empathy. . . .
    S   (Leaning over to see what he is reading and breaking in.): What's empathy?
    E   (Extends his hands, palms up.): Projection, uh, into . . .
    S   (Breaking in again.): Like sympathy to others?
    E   (Waving his arms in relief.): Something like that. (Sighs.) This test is designed to show YOU how well . . .

It sounds as if a bamboozled experimenter is saying to a rambunctious subject, "I'll show *you!*"

will rate the photos. At this crucial point ideally the subject will be receiving almost identical information orally and visually, for he will hear the end points of the scale labeled by the experimenter and will see the end and intermediate points labeled on the scale in front of him. This imperfect redundancy is designed to make certain that the subject understands his task.[10]

At times intended redundancy becomes actual discrepancy. The subject hears and sees different things. The experimenter changes the labeling of the end points of the scale. Sometimes this is done symmetrically, and sometimes it is done asymmetrically.

One experimenter reads, "a — 10 is very extreme failure, and a + 10 is very extreme success. A — 1 rating would be mild failure and a + 1 very mild success." Another reads, "a rating of − 1 means that you have judged the person to have experienced mild failure, while a rating of minus —uh—plus one means that you judge the person to have extreme mild success." A third gets safely through extreme failure, extreme success, and mild failure, only to read, "while a rating of + 10 means that you judge the person to have experienced mild success." A fourth reads, "A rating of − 10 means that you judge the person to have experienced failure." A fifth, "Minus ten means very extreme failure . . . + 10 very extreme success. A − 1, very mild failure; + 1, very mild success."

It is difficult either to predict or to statistically assess the precise effects of these obviously relevant changes, for they are few in number and partially offset by the visual impression the subject receives from the scale taped to the table. But, considering all the attention that has been paid by experimenters to clearly labeling the end points of scales so as to cut down on subjects' idiosyncratic interpretations of words like "extreme" and "mild," it seems safe to say that the experimenters' idiosyncratic interpretations of the end points ("very extreme," "very mild") will introduce unanticipated variance into subjects' ratings.

Again, how general such faulty reading of crucial content is in the instructions periods of psychological experiments is a moot point upon which research might be done. There is a further factor, and its generality is more obvious. To get to it we have to pass from these grossly nonstandardized renditions of the crucial sentences to those which are standardized only in the grossest sense. This will require a brief preface.

Commenting upon Stuart Hampshire's review of Gilbert Ryle's *The Concept of Mind,* John Wisdom confesses that it is difficult for him to

---

10 The imperfectness of the redundancy might be responsible for one of the most deviant set of responses in the experiment. One subject uses only + 1, − 1, + 10, and − 10 in making her ratings. Now it is possible that she is just "the kind of person" who uses the end points of scales. It seems more likely, however, that for some reason she listened instead of looked.

decide the nature of the dispute between Hampshire and Ryle on the basis
of the *content* of their writings:

> What is the dispute between Ryle and Hampshire? One of them
> [Ryle] says, "Our language is riddled with the myth of the ghost in
> the machine"; the other says, "Certainly, certainly, our language is rid-
> dled with the myth of the ghost in the machine." Only the tone of
> voice is different. (Wisdom, 1962, p. 52.)

Actually, if the two were disputing face to face, probably more than
just their tones of voice would be different. Differences in pitch, loudness,
distribution of stress ("Our language is *riddled* . . .") speed of speaking,
and positioning of pauses might also be involved. And there could be differences as well in the nonverbal accompaniments to their words. Ryle might
conceivably bang his fist on the table as he said "riddled," while Hampshire
might produce the "Certainly, certainly" effect by shrugging his shoulders
and extending his hands, palms up, as he began the sentence.

Such examples as these are systematically studied under the rather for-
midable headings of "paralinguistics" and "parakinesics" (Pittenger *et al.*,
1960; Birdwhistell, 1959, 1960). Between them, paralinguistics and parakinesics study the vocal and motion qualifiers which modify the content of
statements made by an individual. These disciplines have begun to system-
atize what comedians and orators, circus barkers and politicians, therapists
and testers and experimenters have exploited all along—that people respond not just to *what* is said but also to *how* it is said.

The fact that "the sound [and motion] accompaniments suggest what
is to be made of the verbal propositions stated" (Sullivan, 1954, p. 7) allows the experimenters in these crucial sentences to attempt to influence
the subject's rating of the photos *without violating the script they have
been provided.* How is this done?

Let us consider, for ease of presentation, paralinguistic and parakinesic
matters separately; and let us develop composite pictures of plus and minus
stressers.[11]

In the following two types of renditions of the crucial sentences, the
words and syllables which receive primary stress are capitalized. Certain
other relevant features of vocal behavior appear in parentheses.

---

[11] This is the only place in this chapter where I have not transcribed directly from
specific films but made composite pictures based on plus and minus tendencies that
come out in different films. I do this because of the extreme difficulty in getting my
point across without recourse to some specialized notational system which only
about ten people in the world would be able easily to follow. However, an unfortunate consequence of the composite technique is that it reduces eighty-six variations to two groups. Pete Wagschal made some of the observations used here.

(E enunciates each word distinctly.) A rating of MINUS ten means that you judge the person to have experienced EXTREME FAIL-URE. (E pauses; his voice lowers now and speeds up.) A rating of plus ten means that you judge the person to have experienced extreme success. (E pauses briefly; his words now are enunciated slowly, distinctly, and more loudly.) A rating of MINUS one means that you judge the person to have experienced MILD FAILURE (E pauses; his voice speeds up), while a rating of plus one means that you judge the person to have experienced mild success.

Compare:

(E begins in a low, quick monotone.) A rating of minus ten means that you judge the person to have experienced extreme failure. (E pauses briefly; he begins now to enunciate more slowly, loudly, and distinctly.) A rating of PLUS ten means that you judge the person to have experienced EX-TREME SUC-CESS. (E pauses; his voice speeds up; he slurs his words.) A rating of minus one means that you judge the person to have experienced mild failure (E pauses briefly; his voice slows down, gets louder, and he enunciates more distinctly), while a rating of PLUS one means that you judge the person to have experienced MILD SUC-CESS.

The experimenters have violated the spirit but not the letter of their task. They have read the same words, but they have not read them in the same way. Nor have their subjects, who have heard the same sentences, received the same messages.

Moreover, again without deviating from the content of the standardized instructions, the experimenters differentially stress parts of the crucial sentences parakinesically. Consider the following composite picture of a minus stresser:

A rating of − 10 (E touches the − 10 end of the rating scale and leaves his pencil on it) means that you judge the person to have experienced extreme failure. (E pauses, removes the pencil from the rating scale, looks up, and exchanges a glance with the subject.) A rating of + 10 means that you judge the person to have experienced extreme success. A rating of − 1 (E looks up, raises his eyebrow, points emphatically to the − 1 on the rating scale with his pencil, and smiles) means that you judge the person to have experienced mild failure (E glances at S), while a rating of + 1 means that you judge the person to have experienced mild success.

A plus stresser simply makes the same or equivalent moves on the plus sentences:

A rating of − 10 means that you judge the person to have experienced extreme failure. A rating of + 10 (E touches the + 10 end of the scale and leaves his pencil on it) means that you judge the person to have experienced extreme success. (E pauses, removes the pencil from the rating scale, and looks up at the subject.) A rating of − 1 means that you judge the person to have experienced mild failure, while a rating of + 1 (E pauses, looks up, points with his pencil emphatically to the + 1 on the rating scale, and smiles) means that you judge the person to have experienced mild success. (E pauses, removes the pencil from the rating scale, looks up, and exchanges a glance with the subject.)

XII

You are to rate each photo as accurately as you can. Just tell me the rating you assign to each photo. All ready? This is photo number one.

These final sentences of the instructions period provide a transition from the crucial sentences to the photo-rating period. As such, they will concern us as little as they seem to concern the experimenters, who usually hasten on to the rating period.[12]

Additions and omissions destandardize the readings of this section of the instructions. Two experimenters add last-minute instructions on how to use the scale.

> E_1: Just tell me the rating you assign to each photo. (E_1 puts down the instructions sheet and looks at the S.) Plus one or whatever you think it would be.

> E_2: Just tell me the rating you assign to each photo. Are you ready? You just say plus one, plus ten, or minus ten, you see?

A few experimenters add the comment, which is included in the instructions to them, "You have about five seconds per photo," to the end of the instructions to the subject. This usually happens if the experimenter has had a slow-poke or two already and hence is spurred to take preventive action.

Those experimenters who omit instructions most frequently leave out the last two sentences, "All ready? This is photo number one." In four of

[12] Exceptions are provided by those experimenters who engage in overtime interactions with the subject during the "break" between the three "acts" of the experiment. The overtime interaction is a rather common phenomenon in these sessions. It is as if the intermissions become temporal "back regions" in which the experimenter can forget the script and improvise a little. Some of the overtime interactions are more lengthy and more charming than those quoted in this paper. However, the poor quality of the sound track makes it difficult to do more than gather the sense of these pow-wows.

the dyads, "All ready?" is omitted; and in fifteen, "This is photo number one" is omitted.

The "all readies" which *are* said range from "Are you ready?" accompanied by a pause, a look, and a smile, to a perfunctory "All rightie" to no one in particular as the experimenter picks up the first photo.

XIII

With the experimental sessions now anywhere from 83.2 to 148.8 seconds old, we come finally to that part of the experiment with which the texts are most concerned—that period in which the experimenter presents the stimulus and the subject makes his responses. In this experiment the intended stimuli are the ten photos, which have been standardized so that their mean rating is zero. It is in this period of standardized research that all the variance is supposed to be found—that is, of course, the variance introduced by the individual differences between subjects and/or treatment conditions.

Unintended stimulation in this phase of the experiment is introduced by the different ways in which the experimenters present the stimuli. Some experimenters hold the photos by one of the lower corners, some by one of the sides, some by cupping the photos in their hands. Some experimenters stand the photos on the table; some hold them at the subject's eye level; some hold them at their own eye level; some hold them midway between their eye level and the subject's. Some experimenters hold the photos near their own body; some thrust them far out toward the subject. Some experimenters tilt the photos toward the subject, some away from the subject. Some experimenters raise and lower the photos quickly, and some do it leisurely. The permutations of these presentations merely begin to define the range of differences in stimulus presentation.

There are also variations in what the experimenters do while awaiting the subjects' responses. Some experimenters rest their chin on the palm of their free hand and stare boredly into space. Some keep their heads buried in the paper on which they will record the rating. Some watch the subject throughout the latency period before the response is given. If, as many do, the subject begins to smile, giggle, or laugh, while trying to decide on the rating to give, some experimenters join in the fun ("mutual flooding-out") and some do not. And of course some experimenters (I am tempted to say all) vacillate in their mode of presentation, not only from subject to subject but also from photo to photo:

> As he says, "All ready?" the E picks up the pack of photos in his right hand. S scratches her leg. E says, "This is photo number one," and picks it up by the bottom. He holds it just barely above the table top and looks all the while directly at the S. S meditates. E looks down to

his data sheet. S scratches her leg and then her nose. S gives her rating. E raises his eyebrow, fiddles with his ball-point pen, and records the rating. As he shows her photo number two, he doesn't look at her. Then, as she deliberates, he does look up at her. On number three he keeps his eyes glued to the data sheet. He is now holding the photos near her eye level. He doesn't look at her at all while she is rating photo number four. As he shows her number five, he looks up at her for a second. During number six he doesn't look at her but rests his chin on his free hand. During number seven he watches her from the time the photo is raised to the time she makes her rating. He looks at her as he raises number eight and smiles when she smiles but then looks away. He alternates, looking at her during number nine but not during number ten.

Another unintended variable is the amount of time allowed the subject for each rating. The experimenter has been instructed to allow no more than five seconds per photo. Besides requiring a time judgment, this order requires of the experimenter, if the subject has not yet given a rating when the five seconds are up, an act of socially approved aggression—putting the photo down, saying "Time," or the like. This proves to be very difficult for these experimenters to do—and so presents a minor tribute to that theory of face-to-face interaction which underlines the extent to which participants will try to de-stress any potentially challenging aspect of an encounter (Goffman, 1955).

In most cases a subtle tug of war develops.[13] Some experimenters, judging the time to be up, lower the photos little by little in hesitant, jerky movements, until the subject finally makes his rating. Some tap their pencil impatiently on the rating sheet or twiddle their thumbs. Some take to glancing up at and away from the subject several times. And others just sit and wait, giving the subjects all the time in the world.

Those experimenters who engage in some verbal exchange with the subject during the rating period constitute a final deviant class. The rating period is supposed to involve a silent experimenter standardly presenting a standard stimulus to a verbally responsive subject. But this is not always the case. Some experimenters preface each photo with "This is photo number . . ." Some repeat each of the subject's ratings. And some do both:

E: Photo number one.
S: Minus two.
E: Photo number two.

[13] The experimenters' behavior here is reminiscent of the situation in which someone says playfully, "You'd better do such and such before I count to five" and then counts, "One, two, three, four, four and a half, four and three quarters," etc. The point is that the experimenters achieve this effect in different ways.

S: Minus two.

E: Minus two. Photo number three.

S: Plus four.

E: Photo number four.

S: Plus three.

E: Plus three. Photo number five.

S: Plus three.

E: Plus three. Photo number six.

S: Minus seven.

E: Number seven.

S: Minus two.

E: Photo number eight.

S: Plus five.

E: Plus five. Photo number nine.

S: Minus five.

E: Minus five. Photo number ten.

S: Uh, plus two.

E: Plus two.

XIV

The task is done. No further variation in the way the experimenters treat their subjects will affect their responses in this experiment. But how about a later one?

All the experimenter has to do now is say good-bye. His instructions tell him, "Say hello and good-bye to the subject and nothing else except what is printed on the instructions sheet." But a bare "good-bye" seems to end a relationship on a rather inconclusive note. The subject has given of his time to fulfill an invitation. It is only social, then, for some experimenters to say at the close of the session, "Thank you very much," "That's all there is to it, Laura," "OK, Cindy, very well done," "OK, Diana, that's all." The subject (especially when she is young and pretty) is sent back out into the "real" world with a warm smile and a sense of having been appreciated.

Exceptions occur in those rare cases in which the experimenter follows his instructions to the letter. As it is, only one experimenter literally says "Good-bye," but others utter a noncommittal "OK" or "That's it." In some cases they don't even look up as the subject leaves.

Why might these unlike leave-takings be important? One reason that some experimenters prefer using animals as subjects is to be able to control the individual differences associated with the disparate past experiences of human subjects. Now it stands to reason that, among these disparate past experiences, disparate past experiences in *experiments* will be especially relevant. Hence, especially since these warm and cold farewells usually conclude warm and cold interactions respectively, they might differently influence the subjects' future expectations about, first impressions of, and behavior in later experiments—as well as those of the college friends to whom they communicate their experience in a psychological experiment.

XV

Although the experimenter and subject have finished their parts, let us bring them back for a brief encore. We will call it "Sex and the Psychological Experiment."

I have made reference in passing to several deviations from the experimental instructions and variations in experimenter behavior which occur when male experimenters interact with female subjects. Male experimenters are more likely to smile while greeting female than male subjects, and they are more likely to use a female's name ("This one here, Phyllis") or an affectionate equivalent ("dear") at some point in the experiment than they are a male's. They are more likely to smile at a female subject at the end of the experiment than at a male, and they are more likely to use the subject's name in saying good-bye if it is a she than if it is a he. I now want to suggest a bit more about sex differences in the experimental interaction and their possible implications.

In one of their studies, Rosenthal and his associates at North Dakota found in one case that a female subject on a post-experimental rating form concerning subjects' awareness of verbal conditioning made clear reference to the sexual implications of being alone with a male in a small room and described her male experimenter in inordinate detail (Rosenthal *et al.*, 1963c). The authors note that the experimental interaction lasted only about five minutes and that this "seems to be an unusually short period for the development of 'transference' reactions toward an experimenter." I would suggest that to bring an already overworked concept such as that of transference (Jackson and Haley, 1963) into the discussion probably obscures more than it reveals. Instead, in keeping with the focus of bringing both members of the dyad back into the picture, I would wonder whether this experimenter did anything differently from other experimenters to merit such attention. The films indicate that some of our male experimenters paid more attention to their job and some more to the sex of the subject than did others. A pilot study in which "subjects" act as participant-observers and monitor experimenters' behavior suggests that this result is not unique. It is a convenient fiction to believe that the sex of the subject does not alter the behavior of the experimenter.

But there exists an entire research literature on sex differences (see, for example, Terman and Tyler, 1946). This literature focuses on the question of what males and females do differently. These differences are measured by their differential responses to the stimuli in tests and experiments.

However, in this experiment male and female subjects are treated differently by male experimenters. What if this is true in other studies as well? To the extent that the literature on sex differences is based upon empirical research, it usually presumes some "constant," some "same experimental situation" to which both sexes are responding. However, is there such constancy?

The evidence in this experiment is that there is not. To give but one interesting example, male experimenters look significantly more often at female subjects than they do at male subjects, but they exchange significantly more glances with male subjects than they do with female subjects. These data suggest a complicated variability in visual behavior in which when the male experimenter looks up, as he often does, the female subject tends to look down or away, whereas on those less frequent occasions when the male experimenter looks up at a male subject the latter does not evade his glance. Here, then, we have a new sex difference to add to the literature: the sex of the subject affects the behavior of the experimenter. The question is: once we know this can we quote from the research literature on sex differences quite as confidently as we did before?

XVI

In concluding this chapter I want first to quickly review its contribution to the major goal of this part of the thesis: the establishment of the generality of experimenter variability, experimenter effect, experimenter bias. Then I will make a preliminary assessment of the light it throws upon two issues about which I will have more to say in Part IV—the role of the psychological experimenter and the philosophy of the psychological experiment.

Throughout this chapter the question I have endeavored to keep uppermost in the reader's mind is: how much of this extemporaneous experimenter behavior is peculiar to the specific case under study? To help answer this question I have suggested dividing the improvisations into roughly two groups. The first group represents deviations from accepted experimental procedure. It is difficult to say how general such deviations are in psychological experiments, for there has been insufficient monitoring of them. The second group represents behaviors upon which accepted experimental procedure has thus far made no pronouncement. In this group I include the experimenter's kinesic and vocal behavior. I think that, in the absence of agreed-upon standards of kinesic and vocal behavior, it is possible to deduce that experimenter variability in these modalities is quite general. And there is no reason I can see to suspect that such variability makes a difference only in this experiment. How much difference it makes in other experiments is, to use what the reader should now realize is a misleadingly simple phrase, "an empirical question."

But why has experimental psychology been so lax in developing standards for the nonverbal aspects of experimenters' behavior? I suggest that the laxity is partly a result of failure to see that the psychological experiment is a social interaction. Only after it is viewed in this light can we bring to bear upon the psychological experiment what we know about interactions and conversations in general. As Birdwhistell states, "probably no more than 30 to 35 per cent of the social meaning of a conversation or an interaction is carried by the words" (1959, p. 13).

Now, as to the role of the psychological experimenter and the philosophy of the psychological experiment. I have been concerned with a discrepancy between the ideal and the real. Psychological experiments are supposed to be standardized, controlled, replicable, objective. These experimental sessions were unstandardized, uncontrolled, different, heterogeneous. Psychological experimenters are supposed to be inflexible, mechanical, "programmed," standardized in their behavior.[14] These experimenters improvised and ad-libbed and were nonconforming, different, variable in their behavior.

The resemblance between this experiment as observed and the experiment as it is usually reported is at best a likeness between distant relatives in an extended family.

What seem to be standardized are our collective illusions about the "standardized" experiment and the "standardized" experimenter.

Keeping this discrepancy in mind, let me now review the claims and realities concerning the behavior of experimenters from the standpoint of role theory. Translated into role language, the ideal of experimental control requires that as soon as he enters the "lab" the experimenter must embrace the experimenter role and discard all other roles. He is supposed to act solely in accord with the normative demands encumbent upon anyone who assumes the status of experimenter. All his additional roles become oppositional roles which he must leave outside on the coat rack when he dons his symbolic white coat.

But the normative demands that have been written for him have been based on an incomplete analysis of the experimenter's role. The role prescriptions have been derived from a *natural-* rather than a *social-*science

---

[14] Riecken says: "Finally, let us note about the experimenter that he is inflexible in his behavior. *Ideally*, at least, the experimenter's every move in an experiment has been predetermined and can be said to be 'programmed' . . . He has a script that provides lines and business. The script cannot be revised or adapted to meet the exigencies of particular subjects or events . . . his activities are, indeed, a mechanical program of activities." (Riecken, 1958, pp. 12–13, my emphasis.)

perspective on the psychological experiment. They refer to his role as stimulus presenter but neglect the fact that he is also a host, an interviewer, a party to a two-person interaction. Hence, the rules that would tell him how to behave in some of *these* functions—how to greet subjects, whether to look and smile at them, etc.—remain unwritten, and so, given this blurriness of the norms, one finds creativity where one is supposed to find conformity.

This creativity takes the form of *role distance*, a concept suggested by Goffman in order "to adapt role concepts for use in close studies of moment-to-moment behavior" (1961). Role distance—a previously unheard-of concept in role analysis—refers to "one type of divergence between obligations and actual performance." This type of divergence occurs when the role player steps out of the role he is supposed to be playing at the moment and into one of his other roles.

Goffman elucidates: interactions are "multi-situated." The participants in any one interaction also enact a number of other roles in the society at large. For example, the experimenter may also be a professor, a hypnotist, a therapist, a graduate student, etc. These additional roles cannot be entirely excluded from the interaction. Every now and then the role player slips back into a role which is supposed to be temporarily subordinated. In Goffman's inimitable phrasing, despite whatever discipline he is supposed to maintain over nonrelevant role behavior, he "stands guard at the door of the tent but lets all his friends and relatives crawl in under the flap." (See also Strauss, 1959.)

Does the concept of role distance apply only to degrading roles? Goffman thinks not. He writes that "roles certainly differ according to how seriously and fully the performers must stick to the script. [But] even in the most serious roles, such as that of surgeon, we find that there will be times when the full-fledged performer must unbend and behave simply as a male." We have seen that male experimenters are not above doing the same.

The concept of role distance allows us to reach by way of social-psychological theory the same conclusion we reached by way of observation; that is, the ideal experimenter is supposed to be a wooden soldier who thoroughly disciplines any nonrelevant role behavior (e.g., smiling at pretty girls). Of such an ideal Goffman warns:

Perhaps there are times when an individual does march up and down like a wooden soldier, tightly rolled up in a particular role. It is true that here and there we can pounce on a moment when an individual sits fully astride a single role, head erect, eyes front, but the next moment the picture is shattered into many pieces and the individual divides into different persons holding the ties of different spheres of life by his hands, by his teeth, and by his grimaces. (Goffman, 1961, p. 143 and *passim*.)

Applying it to most roles, the concept of role distance shows up the inadequacy of the going role theory. But in the case of the experiment, it also shows up the unreality of the going philosophy of experimentation. For when the experimenter exhibits role distance, experimental conditions become destandardized. The experimenter's uncontrolled nonverbal behavior insures that experimental observations are made under uncontrolled conditions.

So we have moved from the role of the experimenter to the philosophy of the experiment. I wish to make two points in conclusion.

First, psychologists traditionally consider that the variance in the responses of subjects in the same treatment condition is the result of individual differences among *subjects*. These individual differences are conceptualized as intervening variables. They are considered the sole source of error variance in experiments.

But psychologists have located error variance *within* the subject too quickly. There is enough variability in the interaction between experimenter and subject to account for some unknown amount of it. This entire chapter can be seen as a specification of dimensions of sources of error variance in the experimental conditions themselves.[15] Recognizing that the unstandardized aspects of the interactions of experimenters and subjects represent interpersonal "intervening variables" allows us to reduce the explanatory burden placed on the statistical intervening variables by putting some of the variance in experimental results back into the social environment.

Second, and finally, the philosophy of the psychological experiment must come to terms with the social nature of the psychological experiment. The standardization myth resulted from the direct transplanting into the soil of psychology of a philosophy of experimentation which had flowered and borne fruit in the quite different climate of the physical and natural sciences. In its eager acceptance of this way of looking at and talking about the psychological experiment, psychology skipped the natural history stage. Proscription preceded description. As a result, we know more about what is supposed to happen in a psychological experiment than we do about what does happen.

I am trying to say that although an experimenter-subject dyad may be viewed as a tight little island of social interaction cut off from the mainland of everyday social gatherings, it is an island to which the population of two carries its entire interpersonal repertoire. A philosophy of science based

---

[15] Alternatively, as Eugene Gendlin first suggested to me, it can be seen as an attempt to suggest the interpersonal dimensions which might have to be considered in a definition of "empathy."

upon the natural and physical sciences and taking as its unit the monad rather than the dyad cannot fully comprehend experiments in which inter- actions such as the following, transcribed from one of the filmed experi- mental sessions, regularly take place:

S: (Sneezes.)
E: *Gesundheit.*
S: Thank you.
E: You're welcome.

6

Examiner Difference: Does It Make a Difference?

In the preceding chapter I attempted to establish the generality of experimenter variability by means of an analysis which was theoretical, deductive, and oriented toward variability in experimental procedure. Although the reasoning was accompanied by detailed observations of an experiment, it did not depend upon those observations. From the gap between the traditional typification of psychological experimentation and the nature of social interaction, it could simply have been deduced that, in general, experimenters will differ in the manner in which they behave in the psychological experiment.

The present chapter, in contrast, will attempt to establish the generality of experimenter variability by means of an analysis which is empirical, inductive, and oriented toward variability in experimental results. The answer to the question whether experimenter effects and biases are indigenous to this particular task or set of experimenters is simply—no. Bodies of literature exist which show that psychological experimenters sometimes obtain significantly different results from comparable subjects. A review of one part of this literature will inductively buttress general notion (c) by presenting twenty or more independent confirmations of it.

There are at least three more or less well-defined "areas" of the literature which could be reviewed. One is the entire research program of Robert
Rosenthal, out of which my work grew. Fortunately that research has been
collected in a single volume and so is readily accessible (Rosenthal, 1966).

A second less well-defined "area" consists of the various studies of traditional experimental tasks which have indicated the influence of the experimenter on the results of the research. Some of this work has already been
alluded to in passing and much of it will be referred to again at the end of
this chapter. Unfortunately this rapidly growing body of evidence has not
as yet been collected, so to speak, under a single roof, for the evaluation of
the curious and the skeptical.

The third area, the area I will review in some detail, is that of psychological testing. I will discuss studies of so-called "examiner differences" and
"examiner bias" (or "influence") in intelligence tests, the Rorschach, and
the Thematic Apperception Test. Of the two more or less distinct traditions within the testing movement—the psychometric and the psychodiagnostic—the intelligence test stems from the former and the Rorschach and
TAT from the latter. I have purposely included tests from both traditions
so as to increase the generality of the results.

It is worth noting that although the two traditions differ in many respects—so many respects, in fact, that one is surprised to find any common
denominator—they have in the past been in agreement with each other,
and with experimental psychology, on the issue of the place of the examiner. His place was a nonplace. In the indices to early psychometric texts one
finds no reference to "the tester"; in the indices to early psychodiagnostic
texts one finds no reference to "the examiner." Both traditions have shared
with experimental psychology what I shall now call "the dogma of immaculate perception"—the underlying assumption being that the observer's contribution to his observation is nil.

As Julian Wohl puts it, in the psychometric tradition the tester was
originally considered to be:

> . . . an impersonal factor in a mechanized measuring process . . . the
> least significant element in the testing process . . . The psychometric
> tradition [saw] the actors in [the testing] interaction as responding
> to each other ideally not at all . . . An underlying assumption fol-
> lowed here [was] that one can have measurement or observation with-
> out this creating a disturbance or effect on what is being observed or
> measured. (Wohl, 1963, p. 360.)

In a similar way, the X-ray theory of projective testing (Frank,
1939) assumed that, regardless of who the examiner was, unconscious tendencies existing within the testee would emerge from the nether regions of
the personality, seeping out like the fumes from a long forgotten under-

ground wine cellar, and impress themselves upon the unstructured stimulus presented by the test materials. As in the case of the psychometric tradition, the focus was on the subject and the test materials, and the unit of study was the individual rather than the social interaction. The examiner was relegated to some shadowy background position and treated as a nonperson. It was (and still is) customary for a patient in a clinical setting to be tested by just one examiner. To reiterate a point made in the opening pages of Part I, this procedure implicitly assumes that examiners retain their anonymity in the testing situation, and that therefore different examiners would elicit identical protocols from the same subject.

This earlier theory of psychological testing is in the process of being superseded by a theory in which the examiner "is given full equality with the testee and the test as a determinant of the outcome of the testing situation" (Wohl, 1963, p. 363). In retrospect it looks to Wohl as if the former ideal of objectivity in "*experimentation* and testing" which was "defined implicitly as the observation of behavior without an observer" was "a false objectivity" and "epistemological nonsense" (p. 364, my emphasis).

Note that Wohl refers here to the false ideal of objectivity in both "experimentation and testing." Bracketing the two represents an almost unique insight on his part that the transformation in testing philosophy which was produced to some degree by the results of studies such as the ones I will presently review has implications for the philosophy of psychological experimentation as well as for the philosophy of psychological testing.

This is an important point. I indicated in the historical introduction[1] that this so-called "examiner difference" literature represented one of the early areas within psychology in which systematic study of the personal equation reappeared after its lengthy eclipse. However, until now the significance of this literature for experimental psychology has been misconstrued. As I put it earlier, distance precluded insight. The consignment of these studies to the cubbyholes labeled "*examiner* difference" and "*examiner* bias" indicted clinical psychologists and let experimental psychologists off scot free. It was a case of "them," not "us."

If this consignment were just, then my reviewing this literature would not contribute one whit toward establishing the generality of *experimenter* variability. But, since I obviously think it will, I had best indicate right away the fallacy in the way the so-called "examiner difference" literature has been interpreted.

It seems that the occupational rivalry between experimenters and clinicians has led to an obfuscation of the implications of the "examiner difference" literature. In the opening sentence of one of his review articles, Ro-

[1] See Chapter 1, section IX.

senthal writes that "more than thirty years ago . . . we began as *clinical* psychologists to examine experimentally our personal effect upon our patients' performance in a clinical test or task" (1963c, p. 324, emphasis in the original). For my purposes the key word in that sentence is not "clinical" but "experimentally." It implies that much of the literature which has been assigned to the category "*examiner* differences" was from the start a literature on "*experimenter* differences" as well.

Let me elucidate this point. The following four types of design can be found in the "examiner difference" literature:

1. A gives B a psychological test. A is working in a clinical installation; B is a patient. Later on, C comes along and takes the test protocol from the files. He adds it to other protocols obtained by other people in the installation. He then publishes a correlational study on "examiner differences."

2. A gives B a psychological test. A is working in a clinical installation; B is a patient. C has placed A in a treatment condition. C may be A's teacher, supervisor, or some official in the installation. A does not know that he is collecting data for an experiment. C has placed other people in the installation in other treatment conditions. He then collects the data and publishes an experimental study of "examiner differences."

3. A gives B a psychological test. A is working in an academic setting; B is a *subject*. He comes in not for diagnosis but as a paid or voluntary participant in research. Although C misinforms him as to the exact nature of the study, A does know that it is an experiment. C similarly misinforms the other "experimenters" whom he has recruited. C then publishes the results as evidence for "examiner differences."

4. A gives B a psychological test. A is working in an academic setting; B is a subject. Either A is told that he is participating in an experiment on "examiner differences," or A will himself be the author of the study.

The typology is not exhaustive. However, it will do. In the last two cases it is clear that differences between data-collectors in obtained results should properly be called "experimenter differences," whereas in the first two cases they could be called "examiner differences."

In other words, some of the evidence that examiners influence the results of the tests they give comes from *experiments* on psychological testing. In these cases there is a peculiar overlapping of roles. The person who gathers the data is at once an "examiner" and an "experimenter." The tasks are at once "tests" and "experiments." Thus, these results could have been counted as evidence for experimenter influence as well as for examiner influence. But since experimenters were more inclined to discover what they considered to be covert dealings in the transactions of clinicians than in their own, this double-edged nature of the results of experiments on examiner influence has passed relatively unremarked.[2]

[2] This redefinition of some of the "examiner difference" studies allows us to look

In what follows I will review studies which fall properly in the "experimenter difference" literature and studies which fall properly in the "examiner difference" literature. The former studies will be cited in line with the primary goal of this part: to establish the generality of the experimenter's contribution to his research results. The latter studies will be cited in order to make it clear that examiner effect and bias are as real as experimenter effect and bias. This will also allow me to say something about effect, bias, and clinical practice.

II

In an early study in an area which in the 1960's has become one of vital concern, Herman Canady sought to answer the questions: "To what extent do we know that the results of intelligence tests given by white examiners to Negro children are reliable? Can a white examiner get 'en rapport' with Negro children? Would there be conspicuous differences between the scores obtained by a Negro (N) examiner and a white (W) examiner giving tests to the same group of Negro children? What is the frequency or extent of error, if any, made by white examiners in testing Negro children?" (Canady, 1936, p. 208.)

To study these questions he did an experiment. He had seventy-three pairs of intelligence tests given to forty-eight Negro and twenty-five white elementary school children. The examiners were twenty white graduate students in psychology at Northwestern, all of whom had been trained in the use of psychological tests, and one similarly trained Negro examiner who was Canady himself. All examiners knew that an experiment was going on. The Stanford version of the Binet-Simon scale was used since its test-retest consistency was reported as between .85 and .90.

Each child was given the test twice, with the interval between testing sessions varying from a day to a year. The person doing the retesting was ignorant of the results of the previous test. Twenty-three Negro children and eighteen white children were tested first by a Negro and second by a white examiner. The remaining twenty-five Negroes and seven whites were tested first by a white and second by a Negro examiner.

Canady's hypotheses were: "If there were a tendency for the Negro children tested first by (N) to test higher than those tested second by

---

at them as a sub-set of the second "area" mentioned previously. They are studies of one kind of experimental task—the psychological test—which have indicated experimenter influences. Rosenthal has a rather different rationale for including studies of "examiner differences" in his review of "experimenter attributes as determinants of subjects' responses." (See Rosenthal, 1963c, p. 324, footnotes 2 and 3.) It is worth noting that if one accepts Rosenthal's rationale *all* studies to be reported can be considered relevant to the question of the generality of *experimenter* variability.

(W); and for those tested second by (N) to test higher than those tested first by (W), then we would infer that this gain in IQ was due to the personal equation of examiners. If there were a tendency for the white children tested first by (N) to test lower than those tested second by (W), and those tested second by (N) to test lower than those tested first by (W), then we would infer that this loss in IQ was due to the personal equation of examiners" (p. 214).

Canady's hypotheses were borne out for three of the four conditions: Negro children tested first by (N) scored significantly higher than when tested later by (W); Negro children tested first by (W) scored significantly lower than when tested later by (N); white children tested first by (N) scored significantly lower than when tested later by (W). The fourth treatment condition, in which the number of cases was only seven, did not produce any differences.

The largest change was a gain of twenty-eight IQ points made by a white child who was tested early in the month by a Negro examiner and late in the month by a white examiner. Overall, however, the results when the Negro child is tested first by a Negro examiner and second by a white examiner are the most interesting. One expects IQs to go up on retesting if there is any change at all. But twelve of the Negro children lost IQ points on being retested by a white examiner, whereas only seven gained. Canady concludes that "an average increase of six points in IQ was found for the Negro children under (N) and an average decrease of six points for the whites under (N)" (p. 218).

For some time, little of the considerable amount of IQ research which was concerned with Negro-white comparisons followed Canady's example of assessing the effect of the race of the examiner. In their review of Negro-white comparisons, Ralph Dreger and Kent Miller write that at times "the color of the examiner has been taken into account in assessing results; in others this factor has been ignored" (1960, p. 372). They look with some suspicion at a study of 420 Negro children aged six to twelve from towns in five states in the deep South to whom the WISC was administered. The author of the study administered 342 of the tests and reported that "excellent rapport was obtained." Dreger and Miller wonder how "in the light of the conspicuous Southern accent of the chief white examiner" this feat was accomplished (p. 367).

Historical conditions in the United States in the 1960's have produced renewed interest in Negro-white differences and similarities and the methodological problems of assessing them (e.g., Pettigrew, 1964b). A considerable literature on the cultural biases in IQ tests has accumulated (see Riessman et al., 1964, pp. 248–58) and a set of guidelines for testing minority group children has been formulated (SPSSI, 1964). A part of this trend has been to abandon the model of the monad in at least this research area and focus attention on the effect of the race of the examiner on the results. To take but two examples, in a study of southern Negro college students, it was found that when a digit-symbol substitution task was presented as a test of eye-hand coordination, "Negro subjects scored higher with a white administrator than they did with a Negro administrator. But when the same test was described as an intelligence test, there was marked impairment of performance with the white tester, while subjects who were tested by the Negro experimenter showed a slight improvement" (Katz et al., 1964, p. 54). Going a long way down the age scale, in the retesting of Negro infants by white examiners on the Gessel Developmental Examination it was found that on the third retesting (about age two) they fared poorly in comparison with white infants, whereas on the first two testings the groups were on a par. After considering a remark made by one of the Negro mothers, the authors divided the total Gessel score into verbal comprehension and verbal responsiveness components. They were then able to note that for the Negro infants only the latter had fallen off vis-à-vis white infants. They conclude that "early awareness of racial differences and loss of rapport" caused this inhibition of responsiveness (Pasamanick and Knobloch, 1964, p. 268). It seems that Negroes learn very young to "play Negro" (Pettigrew, 1964a, p. 116) with a white examiner.

Should whites then test whites with white IQ tests and Negroes test Negroes with Negro IQ tests in a separate but equal solution to a methodological problem which in the racial area is becoming increasingly visible? One case study makes it clear that it is not the color of the examiner alone that can cause examiner difference or examiner bias. I quote it in detail since it is one of the few statements in the literature that goes beyond the effect of the particular examiner to consideration of the influence on test results of larger and also more subtle factors such as the setting, the interaction of staff members, and the subject's perception of these:

> A few years ago a birthday party for a member of the staff at a well-known psychological clinic played a novel role in the test performance of a Negro child. Prior to the party this boy, whom we shall call James, had been described on the psychological record as "sullen, surly, slow, unresponsive, apathetic, unimaginative, lacking in inner life." This description was based on his behavior in the clinic interviews and on his performance on a number of psychological measures including an intelligence test and a personality test. His was not an unusual record; many culturally deprived children are similarly portrayed.
>
> On the day of the birthday party, James was seated in an adjoining room waiting to go into the clinician's office. It was just after the lunch hour and James had the first afternoon appointment. The conclusion of the lunch break on this particular day was used by the staff to

present a surprise birthday cake to one of the clinicians who happened to be a Negro. The beautifully decorated cake was brought in and handed to the recipient by James' clinician who was white, as were all the other members of the staff. The Negro woman was deeply moved by the cake—and the entire surprise. In a moment of great feeling, she warmly embraced the giver of the cake. James inadvertently perceived all this from his vantage point in the outer office. That afternoon he showed amazing alacrity in taking the tests and responding in the interview. He was no longer sullen and dull. On the contrary, he seemed alive, enthusiastic, and he answered questions readily. His psychologist was astonished at the change and in the course of the next few weeks retested James on the tests on which he had done so poorly. He now showed marked improvement, and she quickly revised not only the test appraisal of him on the clinical record card, but her general personality description of him as well. (Riessman, 1962, pp. 49–50.)

Riessman concludes in italics that *"the test is a social situation."* He goes on to say that "the testing situation . . . reflects a relationship between people, a relationship that is often remarkably subtle. And when anything hampers this relationship, the result is likely to show in the test score itself. This can occur on an individual test as well as a group test, an IQ test as well as a personality test, a subject matter examination as well as a psychological measure" (p. 50).

Everything Riessman says of a psychological test is applicable to a psychological experiment as well. Studies of research have shown that the race of the experimenter can make a difference (Rankin and Campbell, 1955; Trent, 1954; Katz, 1964; Katz, *et al.*, 1964). Perhaps it takes a time of historical crisis for a particular variable such as race to become sufficiently salient so that researchers will begin to study the effect of the race of the researcher himself on results in research on race.

Canady's work was on the intelligence of Negro children. It has taken time, but work on Negro intelligence in general is now taking into consideration the effect of the examiner. Only a minority of studies of the intelligence of *children* have followed Canady's paradigm (e.g., Sacks, 1952). In his review of research with the WISC, William Littell notes that "the possible effects of differences in the examiner's technique of administration is another problem area which has not received the attention it merits, as is the whole field of possibilities arising from the relation between the examiner and the child . . ." (1960, p. 146). He goes on to suggest that patterns of subtest variations may reflect variations in the ability, comfort, and expectations of the examiner with various subtests, as well as differential abilities of the subject. This possibility bears upon the question of the diagnostic validity of WISC subtest deviations.

Some work has been done on specific subtests. Edwin Cohen reasoned that different IQ testers "may affect the anxiety or motivation of the subject differently, producing changes in test results. For example, if an examiner arouses anxiety in a subject by his attitude, mood, comments, etc., the subject might do more poorly on digit span. . . ." (Cohen, 1950, p. 150.)

Cohen did not experimentally test this hypothesis. Instead he did a study to find out whether different examiners tend to get different subtest scores, on the average, for certain subtests. He collected a minimum of seventeen scored IQ tests from each of thirteen examiners. The only difference found was that "subjects tested by examiner A made significantly higher scores on arithmetic than would a random sample of clinic subjects of the same intelligence level" (p. 152).

Robert Young did an experiment which might really have been a test of Cohen's hypothesis. He selected forty-eight "experimenters" at random from introductory psychology classes. Personality measures on these experimenters were obtained by the Worchel Self Activity Inventory. Each of the experimenters then administered the digit-span test to one of forty-eight subjects also selected on the basis of personality measures. Reliable differences in the performance of the subjects were found to be a function of the experimenter and of the sex of the subject. "Subjects with 'poorly adjusted' experimenters performed better than subjects with 'well-adjusted' experimenters. . . ." (Young, 1959, p. 375.)

Some of the most clever experimentation in the area of examiner differences on intelligence tests has been performed by Joseph Masling (1959). He had eleven graduate students who had given from ten to two hundred Wechsler-Bellevues administer the Information, Comprehension, and Similarities subtests under the guise of interest on Masling's part in the comparability of various short forms of the W-B. The examiners were told that their subjects would be undergraduates completing their assignment of participating in psychological experiments. The examiners knew they were experimenters. The examiners were asked not to "bias" their results by "communicating with each other" and to urge the subjects not to discuss the study with their friends.

Actually the subjects were two "attractive female accomplices" of Masling who acted in either a warm or cold role toward the examiners, giving memorized answers, fourteen of which had been devised so as to be difficult to score. Each session was taped so as to be certain that the answers given were the same and that only the style of intraction differed.

Each accomplice played five warm and five cold roles, and each examiner saw one subject who acted warm and one who acted cold.

In scoring the responses, the examiners tended to be more lenient to the warm subject than to the cold one ($p = .056$), to give more reinforcing comments to the warm subject than to the cold one ($p = .025$), and to give more opportunity to clarify or correct responses to the warm subject than to the cold one ($p = .025$). More experienced examiners were as much influenced by the atmosphere of the interaction as were less experienced examiners.

Besides the statistically significant results due to the treatment conditions, Masling also reports results which indicate that there are individual differences in the way the examiners proceeded and the results they obtained. In fact, "the differences between conditions seemed much smaller than the differences among examiners" (p. 339). Examiner one made a total of fourteen remarks to his subjects, while examiner seven made sixty-four. Examiner eight's scoring favored the warm condition by 4.8 points, while examiner five's scoring favored the cold condition by 4.8 points. These individual differences are reminiscent of the ones reported in the previous chapter for the person-perception experiment.

It is important to note that in most of these studies it would be just to call the data-gatherers, as Young does, experimenters. However considered as experiments, the methodological limitations of this IQ research are painfully clear. Rather than doing research on "the personal equation of examiners," Canady—at best—was working on the "racial equation" and that with N of 1 for his Negro condition. He does not report between-examiner differences within the treatment condition "white examiner" and so no personal equation can be computed.

In using untrained undergraduate experimenters who administered just one subtest out of context, Young violates most principles of representative design (Hammond, 1954), and so generalization to clinical realities from his study of normal subjects is dangerous.

Masling is well aware that "the artificial nature of this study—the use of accomplices and relatively unsophisticated examiners, the extreme nature of the interaction, the use of ambiguous responses—together with the inadequate sampling of both the examiner and accomplice population—limits severely the generalization of these findings to non-laboratory settings" (1959, p. 340).

Furthermore, only Masling's study adequately sorts out the effect of examiner differences in administration from examiner differences in scoring.

Let us see whether the research using projectives tests is any better.

III

Emmett Baughman writes that "*a priori* one has reason to expect that projective data will be much more influenced by the relationship between S and E than will the information received in the more traditional psychometric examination. To indicate the capital of Italy is one thing; to reveal personal material is quite another, especially when one has only the vaguest idea of its real meaning and how it is going to be interpreted and used. . . ." (Baughman, 1951, p. 243.)

Notice that the fact which is usually cited in order to explain why Rorschach responses are relatively free of examiner influence—the unstructured nature of the test as opposed to the structured interview or the structured intelligence test—is the reason cited by Baughman in his argument for *a priori* consideration of examiner influence as greater on the Rorschach than on the objective test. Perhaps it is the competition of these hypotheses that has led to the large number of studies of examiner influence on the Rorschach.

The earliest studies were concerned simply with establishing by nonexperimental methods the fact of influential examiner differences. Baughman (1951) selected 133 Rorschach protocols from the files of a VA clinic. The protocols had been secured and scored by fifteen examiners. The patients had been assigned on the basis of examiner load. Baughman did a frequency analysis of the data with the null hypothesis being that on each scoring category each examiner would have as many scores above the median value for the total group as below, except for the operation of chance factors. The null hypothesis could safely be rejected. Twelve out of twenty-two scoring categories differed significantly at the .001 level and four more at the .05 level.[3] The examiners who contributed most to the variability, incidentally, were also the examiners who saw the largest number of patients.

Baughman was not certain that the subjects had been randomly assigned to the examiners, did not control for differences in the total number of responses, and did not separate administration from scoring effects.

David Berger improved on Baughman's procedures. The personal Rorschach of each of eight psychology interns was obtained and rechecked for consistency of scoring. These were Rorschachs taken by the interns when they were still freshmen in college and so "essentially unschooled and naïve in Rorschach doctrine and lore." (Berger, 1954, p. 245.)

A sample of the Rorschach records of patients examined by these eight interns was then collected. The complete sample of patients tested was evaluated to determine whether any difference existed in age, IQ, or diagnosis for those patients seen by each of the eight examiners. No significant differences were found.

The personal Rorschachs of the eight examiners were ranked on various scoring dimensions and percentages. The latter was done in order to correct for differences in the total number of responses. The Rorschachs they elicited were similarly ranked. The rank of each examiner on each of

[3] For the specific scoring categories influenced in each study see Friedman (1965). Suffice it to say that every scoring category has been affected in at least one study.

the twelve Rorschach scores of his personal Rorschach was compared with his rank on each of the twelve corresponding median scores of his elicited Rorschachs. For the number of populars, the rank-order correlation was .86, an occurrence which could happen by chance but once in a hundred times. For the number of space responses the correlation was .80 ($p = .03$). In Rosenthal's terminology, "model bias" had been demonstrated.

Berger did not have the patients' Rorschachs rescored. Hence, whether we have here a model bias in eliciting, recording, or scoring responses cannot be decided.

Robert Gibby, Daniel Miller, and Edward Walker corrected this oversight. Their subjects were male veterans between the ages of twenty-five and thirty-two, all of whom were functional rather than organic cases, and who were the most recently seen patients of twelve examiners, all of whom had had a minimum of two years' testing experience, used Beck's administration of the Rorschach, and had tested at least twenty patients. The assignment of patients was probably random since "it is determined by the day of the week when the patients are first admitted. Since there is no policy of scheduling any particular type of complaint on a given day, each psychologist had an equal chance of being assigned patients in all the diagnostic categories." (Gibby et al., 1953, p. 425.)

The obtained Rorschach records were coded and scored blind by one of the authors with a randomly selected sample of records scored by a second person for reliability purposes. Hence, any significant differences between examiners refer to examiner differences in elicited responses free of examiner variance in scoring.

Of nine absolute scores, three differed at the .05 level. "This is approximately seven times the number of significant variances that might occur by chance" (p. 426). Variances were also calculated for proportions with total number of responses taken as the denominator. When this was done, three were again significant beyond the .05 level.

The authors note that "in the case of [the scoring category] F, there is considerable range of means, from 10.0 to 20.8. If F is given its conventional interpretation as an indicator of control, the possibility arises that when testing members of a homogeneous population some examiners will elicit protocols which indicate overconstriction while the records obtained by others will indicate weak control" (p. 426). Thus the results are both statistically and diagnostically significant.

Another early study that separated administration from scoring effects was that of Richard Sanders and Sidney Cleveland (1953). It has the further advantage (and disadvantage) of having attempted to assess the personality differences among examiners which relate to differences in elicited responses by a mechanism more complex than that of a model bias.

After having obtained a personal Rorschach from each examiner-to-be,

Sanders and Cleveland trained nine graduate students in the administration of the Rorschach. Each of the nine then administered twenty Rorschachs to undergraduate subjects. Presumably the examiners knew the data was to be used for research rather than clinical purposes. At the end of each testing session the subject filled out a questionnaire rating the examiner on overt hostility and covert anxiety. The questionnaires were filled out only after the examiner had left the room and were placed in a sealed envelope. Indications of the examiners' covert hostility and covert anxiety were obtained by rating their personal Rorschachs.[4]

All records were scored blind by the authors and reliability of scoring around .90 obtained. Of twenty variables, nine were found to be related to examiner differences.

The findings as to the personality correlates of these differences were as follows:

1. Examiners ranked high on overt anxiety elicit from their subjects significantly more general responsiveness, more oppositional trends, and more responsiveness to external and emotional stimuli.

2. Examiners with high covert anxiety elicit significantly more human responses, more human movement, higher hostility-content scores, and a smaller percentage of animal responses than do examiners ranked low on covert anxiety.

3. The more overtly hostile examiners get Rorschachs suggesting passivity and stereotypy. Compared to examiners perceived as least hostile, those who are described as overtly hostile elicit significantly less hostile content and fewer human responses. The more overtly hostile examiners get slower reaction times than the less overtly hostile examiners.

4. Compared to examiners who rank low on covert hostility, the examiners high on covert hostility elicit significantly fewer animal responses, more hostility, more content categories, and more human responses.

The authors present no theoretical framework within which these particular relations between examiner attributes and Rorschach responses could begin to make sense.

Having established the existence of examiner effect on the Rorschach, researchers have zeroed in on selected examiner variables and selected portions of the Rorschach which they may affect.

A number of studies have investigated the effects of sex differences

[4] An interesting point here is that Sanders and Cleveland do not seem to have checked to see whether the personal Rorschachs which they had elicited from examiners showed any significant between-author differences. It is somewhat paradoxical that a study of examiner difference on the Rorschach should use the examiner's own Rorschach as a criterion for judging his covert hostility and covert anxiety. For, by the logic of the study, would not *that* Rorschach *also* depend upon who the examiner's examiner was?

between examiners. The results of the studies are ambiguous. Priscilla Alden and Arthur Benton (1951) selected one hundred Rorschach records from the files of a VA hospital. All the test subjects were males. Fifty of the examiners were male, and fifty were female. Alden and Benton found no significant differences in either overt or covert sexual responses that could be attributed to the sex of the examiner.

Henry Curtis and Elizabeth Wolf had different results (1951). They obtained the records of 368 male veterans tested by three female and seven male examiners. Comparing overt and covert sex responses given to each sex, they found statistically significant differences in both.

In an experimental study, Albert Rabin, William Nelson, and Margaret Clark (1954) found that sometimes the sex of the experimenter makes a difference and sometimes it does not. Subjects who had waited for the Rorschach examination in a room decorated with anatomical charts did not differ in the number of anatomical responses given to male and female experimenters. But those male subjects who had waited in a room decorated with pictures of nude women gave significantly more sexual responses to the male than to the female experimenter. The authors conclude that the female experimenter had an inhibiting effect upon the verbalization of sexual responses. Unfortunately they report no reaction times or eye movements by which we might check this conjecture. Furthermore, since the study uses an N of 1 for the experimenter condition "male" and N of 1 for the experimenter condition "female" and since few clinicians have their patients await the Rorschach in the Playboy Club, the generalizability of these results to the clinic is limited.

Another group of studies are those which have systematically varied aspects of the Rorschach administration which are probably unsystematically varied by different examiners in different ways in their everyday work. These studies tend to be experimental.

In an elegantly designed study, Edith Lord (1950) had each of thirty-six college students tested under three conditions of Rorschach administration—positive, neutral, and negative—and by each of three female examiners. The examiners knew they were experimenters. The order of examiner and type of administration were both counterbalanced. In the positive interaction the examiner was warm and charming; in the neutral interaction the examiner was efficient and businesslike; and in the negative interaction the examiner was harsh and demanding.

The results indicate that, while styles of administration made a difference, individual differences between examiners were even more noteworthy. The effect of the rejecting, disapproving test atmosphere was to produce a performance that was "less imaginative, less responsive, more stereotyped, and characterized by more self-questioning and more resistance against feelings of inadequacy" (Ainsworth, 1954, p. 459). In the warm, accepting test atmosphere the protocols were richer and showed a fuller use of the blot material.

However, "the effect of the artificially altered test atmosphere was much less than the effect of the examiners themselves" (Ainsworth, 1954, p. 460). Lord shows this by an exhaustive scoring-category comparison of the protocols obtained by the three female examiners. One seemed to produce Rorschachs indicating a threatening and frustrating situation. Another's elicited protocols implied an intellectual challenge but with considerable rapport. The third examiner evoked well-controlled emotionality. Lord obtained independent descriptions of the three examiners. These fit rather well the descriptions she drew out of their subjects' Rorschach responses.

Some idea of the extent to which the supposedly stable aspects of the Rorschach are susceptible to differences between examiners and differences between styles of administration can be gathered from the following aspect of Lord's data: Only fourteen of the thirty-six subjects maintained a constant experience balance (M: sum C ratio) through all the variations in the testing situations. Approximately two thirds of the subjects reversed their M: sum C ratio from one administration to the next or from one administrator to the next. As Lord puts it, "the proportion between M and sum C was exceedingly shifty . . ." (1950, p. 9).

Considering the clinical emphasis often placed upon the experience balance, it would seem that these results are diagnostically as well as statistically significant.

In the person-perception experiment reported in Part II we have seen that experimenters vary in the fidelity with which they read the mimeographed instructions. Examiners probably vary even more than do experimenters in this aspect of their task because there are different "standard" Rorschach instructions. The variety of verbal directions is probably limited only by the number of testers. By virtue of these variations in instructions examiners probably project different definitions of the testing situation. Hence, the results obtained in an experiment conducted by Edith Henry and Julian Rotter (1956) are worth noting. It was intimated to one group of undergraduate subjects that the Rorschach had been used in mental hospitals to detect imbalances in a person's emotional life. Another group received the regular Klopfer instructions. The former group responded with fewer responses, more popular, animal, and form responses, and better responses than the latter group. In general they produced sparse, "safe" records.

It has been hypothesized that examiners differ in the way they conduct the Rorschach inquiry. To find out whether there was in fact differential examiner influence on the Rorschach inquiry, Gibby conducted an experiment in which there were two experimental groups. The twelve examiners in one group were randomly assigned 240 patients at a VA installation. They administered the Rorschach with a nonstandardized inquiry. Nine other examiners tested 135 patients with a standardized inquiry which allowed them to ask only, "Where in the blot is . . . ? What about this blot makes it look like . . . ? What else about the blot makes it look like . . . ?"

All protocols were scored twice by someone other than the examiners. First they were scored only for the free-association or performance-proper phase. Then, taking into consideration the changes brought about in the inquiry, they were scored again. Variability in the total number of responses was controlled arithmetically by calculating percentages. The difference from free association to inquiry was expressed for each determinant in arc-sine units. The distribution of these differences was then calculated for each determinant in the case of each examiner and compared through the analysis of variance technique. The hypothesis tested was that "there are significant differences among examiners in mean change between free-association scoring and final scoring following the inquiry . . ."

Using the nonstandardized inquiry, significant between-examiner differences in mean change were found for seven scoring categories. Using the standardized inquiry, significant between-examiner differences in mean change were found for six scoring categories.

These results indicate that merely standardizing the words which the examiner is supposed to say in the inquiry does not eliminate examiner effects in the inquiry. This finding makes sense in light of the earlier discussion of paralinguistic and parakinesic differences in the various phases of the experiment. "Body English," so to speak, seems to be at work here too.

Gibby concludes:

> The Rorschach psychogram needs to be considered as being a function not only of the characteristics of the subject, but also as a function of the characteristics of the examiner. These are expressed in the interaction which occurs at various levels, conscious or unconscious. The particular training of the examiner, his "set" toward the S and his inclinations which are determined possibly by the response pattern of the S, are conceivably forces which all affect the Rorschach inquiry. But above and beyond these still remains the factor of the total stimulus value of the examiner to the patient in the production of the inquiry which determines the final psychogram. (Gibby, 1952, p. 452.)

In another study of the Rorschach inquiry, Melvin Zax and George Stricker began by noting that experts differ in the degree to which the inquiry *should* be structured. They concluded from this fact that it is likely that examiners will differ in the extent to which they do structure the inquiry. Then they set up the following experiment. Five examiners each gave fifteen Rorschachs to normal college students for research purposes. Each subject's Rorschach was rescored three times: first for just the free association, then for the free association plus the standard Sarason inquiry, and finally for the free association plus Sarason inquiry plus a more structured inquiry.

The null hypothesis was that the levels of inquiry structure had no effect on the tendency to produce the various determinants. It could be safely rejected since on seven of the eight selected determinants there were significant differences in the level of inquiry at which they were elicited. Of seventy-five subjects who ultimately gave shading (FY) as a determinant, fifty-seven did not do so until the final or most structured inquiry. Zax and Stricker maintain that different clinicians reach this tightly structured inquiry at different paces. "Such findings have clear implications for the clinical use of the test. They would suggest that in the absence of a standardized inquiry the FY index is highly unreliable." (Zax and Stricker, 1960, p. 331.)

It is possible that examiners also differ unwittingly in their gestural and verbal reactions to the Rorschach responses as they are given in the performance proper. A few studies have experimentally varied these usually uncontrolled reactions to see if they can serve as reinforcers for specific classes of responses.

Thomas Wickes used thirty homemade inkblots, two examiners (one of whom was Wickes himself), two experimental groups, and one control group. His subjects were college students. In the first experimental group the first fifteen cards were presented in the standard manner; with card sixteen the experimenter began to say "Fine" to the first movement response, "Good" to the second movement response, and "All right" to the third. In the second experimental group, with card sixteen the experimenter began to make various postural and gestural changes, nodding his head three times to the first movement response, smiling on the next, and leaning forward in his chair after the third. In the control group the thirty cards were administered to all subjects "in a manner as nearly identical as possible." (Wickes, 1956, p. 24.)

The findings were as follows. The group which was verbally reinforced made significantly more movement responses to the second fifteen cards than to the first fifteen ($p = .025$). So did the nonverbally reinforced group ($p = .005$). There was no difference in the control group in the number of movement responses given in the first and second half. Wickes concludes: "It is indicated that examiners need to be more careful of what they say and do, in a perfunctory manner, when they are engaged in testing" (p. 25).

Some of the artificiality introduced into Wickes's study by the use of homemade blots was removed by Max Magnussen. His subjects were thirty-three males coming for personnel evaluation. The author seems to have doubled as examiner and experimenter. Using the regular Rorschach blots, he reinforced popular responses. In the verbal reinforcement condition he said "Uh-huh" after each popular response. In the nonverbal reinforcement condition he nodded his head once after each popular response. "Under the control condition the test was administered with a conscientious attempt not to provide any cues or reinforcements." (Magnussen, 1960, p. 168.) Both the verbal- and the nonverbal-reinforcement group produced more popular responses than did the control group ($p = .05$).

Moving yet a step closer to clinical actuality, Richard Gross (1959) employed as subjects patients on a psychiatric ward of a university hospital. Again it seems that the author was also the examiner and the experimenter. In one treatment condition (VR) he reinforced human content responses with a verbal "Good." In the second experimental condition (NVR) he nodded after human content. In the control (C) group the cards were administered with an attempt not to offer any cues.

"The (VR) group gave more human responses than the (C) group at the .05 level of significance. The (NVR) group yielded more human responses than the (C) group at the .02 level. The (VR) and (NVR) groups did not differ significantly from each other." (Gross, 1959, p. 67.)

Gross concludes that to guard against assigning to the personality of the examinee Rorschach results which are in fact contingent upon the behavior of the examiner, one has to know about even "minimal or unconscious cues of the E" (p. 67). It should be kept in mind that in everyday clinical practice one does not usually know anything about the testing situation which the examiner does not or cannot report.

Before passing on to the literature on the TAT, let me say a few words about these Rorschach studies. Note that most are studies of *examiner effect*. There are no studies of *examiner bias* in the sense in which the term is used in this thesis—i.e., giving expectancies to examiners and seeing whether they then elicit, score, and/or interpret results in such a way as to fulfill their expectancies. This is a point to which I will return later when I discuss clinical practice.

Note also that the studies tend to be concerned with examiner variability in obtained results—which may or may not be related by the authors to variability in examiner attributes. I have not come across any observational study of variability in examiner procedure on the Rorschach. In fact, some studies simply assume that this variability occurs and try only to show that it can affect the supposedly stable aspects of the test. Moreover, when links are forged between examiner attributes and subjects' responses, they are usually not derived from any theory of social interaction or any broader consideration of the social setting and purpose of psychological testing. I will return to this point later also.

Finally one has to be aware of the possibility of experimenter bias in the examiner-differences literature. For example, take the reinforcement studies. The experimenters assure us that they made conscious efforts to stick precisely to the experimental design as reported. But the author of the study was also usually the examiner. He knew the hypothesis he was testing. He knew the results he expected to get from each treatment condition. And he knew, perforce, which condition each subject was in. Despite all the good intentions in the world, this situation maximizes the possibility of bias.[5]

IV

TAT interpretation is a peculiar phenomenon. In many ways it is a faithful representation of the two cultures of American psychology. Clinical psychologists use the TAT to get at enduring, stable, long-term concerns, strivings, and dispositions of their patients. But David McClelland's research and theory oriented rationale for the test stresses its great sensitivity to situational changes: "To anticipate a little, the sensitivity of fantasy is both its greatest strength and its greatest weakness: strength because it picks up *slight* motivational variations, weakness because it picks up variations in other factors as well" (1958, p. 32).

Does it pick up variations in examiners? There seem to be fewer studies of this question with the TAT than with the Rorschach.

Rodney Clark (1952) found that male subjects gave more sexual responses and more guilt responses on the TAT to a male examiner than to an attractive, rather seductive, female examiner.

Lewis Bernstein (1956) varied the "examiners" rather drastically. Using sixty-eight students as subjects, he split them randomly into two groups. For one group the experimenter was present while the subject took the TAT. For the other group the experimenter was absent and the subject heard the instructions from a tape recorder. Bernstein found that TAT stories written with the experimenter absent more frequently contained sad themes, sad outcomes, and showed greater subject involvement than stories written with the experimenter present in the testing room. Bernstein goes on to suggest that clinical examiners are "differentially present" in the degree to which they hover over their patients while the latter take the TAT.

---

[5] It is as if psychological testers were given an expectancy as to the classification in which their patients (and that itself is a classification) fell and then, expectancy in mind, proceeded to do their job. And of course that is how it often happens. See section VI.

George Turner and James Coleman (1962) examined the TAT stories given to cards one and 13MF by 204 patients who had been randomly assigned to twenty-four examiners. The stories were scored for the number and type of thought units and the number and type of affective units. Results showed that there were significant differences between examiners in the number of "storytelling" thought units elicited ($p = .04$) and in the number of "warm" affective units elicited ($p = .01$). The authors conclude that since "storytelling" and "warm" units are important for the assessment of personality, it seems that some examiners will obtain diagnostically richer protocols than others from comparable patients.

Does the race of the examiner make a difference in TAT studies? Dreger and Miller comment that one difficulty in interpreting TAT results which indicate that the race of the subject makes a difference "comes from our not being able to know whether the examiner was white or Negro" (1960, p. 377). They review one TAT study (Abel, 1945) which found that with a white female examiner, white males and females and Negro females were more communicative than Negro males. They comment that it "scarcely seems surprising in the light of other research on the TAT and some knowledge of Negro-white sociodynamics that Negro males were inhibited in the presence of a white female examiner; but possibly we are engaging in ad hoc reasoning" (p. 376).

James Milam considered "the critical examiner-subject relationship as a factor influencing the fantasy processes of the subject" (1954, p. 221). He varied this systematically by administering the TAT in a hostile, neutral, and positive way to thirty-six college subjects who were randomly assigned to these three conditions. He used TAT cards one, 7BM, and twenty and studied as his dependent variables story length, the attitudes manifested in the story, and the amount of anxiety the story hero showed. "Variance due to examiner role was found to be significant at the .01 level for all three measures."

Subjects treated negatively left out story elements and showed negativism when questioned about them. The most severe perceptual distortions occurred in this group. Heroes frequently came into conflict with other story characters and showed strong hostility and aggression. They also displayed marked anxiety. They either fought and destroyed others or became depressed and suicidal and withdrew from social structures.

Subjects treated in a positive way produced long, well-elaborated stories. Their heroes showed little hostility or aggression and experienced little anxiety. Positive feelings in the hero and other characters predominated.

Subjects treated neutrally produced stories that were brief and to the point. Their heroes experienced mild emotions or none at all.

Milam concludes: "the hero-press interdynamics in TAT stories tend to approximate the subject-examiner interdynamics in the testing situation" (p. 226).

V

Having elicited and scored the testing protocol, the clinical psychologist has left the job of interpretation and diagnosis. Similarly, after having elicited and statistically manipulated the subjects' responses, the experimental psychologist has left the job of interpreting the results. The topic of interpretation error in psychological experiments has been discussed elsewhere (Rosenthal, 1963e). Interpretation error in psychological testing is especially interesting when it is nonrandomly distributed. As Jean McFarlane put it, "interpretation in the hands of the clinically inexperienced, the doctrinaire, or the methodologically uninformed easily degenerates into nothing more than one more projective tool—to wit, one which discloses the organizing dynamics of the interpreter . . ." (1942, p. 405).[6]

A few examples follow.

Richard Filer (1952) found that the three most frequently mentioned mechanisms of defense in the reports of thirteen male clinicians were more characteristic of the examiner than of the test subject.

Elizabeth Mintz has noted that there have been many studies of the relation between personality and perception but not

> insofar as they affect interpretation of projective tests by clinical psychologists . . . We cannot confidently predict simple, direct relationships between the degree to which a psychologist possesses a given trait and the tendency to exaggerate the importance of this trait in a patient. Such variables as insight, anxiety, and kind of defense need to be taken into account. If assimilative projection contributes to diagnostic errors, a psychologist might erroneously perceive a patient as resembling himself in traits of which he is aware. If projection in the classical psychoanalytic sense takes place, a psychologist might erroneously attribute to a patient a trait which he himself unconsciously possesses. Perceptual defense might cause the psychologist to overlook problems similar to his own. And, finally, perceptual vigilance might oversensitize a psychologist to problems resembling his own, which would actually exist in the patient. (Mintz, 1957, p. 123.)

She tested these notions on diagnosticians at four VA installations. The examiners had on the average five years of diagnostic experience. They were to judge from a Rorschach and TAT how a patient would answer

[6] In his review of the literature, Masling misquotes "projective" as "predictive" (1960, p. 74).

certain sentence-completion test items. Mintz also obtained from these judges self-reports on such variables as their present financial condition and how they felt about it.

She found a correlation between admission of money worries on the part of the clinician and exaggeration of the importance of money problems to the patient ($p < .01$). She also found a high correlation between the amount of hostility possessed by the judge and diagnostic errors on this variable. The first of these errors she interprets as a function of assimilative projection of conscious anxiety; the second as a function of the examiners' low self-understanding. "Twenty per cent and 25 per cent of variance in diagnostic errors on these respective variables could be considered as related to variance in personal anxiety and lack of self-understanding on the part of the psychologists" (p. 128).

Perhaps the most ingenious and least ingenuous work in this field is that of Masling (1957). He used as his examiners the eight graduate students in his seminar on projective techniques. The subjects were the two "attractive female undergraduates" of his previously cited study. They again played warm and cold roles, this time having memorized two protocols for a sentence-completion test with equal numbers of operationally defined "sick" and "healthy" responses. Their interactions with the examiners were taped in order to be certain of their having given standardized content. Each examiner saw one accomplice in a cold role and one in a warm role in a counterbalanced design.

The examiners then wrote up regular testing reports whose thought units were categorized as positive, negative, or neutral. Masling's hypotheses were (a) when an examiner tests several subjects he will make more positive statements about the subjects who act warmly toward him than about those who act coldly, and (b) when a subject acts interested in an examiner more positive statements will be made about her than when she acts disinterested. Both hypotheses were supported.

Matching Masling's work for both ingenuity and deception is that of William Haase which adds the socio-economic to the psychodynamic and social-interaction perspectives on examiner bias. Haase notes that most of the literature on examiner bias has dealt with personality variables which are conceptualized as "within" the examiner. Far less attention has been paid to socio-economic factors and prejudices.

Haase employed in his study seventy-five psychologists at various levels of experience. He constructed four pairs of Rorschach records so that their psychograms and content were equivalent but not identical. To each of these he appended a social-service history of the fictional "patient." The only factors distinguishing these social histories from one another were socio-economic ones. By this variation, Haase presented to his psychologists the equivalent Rorschachs of "lower-class" and "middle-class" patients. He wanted to know whether this differing socio-economic set would influence the examiners.

Haase does not present his data in a form amenable to a study of examiner effect. But as far as examiner bias goes, the results are quite conclusive. Sixteen different middle-class set, lower-class set comparisons were made with three statistical techniques. "In every case except one [these were] biased in favor of the middle class with a $p > .01$." (Haase, 196, p. 243.) Haase found that the clinicians' impressions prior to diagnosis, the diagnosis itself, and the predicted prognosis based upon equivalent Rorschach records all tended to favor the middle class. To McFarlane's warning that a projective tool may easily degenerate into one that discloses the dynamics of the interpreter rather than the subject, we may now add, "and discloses his socio-economic attitudes as well . . ." (Haase, 1964, p. 246).

VI

We have now reviewed some of the literature in the areas of "examiner difference" and "experimenter difference." It might be useful to treat them separately in this conclusion.

From the point of view of *examiner* difference one of the most remarkable things to me about this literature is the rather minimal impact it has had on actual clinical practice. I refer to the fact that in my experience patients are still tested by but a single examiner who in his testing report generalizes about *their* needs, *their* defenses, and *their* pathologies. Of course, the examiner is now supposed to be aware of his position in the testing situation. But one wonders whether mere awareness is enough. The solution which the examiner-difference research implies—having each patient tested by more than one person—has not been carried out on any large-scale basis.

In fact, the general isolation of this research from clinical realities is rather remarkable. Besides its minimal impact upon clinical practice, there is the further matter of its minimal approximation to the social situation in which psychological testing is usually carried out. Two factors in this non-representativeness of design should be mentioned: the absence of studies of examiner bias and the absence of consideration of the larger social structure in which diagnosis usually goes on.

The two are intimately related. The case could be made that examiner bias (in a sense directly analogous to the sense in which I use the phrase "experimenter bias") plays a considerable part in psychological testing. For example, the referral to an examiner often will contain some sort of preliminary diagnosis of the patient. Or sometimes it will contain the intake interview, presenting complaints, childhood history, etc. In either case, some specific or general expectancies are conveyed to the examiner by this information. In fact, simply knowing that the patient has been referred for psychological testing—especially when the patient has been admitted to a mental institution—is enough to arouse in the examiner at least the general expectancy that the examinee is mentally ill.

In other words, the examiner often has some expectancy about what the results of the tests will show. But having an expectancy is not enough. Is there any reason to believe that the examiner may be influenced by this expectancy? To answer this question let us consider the larger social structure in which testing takes place.

An immediate problem is that these social structures are quite diverse as are the various role positions held by "the tester." For simplicity let us consider the situation in which the tester is a psychology intern in a medically dominated installation—a not uncommon social situation.

In these institutions testing usually serves a dual function—diagnosis of the patient and socialization of the tester. The tester is an intern. He is the low man on a second-class totem pole. He is in an insecure position. His proper conduct as an intern may represent the last hurdle along his rocky road to a degree. He wants to please—both his patients and (more importantly, at times) his superiors.

It is likely that just as the tester will place the patient under personal scrutiny, so the tester himself will be under personal scrutiny in the institution. And it is likely that the same sorts of judgments—those relating to his personality characteristics, emotional problems, mental health, or mental illness rather than, say, his politics, religion, athletic ability, values, or morals—will be the outcome of the scrutiny in both cases.

One sign of his own mental health may be how well the intern carries out the job of assessing his patients' mental illness. And here is where that expectancy comes in. For, in the absence of any independent yardstick, the criterion of how well he does the job will usually be one of *consensus*— among those who are doing the socializing and who may be responsible for or influenced by the expectancy the tester was given.

Thus it is apparent that for this case, at least, the social structure of the institution within which the testing goes on may contain subtle pressures which are conducive to the occurrence of examiner bias. I suspect that more complex but basically similar analyses would hold when the tester has a different role (e.g., staff psychologist) or the testing takes place in a different kind of institution (e.g., an army hospital).

It is surprising that a speculative reconstruction of the realities of clinical practice such as this one has not led to research in which, say, a false expectancy is given to the intern by his supervisor, or a normal subject is slipped into his regular testing schedule by the people who are doing the socializing. One might wonder how many such ringers would be caught by an examiner if all of his significant others were trying to have him fulfill their false prophecy.[7]

So much for examiners; now back to experimenters.

In this part of the book I have been attempting to establish the generality of the notions that (a) psychological experimenters behave differently from one another even though they are not supposed to do so; (b) experimenter effect occurs and can be mediated by aspects of these procedural variations; (c) experimenter bias occurs and can be mediated by aspects of these procedural variations.

Different parts of these two chapters have been directed at different parts of these interrelated notions. As I mentioned at the beginning of the chapter, two other sets of studies could have been reviewed to bolster the case still further. One is the work in the research project of Robert Rosenthal which has yielded thus far more than twenty demonstrations of the occurrence of experimenter bias. The other is the growing literature within various sectors of experimental psychology which attests to various aspects of the impact of the experimenter on experimental results.

Let me make a brief note about the extent of this literature. If it is organized in terms of problem areas, then studies of at least verbal conditioning (Sarason, 1964), sensory deprivation (Orne and Scheibe, 1964), hypnosis (Orne, 1962), attitude change (Rosenberg, 1965), need achievement (Birney, 1958), and extrasensory perception (Schmeidler and McConnell, 1958) can be added to Rosenthal's studies of rat learning and person perception and the studies of various psychological tests reviewed in this chapter. If it is organized in terms of so-called experimenter characteristics, at least sex (Binder, McConnell, and Sjoholm, 1957; Stevenson, 1961), race (Trent, 1954), status (Matarazzo *et al.*, 1960), warmth (Reece and Whitman, 1962), likeability (Sapolsky, 1960), and hostility (Sarason, 1962) have been found to be response relevant in certain kinds of studies.

No attempt to be exhaustive has been made in this list of citations. The intersections of problem areas and experimenter and social-interaction variables have not been sufficiently studied to warrant statements about them. Moreover, one must always bear in mind that studies exist in which

---

[7] I know of only two studies in which such social considerations are treated (Levy and Orr, 1959; Appelbaum and Siegal, 1965). Another important kind of research would be a motion-picture study of the mediation of examiner effect and examiner bias. The usual research focusing on the relation between almost randomly selected and inadequately defined examiner personality attributes and the specific scoring determinants favored on the Rorschach has produced a literature so cluttered with ambiguous results which are unrelated to the larger social situation of psychological testing that it is not surprising how ineffectual in changing clinical practice this research has been. The fact that most diagnostic tests are scratch tests for the presence of pathology with only a residual definition of normality should also be taken into consideration in terms of the bias present in the overall testing situation.

the identity of the experimenter did not prove to be an important consideration (e.g., Ferguson and Buss, 1960).

Despite these occasional negative results, when all these studies are added to the studies and reasoning presented here, I think it is safe to conclude that, to put it negatively, there is no guarantee that any specific psychological experiment ever done was completely free of experimenter effect, experimenter bias, and/or variability in experimental procedure. Or, to put the same thing positively and to paraphrase Rosenthal (1963a, p. 217), experimenter effect, experimenter bias, and variability in experimental procedure are fairly general and fairly robust phenomena.[8]

[8] If I had to put them in the order of their generality and robustness I would say: first, variability in procedure; then, experimenter effect; and finally, experimenter bias. This is because there can be variability in procedure which does not affect the specific response category under study. And there can be variability in procedure which affects the specific response category under study but is not related to the experimenter's expectancy.

IV The Psychological Experiment as a Social Interaction: Broader Implications

The notion came and stuck that a dyadic
relationship, whether transient or enduring,
should be formulated as a single system
. . . I use dyadic interactions as a test of
every formulation or theoretical system I
encounter in the literature.

Murray

Having presented this much of my work one day in a clinical seminar, I prepared to move on to its implications. I was interrupted by a member of the audience who, with a chuckle, said the implications were clear: "I guess it just shows we're all dirty; none of psychology is clean."

I did not feel that was quite the moral. I wanted to reply: it is not so much that we are all dirty but more that our criteria of cleanliness need re-examination. Part IV will elaborate upon this epigrammatic attempt to sketch the implications of this work.

The critical implications are the easiest to focus upon. The superstructure of psychology continues to grow with ever newer specialties and subspecialties of research appearing. Top stories continue to be added to the psychological edifice. New branches of research proliferate, each with its own life history; branches send out twigs; twigs, leaves; leaves, buds; buds, flowers; flowers, fruit.

137

But what of the roots? What of the foundations upon which the skyscraper stands?

We psychologists have expanded with cautious but imperialistic abandon into every nook and cranny of the behavioral universe.[1] Perhaps the time has come now to contract and set our house in order; for the work on the social psychology of the psychological experiment indicates that both consumers and producers of research need to re-examine the "facts" gathered so far in all these specialty areas with questions such as the following in mind: How shall we evaluate the various discoveries of the experimental psychology of social influence once we are aware of the amount of social influence in the psychological experiment? How shall we read and contribute to the psychology of sex differences when we have reason to believe that the sexes have not always been treated in the same way in the psychological experiment? What shall we conclude from the massive literature on experimental and clinical comparisons of Negroes and whites once we are aware of the possible influence on such results of the race of the examiner or experimenter? What shall we accept as valid knowledge in the experimental studies of hypnosis once we are made cognizant of the almost hypnotic control the experimenter sometimes has over the subject? What of the psychology of learning if subjects sometimes learn to give the experimenter what he wants? What of the psychology of individual differences if individual differences among experimenters make a difference?

This list of rhetorical questions, some of which suggest ingenious systematically altered replications after the example of the previously cited work of Orne and Rosenberg, could be extended monotonously for all areas of psychological research. The ultimate defense of psychological experimentation has been that it produces valid knowledge. The ultimate question this work raises is just how valid each unit of that knowledge, accumulated within an inadequate philosophy of experimentation, is.[2]

---

[1] It has often been pointed out that many of the areas originally declared off-limits by certain varieties of behaviorism—thought, dreams, perception, physiology, consciousness—have been reclaimed by simply renaming them thinking behavior, dreaming behavior, perceptual behavior, physiological behavior, conscious behavior. This takes, perhaps, undue advantage of the elasticity of the term "behavior" while allowing the users to remain behaviorists in good standing.

[2] A whole spectrum of speculations and thoughts on just how valid it is were elicited from the readers of the manuscript. Some of the most intriguing were Jay Haley's. I quote, with his permission, from the personal communication pre-

In the sense that it goes to the roots, research upon research is, then, radical. We labor in the basement, examining the very foundations of the building called psychology. But when we find loose stones, cracked cement, quicksand just below street level, what do we do?

This question leads us beyond criticism and into no-man's land. The modesty involved is not false when I say that I have neither easy solutions, recipes, happy endings, nor a clear vision of the morals to be drawn from this work. I referred in Part I to the epistemological dizzyness I encounter when I try to get a clear perspective on its consequences. The fog is too thick. Thus far I get only intermittent glimpses of daylight. I would not underestimate the profound seriousness of the problems raised. I can, however, offer only tentative gropings out of the darkness—and earnestly invite others to help us all along.

Thus, Part IV will not please those who like closed systems. I mean to be provocative, not conclusive. Basically I am asking what are the implications of the banal but, especially in experimental psychology, often unappreciated fact that in our investigations of the behavior of individuals and groups in the social world, our investigation is always a part of and never apart from that social world. I have attempted in Part III to demonstrate that current thinking and research on the social psychology of the psychological experiment concerns, not just this or that species of psychological experimentation or this or that sample of psychological experimenters, but empirical research in general, be it correlational or experimental.[3] I issued a promissory

---

viously referred to: "The *absolutely necessary* premise of testing and experimentation was that the individuals faced the 'same' context. Now what happens when you demonstrate that testers and experimenters *do* bias the responses of the subject and therefore must be included in the description?

". . . the major consequences are two: (a) this way of studying human beings should be discarded, since the basic premise cannot hold, and (b) everything that was found out about the human being by these procedures is now questionable and probably fallacious . . .

". . . If experiments with individuals depend upon the premise that the individuals face the same context, and if they do not because the experimenter influences the subject, then this method of experimentation should go with phrenology . . .

". . . what we know about human beings depends upon our *method* of examining them, and our method of examination depends upon what we think human beings are . . ." (italics in the original).

For some of Haley's profound suggestions as to new directions for psychology, see the works of his cited in the references.

[3] A terminological note: in accordance with contemporary practice, I use "experiment" at times in the restricted sense of research using experimental and control

note, back in the opening pages of Part I, naming some of the larger issues upon which I would attempt to shed some light. Part IV will be but a first payment on that note, a reconnaissance of selected aspects of the territory opened up by the discovery of the contrast between the ideal and the real psychological experiment.

---

groups and more often in a looser sense—as when I follow the practice of referring to "the social psychology of the psychological experiment" as a shorthand form meant to include also psychological tests and other research in which *post hoc* (for example, correlational) methods of control are employed. The same dual use of "experimenters" is employed. Where not otherwise indicated by the text, the more general (and less precise) use of the words is meant.

7 The Scientific Status of Psychology

In his epilogue to the first three volumes in the era-defining series *Psychology: A Study of a Science,* Sigmund Koch asserts that psychology stands poised at the end of an Age—or stage—in its development. According to Koch, the contributors to the study call into question the basic ideology, "the epistemological agreements," "the postulates," the logical and the psychological premises which have ruled psychology for the past three decades—and they "do this in almost every sense in which questioning is possible." The results of the project lead him to believe that "the very canons of analysis which have regulated action in our science for many years" are out of date. Koch contends that "currents of questioning, shifts of judgment, realignments of values, intimations of change are shaping up." He realizes that there will be resistance to such change, resistance from the "many individuals" who will "be shocked at the strong implications generated concerning the inadequacies" of the articulate and inarticulate major assumptions by which the Age has judged psychological research, but he is led nonetheless "to expect a widespread and profound readjustment of rationale and action in our science." He looks out over the contemporary psychological scene and sees

a longing, bred on perception of the limits of recent history and nour-
ished by boredom, for psychology to embrace—by whatever means
may prove feasible—problems over which it is possible to feel intellectual passion.

Psychology seems ready—or almost ready—to assess its goals and
instrumentalities with primary reference to its own indigenous problems. It seems ready to . . . work its way free from dependence on
simplistic theories of correct scientific conduct. (Koch, 1959, p. 783.)

"Simplistic theories of correct scientific conduct"—in these words
Koch evaluates what he takes to be the governing ideology of the Age from
which he sees us emerging. That, as Koch notes in passing, a characteristic
of the Age has been its failure to check upon even the "trans-experimenter
generality" (p. 749) of experimental results is one part of this ideology.
The dogma of immaculate perception, the belief that the data-collector is a
nonperson, the general avoidance of consideration of the social psychology
of psychological research are all part and parcel of that governing ideology,
that unattainable image of cleanliness, those "simplistic theories of correct
scientific conduct."

In terms of the chronology presented in the historical introduction,
the Age began with the importation into psychology of operationism in
order to put an end to the internal warfare between the followers of Watson's metaphysical behaviorism and Wundt's and Titchener's mentalism.
The intervention was remarkably successful. Of course there were some
brief skirmishes about operationism's ability or inability to generate theory
(e.g., Waters and Pennington, 1938). But this resistance was all but
crushed through the wedding of operationism and the intervening-variable
paradigm for theory construction (Tolman, 1936), a marriage which has
endured for three decades and which has produced an uncommon harmony
within psychology concerning its basic logical, methodological, and philosophical ground rules. What Koch now refers to somewhat disdainfully as
the "extrinsic philosophy of science" associated with the interrelated movements of operationism, physicalism, logical positivism, and the science of
science has acted for twenty-five years as psychology's chief legislator and
supreme arbiter for basic questions of meaningfulness, validity, and proper
scientific activity.

The unifying effort of the Age was to make psychology into a *science*.
Of course the urge to make psychology scientific was not new. As Koch
laments, "from the earliest days of the experimental pioneers, man's stipu-
lation that psychology be adequate to science [has] outweighed his com-
mitment that it be adequate to man" (Koch, 1959, p. 784). What *was* new
was the particular image of what psychology had to do to become scientific,

the specific rules of scientific procedure, and the specific criteria by which psychology would be admitted to scientific status.

It would carry us far afield to go into details of this philosophy of science too deeply. Suffice it to say that one cardinal principle was the total applicability to psychology of a conception of science based upon the physical sciences.[1] The unity surrounding this particular version of science was so great that it was easily taken for granted that this was not simply an image of science but Science itself. Thus, Koch's insight that the word "science" has been understood by psychologists in a very special sense is potentially a very liberating reminder, for it unfreezes this confusion of a particular definition for the *ding-an-sich*.

It seems to me, though, that Koch is unduly optimistic in writing his epitaph for the Age quite so soon.[2] His report of the death of the Age may prove, I fear, to have been greatly exaggerated. One must not forget Boring's conclusion to his great work: psychology is getting bigger and better (1957, p. 742). In fact, there are many who believe that psychology has justified itself at the bar of "the traditional criteria against which its progress has been measured" (Koch, 1959, p. 786). It is not likely, while they can still believe that psychology is in the process of living up to the reigning image of science, that they will be easily convinced that reigning

---

[1] For an early but otherwise representative example of this sentiment see Dennis (1926, p. 331): "the fundamental principles of scientific method which rigidly control the physical sciences, control also experimental psychology, and no procedure which does not conform to those general principles is either justifiable or worthy of consideration in psychology." In time "those general principles" changed but not the militancy with which psychological practice was judged by standards set in the physical sciences. Compare Koch (1959, p. 784): "the history of psychology . . . is very much a history of changing views, doctrines, images about what to emulate in the natural sciences—especially physics."

[2] I have resisted the temptation to join in the fun of naming the Age. To be sure, Koch calls it an "Age of Theory" and adds that theory was defined by the Age in a quite special sense—a sense which emulated the conception of theory in physics (p. 784). I have attempted to broaden Koch's catalogue of the characteristics of the Age by showing to what extent its theory of the experiment was another of its simplistic theories of scientific conduct—in this case, a theory too simple to comprehend actual practice. In terms of this broad characteristic, I would date the beginning of the Age from the time when *The Logic of Modern Physics* (1927) became accepted as the logic of modern psychology—an event transitional between Koch's "Age of the Schools" and his "Age of Theory" (p. 731). Koch, by the way, seems to have been convinced by the work he has edited that obituaries are in order for a goodly number of psychological assumptions. Cf. his wish that the symposium on *Behaviorism and Phenomenology* "could be characterized as the death rattle of behaviorism, but this would be a rather more dignified statement than I should like to sponsor, because death is, at least, a dignified process" (1964, p. 162).

image is composed of a set of "reigning stereotypes" (p. 783). Abstract philosophical arguments for a re-evaluation of the criteria by which psychology is judged will not move the average nonphilosophically minded working researcher who is satisfied that psychology has it made.

In other words, there is the danger that important new words such as Koch's will fall on deaf ears. This is particularly likely given his heavy theoretical and philosophical accent. In order to guard against this eventuality, such arguments relating to the philosophy of science need to be bolstered by analyses based upon the realities of science. Psychology's divorce from philosophy has left offspring to whom only data speak. Thus, only after actual psychological research has been carefully measured against the old criteria and—despite the claims made for it—found wanting, will the winds of change be able to drive psychology forward.

Some of the directions in which psychology might profitably go will be indicated in the next two chapters. Right now I want to show how the general notions emerging from the results of the person-perception experiment reported in this book bear on the issue of the extent to which presently accepted ideal scientific criteria have in fact been met by real psychological research.

II

It is the fashion nowadays in some quarters to state that psychology either has met or is on the right track toward meeting the criteria by which its scientific status is to be judged. But is it? Let us compare the real psychological experiment, not against the relatively complex criteria with which Koch is concerned, but against the more basic criteria that one usually finds in basic psychological textbooks.

Morgan considers psychology a science "because it is empirical." He explains that "by empirical we mean that it is founded on experiments" (1956, p. 5). He goes on to distinguish between two kinds of experiments: field experiments and laboratory experiments. Of the two, the latter, of which the person-perception experiment reported here is an example, are considered to be the more scientific.

What, then, is a laboratory experiment? I have asked, answered, and analyzed some common answers to this question previously. Let us now look at some other typical replies.

Festinger writes that a laboratory experiment "may be defined as one in which the investigator creates a situation with the exact conditions he wants to have and in which he controls some, and manipulates other, variables" (1953, p. 137). Control seems to be the chief feature or—as I shall soon make clear—the root metaphor here. Skinner (1947) names control of the variables as the chief characteristic of the experiment. Morgan elaborates upon the criterion of control and uses it to drive a wedge between *inv*aluable experimental observations and *unv*aluable casual or natural observations:

> The experiment is . . . important to science because it provides control. One trouble with casual or natural observation is that we cannot be sure of the conditions leading to a particular result. . . . In an experiment, we can control the conditions that might give us misleading results. (Morgan, 1956, p. 12.)

So far we have seen that psychology is considered scientific because it is experimental. A chief characteristic of the experiment is that it allows controlled observations to be made. Morgan now goes on to write into his definition of the experiment one of the outcomes of this control: "an experiment is, first of all, something we can repeat." He quickly adds—to guard against the possibility of seeing here a royal "we": "the same experiment can be done by different people" (Morgan, 1956, p. 12).

The two characteristics thus added to that of control are replication and intersubjective validity. Dennis's paper on these topics is most comprehensive. He has written:

> Proof in science is merely repeatability . . . what has occurred once under given conditions will occur again if the same conditions are established. . . . The only question concerns the accuracy and completeness of the [public] statement of the conditions. (Dennis, 1926, p. 345.)

How accurate and complete does the public statement have to be? Dennis is quite explicit on this matter. At one point in his essay he writes that for an experiment to meet scientific criteria, "the issue of the experiment must be a statement of the hypotheses, the conditions of test, and the results, in such form that another experimenter, *from the description alone,* may be able to repeat the experiment" (p. 332, my emphasis). A bit later he reiterates this point: "proof is not begun until the conditions of the experiment, as well as the results, are so accurately described that another person, *from the description alone,* can repeat the experiment" (p. 346, my emphasis).

Given his admirably strict notion of how complete the public report of experimental procedure has to be, the purpose of replication becomes, for Dennis, "the necessity, in general, of certifying that the descriptions of conditions and results are accurate to the requisite degree." And so repetition of the experiment by the same experimenter is not sufficient "because of the possibility that the experimenter in the second experiment may not be accurately following his own description, but may be following his first procedure, and therefore may vary from the description in the same way" (p. 346).

Thus, psychology is admitted to the realm of science because its experimental manipulations (a) allow controlled observations to be made, (b) can be replicated by others, and (c) provide facts that can be intersubjectively checked up on.

But do they?

Do they allow controlled observations to be made? In the person-perception experiment the independent variable was to be the expectancy given the experimenter and the dependent variable the subject's ratings of the photos. All other conditions were to be held constant from dyad to dyad. They were not. Viewing the films, we found a whole host of unanticipated variations in the experimenters' procedure. These variations could be divided roughly into two groups. The first were procedural errors on the part of experimenters. The second were procedural variations that could not really be called errors since in these cases no standards of proper conduct have yet been formulated. There were between- as well as within-experimenter differences in both these classes of variations in the experimental procedure.

This means that the subjects did not rate the photos under literally standard conditions. To answer a rhetorical question raised much earlier and to put the results more generally, the control of situational variables was not "tight" enough to insure that the experimental observations were made under controlled conditions.

"But come now," one might object, "isn't it all a matter of degree of control?" Then how much is the requisite degree? Psychological texts are not sufficiently clear about this, but three factors stand out. One is that the degree of control surely has to be tight enough so that unintentional variations in procedure are irrelevant—or very nearly irrelevant—to the subjects' responses.[3] Another is that the degree of control surely has to be tight enough so that any unintentional variations are nonsystematic. And a third is that surely the degree of control has to be tight enough so that the variations cannot mediate the experimenters' own biases.

These factors will now be taken up in turn. First, the improvisations in

[3] Strictly speaking, this formulation holds true as is only for parameter-estimating research. Where there is an experimental and control group, it is not the mean data but mean-*difference* data that are relevant. Therefore, if experimenters behave consistently vis-à-vis subjects of experimental versus control groups, the mean difference may be unaffected by uncontrolled experimenter behaviors even though there may be experimenter effects in the data. It is only where there are significant treatment × experimenter interactions that unintentional variations become relevant to the mean-difference data. See McQuigan (1963) for a discussion of the possible outcomes.

these experimental sessions correlate as much as .46 with the subjects' photo ratings. Hence they are not irrelevant. In fact, a correlation this high is as much as (if not more than) the usual correlation obtained in psychological research between traditional independent and dependent variables.[4] This fact should cause some consternation. So also should the fact that these significant correlations stem from variables in areas (time, exchange of glances) in which no standards of control have been set for psychological experiments. They are not the result of those procedural errors whose generality is debatable.

This is related to the second point. Are these variations nonsystematic? May they legitimately be chalked up to error variance?[5] No. First, some are systematically related to the fact that it has not been recognized that the psychological experiment is a social interaction. This refers to those variations which I have called the interpersonal operations of the experimenter, his "expressions given-off" (Goffman, 1959)—his winks and tics, nods and glances, smiles and gestures. Second, some are systematically related at the one end to the subjects' responses and at the other end to the experimenters' expectancies.

This leads to the third point. The degree of control was not tight enough to keep some of the experimenters from eliciting from randomly

---

[4] For example, compare the correlations of the following subject "attributes" (a usual independent variable in psychology) and experimenter "attributes" (an emerging independent variable in psychology) with the subjects' photo ratings:

Attribute	Photo ratings
S anxiety	− .18
S social desirability	− .17
S sex	.06
E anxiety	.06
E social desirability	− .20
E birth order	.05

None of these is significant, and none approaches the magnitude of the correlation between exchanged glances of E and S in the instructions period and the subjects' photo ratings—which is exactly the kind of correlation never studied. It is unfortunate that the subject "attributes" selected had not been chosen on the basis of theoretical or empirical evidence for their relation to the task. It should also be clear that whether or not correlations of such a magnitude would be found in other studies is an open question that awaits other studies.

[5] In his previously cited article on the new view of psychological testing Wohl writes: "the greater number of relevant variables accounted for, the less variance is there attributable to error. The position of the contemporary tester would be that much of the 'error term' is based upon our ignorance of the effects of certain factors simply because we have been unwilling or unable to evaluate their effects. From the error term should be excluded sources of variance [such as] . . . consistencies which are related to specific characteristics of the examiner." (Wohl, 1963, p. 364.)

assigned subjects the data they expected to get. And—to close the circle—the specific variations which in this experiment mediate bias have in our discussion been related to the unrecognized interpersonal nature of the psychological experiment.

These results indicate to me that far from being an accurate description of what happens in a psychological experiment, the word "control" is instead the root metaphor of experimental psychology.[6] To reiterate an earlier formulation: a psychological experiment is supposed to be a controlled situation in which there are experimental and control groups which allow controlled observations to be made which will lead in turn to the prediction and control of human behavior. But it is easy to forget the "supposed-to-be-ness" of this slogan. For just as, in general, Caucasians are not literally "white" and Negroes not literally "black," so psychological experiments are not literally "controlled." To vary the image: from where we stand the night sky seems placid and peaceful; its stars and planets seem stationary. But this impression is merely a function of the distance from which we view it and the fact that we ordinarily use our eyes and not a telescope. Similarly, at a distance and under casual observation, psychological experiments seem to be the controlled events they are supposed to be, but when they are looked at up close over and over again they reveal a great hubbub of uncontrolled, unstandardized, sometimes unintentional, and usually unreported activity which in turn reveals the unrecognized metaphoric quality of the phrase "experimental control."

The other two supposed characteristics of the psychological experiment are replication by others and the consequent intersubjective nature of the resulting facts. The intimate relation between these two criteria and that of experimental control indicates what should be said about them.

A preliminary point about replication: when Morgan says "the same experiment can be done by different people," it must be understood in what sense the phrase "the same" is to be taken. Psychologists do not in practice ever try to replicate "the same" experiment. They just talk that way. In their discourse, "the same" is, in Ryle's parlance, a "systematically

---

[6] My paradigm on this specific point is Maurice Stein's analysis of the metaphoric quality of modern scientific sociology: "Our research tools have been carefully designed to maximize 'objectivity' and to conceal, if not eliminate, any disfiguring marks that the 'personal equation' of the investigator may have left on his work. Our vocabularies for interpreting and reporting findings have been screened by experts to eradicate all traces of value judgments other than the ineradicable judgment about the undesirability of making judgments. . . . Such antipoetic militancy can only be understood by recognizing that it is actually a defense of a particular poetic metaphor. This metaphor glorifies images of system in various forms ranging from systematic theorizing to systematic research and finally to the study of social systems. With due allowance for poetic license, the root metaphor of modern scientific sociology is clearly the notion of system." (Stein, 1963, p. 173.)

misleading expression" (Ryle, 1951; Wittgenstein, 1958; see also Malcolm, 1962).

To see this at a glance, consider the possible replies to the spoken order, "Say the same thing I say. Say hello." In school lessons the proper response is "Hello"; in party games, "Say hello." The rules operating in the context give the meaning to the word "same." Moreover, one can be particularly peevish in either context and make up the "correct" answer only after the "incorrect" one has been elicited.

The point is that in contemporary psychology experimenters can vary rooms, times, days, seasons, sexes, regions, experimenters, tables, and chairs and still be engaged in replicating, so far as their colleagues are concerned, the same experiment (or standardizing the same test). The rule is, in essence: do not vary anything which makes a difference in the subject's responses; that is what it means to do the same experiment.

But there is a danger that the cart has been put before the horse. For psychologists have not yet adequately staked out the universe of response-relevant contextual variables in the experimental situation. We are in the position of the party wit. After the fact, depending upon the outcome, we can say either that the same experiment was conducted or that it was not. But such a procedure is hardly cricket; it can be as disastrous to psychology as it is advantageous to dull parties.

Suppose now that someone were to attempt to replicate some finding based upon this person-perception experiment or a similar experiment. He would resort to journal write-ups of the methods employed and then try to create the same experimental conditions.

In general, the journal write-ups would make public certain kinds of information—information relating to the materials or apparatus used, the sample of subjects used, and perhaps some very general features of the scene in which the experiment was conducted. There would probably also be a copy of the instructions "all experimenters read to their subjects."

Characteristically certain classes of information would be omitted from the methods or procedure section of the report. Although the reader would learn a good deal about the sample of subjects used, he would learn little or nothing about the experimenter(s). Although he would learn what materials were presented, he would not learn how they were presented. Although he would learn what apparatus was used, he would not know how the experimenter used it. Although he would learn what instructions were supposed to be read, he would not know whether they were so read or how they were read. The reader would not learn anything about what I have baptized "the interpersonal operations of the experimenter." And finally, since experiments are written up as if they are the controlled events they are supposed to be, he would not learn about any uncontrolled aspects.

To return to the results of the person-perception experiment: according to the rather fuzzy rules by which "the same" is presently defined in psychology, if unexpected variations introduce response-relevant nuances, one cannot replicate "the same" experiment unless one replicates these nuances. But psychologists do not, as a rule, report how many glances they exchanged with their subjects while reading the instructions, nor would they have any way of knowing if they decided to. Nor do they, as a rule, report the exact duration of each phase of each experimental session. Hence, working from the public description of the experiment, it is unlikely that another experimenter would replicate the exchange of glances variable or the time variable. But in this experiment they are response relevant— more relevant in fact than the kind of antecedent information about the sample of subjects that is usually reported.[7]

Hence, it would not be surprising to find that from the usual description in the psychological journals a psychological experiment such as this one could not in fact be replicated. Its chances of replication increase as experimenters become more aware of the role played by relevant contextual, scenic, and interpersonal variables in the experiment itself and so write them up in their reports of the experiment and write them into the theoretical systems or frames of reference within which they work and think.

The final question was whether the data obtained in experiments are intersubjectively verifiable. It has already been answered. The growing literature on experimenter effect (e.g., Sarason, 1964) indicates that certain experimental findings in psychology may turn out to be peculiar to certain kinds of psychological experimenters. It is too soon to tell whether this is necessarily so, or whether it is merely a function of the present lack of control of the experimenter's interpersonal operations. In any event, to the extent that relevant experimental procedure is not controlled, not reported, and so not replicated, to that extent our data remain unverifiable by others.

III

It could have been objected anywhere in the preceding discussion that no mention had been made as yet of the criterion of operational definitions. This is particularly striking since the Age of which Koch speaks made so much of them. The signature of behavioral psychology has been placed on a contract with an operational methodology. Surely, in our posting of the criteria in accordance with which psychology is admitted to scientific status,

---

[7] Let us be clear about the problem this raises for experimenters. There is no guarantee that the exchange of glances variable and the time variable will be *the* crucial situational variables in every psychological experiment. Given the present state of our knowledge, I doubt whether one could specify beforehand precisely which interpersonal and situational variables are crucial for which experimental task. The implications of this are discussed in Chapter 9.

top billing should have been given to the circumstance that psychology has operationalized its constructs.

In fact, in "The General Nature of Theory Construction" (1951) Melvin Marx lists control of observations, operational validity of constructs, and testability of hypotheses (including by others) as the three essential features to look for in judging whether a discipline is scientific.

Let us look a bit more closely at this new criterion. Operational definitions are supposed to relate constructs to actual operations. The operational attitude was introduced into physics in order to banish such Idealistic harpies and fairies as Newton's Absolute Time and Absolute Simultaneity to the never-never land from whence they had been called. Psychology was especially ripe for such an attitude. Idealistic definitions of psychological constructs such as "mind," "consciousness," "personality," "ego," and "id" were abundant. After the operational revolution such definitions were to be eschewed and the terms so defined banished from psychological discourse unless they could be redefined by intersubjectively observable operations. Whereas, formerly, in the beginning was the word, now, in the beginning was to be the deed.

The requirement of operational definitions fits nicely with the requirements of controlled observations, replication, and intersubjective validity. Bridgman writes that "in order to be of practical value, operations must . . . be such that they are repeatable . . . (1945, p. 246). Feigl adds, "Since science is by definition a social enterprise it must insist upon operations which are repeatable not only by one observer but in principle performable by any properly equipped observer. A statement is scientifically meaningful only if it is intersubjectively testable" (1945, p. 257). And Melvin Marx, relating these criteria to the special problems created by mentalism, puts it this way:

> Inner needs, phenomenological fields, personality structures, and the like become scientifically productive concepts only in so far as their observational bases can be directly evaluated in some way or the other. . . . [Unless such concepts are operationalized] there does not seem to be any way of testing their validity if science is to be a public and communicable enterprise. (Marx, 1951, p. 14.)

To restate Marx's point in terms of the methodological and epistemological reasons for the replacement of the hypothetical entities of mentalism by the operational definitions of behaviorism: if intelligence is arbitrarily defined in terms whose surplus meanings fit the introspections of the particular experimenter involved, there is no guarantee that what one experimenter means by intelligence and what another means by intelligence will be "the same." The intelligence construct would therefore not be public property, and one could not replicate experiments on intelligence.

Conversely, if intelligence is defined as that which this intelligence test measures, then experimenters will all mean the same thing by intelligence, and by simply purchasing and using the particular intelligence test kit they will be able to replicate and intersubjectively validate studies of intelligence.

Closer to home, if "success perception" or "empathy" is defined by the score obtained by subjects in the present person-perception task, then ideally another experimenter by simply duplicating the faces pictured in the photographs can replicate the experiment or, using the construct-validity technique, can study the "success perception" or "empathy" construct in some new area. The resulting discoveries of the laws of "success perception" or "empathy" will then be public property since the "success perception" or "empathy" operation will be.

These examples provide clues as to what amendments have to be made to these ideas. The question is: does the present approach to operationalization of psychological methodology—which is taken to meet the operational criterion—in fact meet that criterion? The following considerations should indicate the answer to that question.

In a symposium reported in the *Psychological Review*, Harold Israel (1945) raised the important question: what is an operation? This question can be restated: what constitutes an exhaustive description of an operation? Israel noted that Bridgman equivocates in his definitions. First he calls an operation "a unitary event either physical or mental whose nature could be so rigidly and uniquely specified that it could serve as the solid point of reference for the definition of all constructs." Bridgman's definitions of physical constructs follow this definitional practice. He uses the "direct method of supplying an exhaustive enumeration of the component operations in the precise order in which they are performed," so as to rigidly and rigorously define the set of operations which constitute the definition of the construct. However, Bridgman also introduces a second principle according to which "certain operations need not be mentioned when we know from experience that variations in these operations are without effect on the final result."

In applying operationism to psychology, Israel suggests that, given the complexity of human behavior, most experimenters have taken the second of these two roads, without, however, being too clear about how much our "experience" so far can tell us about what operations "are without effect on the final result." But when it takes this course in psychology, Israel concludes, "operational theory becomes involved immediately in the profound psychological problem of the nature of human behavior or what constitutes a unit of behavior." On the molar level, he continues, "it is obvious that the apparently simple and direct procedure of defining constructs in terms of the actual, concrete operations involved is actually a psychological task so difficult that psychology in its present state is hardly prepared to handle it."

Let me now, in terms of the results of the person-perception experiment, try to restate this profound insight.

An operational definition of a construct, first of all, has to refer to what experimenters do rather than what they intended to do or hope they did. But in most cases psychological experimenters simply report what they planned to do. Now, given the range of improvisation involved in psychological experiments, a detailed description of actual operations would prove onerous; but in begging off via routine verbal short cuts and idealized passive-voice constructions ("the Taylor Anxiety Scale was administered"), psychological operationists have skirted the crucial issue Israel raises. Operational definitions which neglect an exhaustive statement of the operations involved usually carry with them implicit theories as to what are the relevant variables to operationize. In formalizing for report only certain of his activities, the empiricist has allowed an implicit theory to determine what he is being empirical about, a theory which in all likelihood has not itself been sufficiently tested according to scientific criteria. In the sentence, "the concept is synonymous with the corresponding set of operations," Israel is arguing that we do not know as yet what constitutes a "set." What in the set is essence and what accident? What is figure and what is ground? Which operations can be abstracted from the package deal and considered the important ones?

The accepted answers to these questions have been related historically to the dominant conceptions of the nature of a psychological test and a psychological experiment and the dominant emphasis on the individual rather than the transaction as the unit of investigation. So long as the tester and the experimenter could be relegated to a shadowy background position, while the subject and the test materials or apparatus inhabited the foreground, the essence of the "set" could be considered to be the fact that a test of a certain name had been administered. The data-collector's interpersonal and non-role-relevant operations could be dismissed as "without effect on the final result," for the data-collector himself was thus dismissed by this conception of the nature of the psychological test and the psychological experiment.

To put it another way, the operationist in psychology has tended to limit his formalizing procedure to a description of the test materials and/or the contents of the pencil and paper task and/or the exact words which were to be said or read from the instructions and/or the mathematical manipulations of the resulting data. The operationist has not in general formalized the experimenter's operations in the subtle modalities of the vocal and the gestural, the olfactory and the tactual, the temporal and the spatial. But do we know that variations in these modalities during an encounter do not in fact change the "set of operations"?

Again, to use what is often a mischievous phrase, the data speak for themselves. It might be customary to define "success perceiving" as the mean of the photo ratings given by an individual to the ten photos. This would be analogous to the operational definition: "His intelligence quotient is his score on this intelligence test." However, we find that "success perceiving" is in fact related to variations in exchange of glances between experimenter and subject and the duration of various phases of the encounter during which the rating task is presented and carried out. At least these nonverbal conditions need to be written into the operational definition of "success perceiving" if we are to hope that a replication of the same operationally defined experimental conditions will produce the same results.

The point is that operations require operators.[8] Bridgman was always unnecessarily obstinate about the fact that for him operations meant *his* operations. He carried this admonition to an extreme and ended up with a conception of the essentially private nature of the experiences of the scientist. But his psychological interpreters went too far in the opposite direction. They defined the experimenter out of the experiment. They systematically ignored what may be called—without my being unduly metaphysical about it—the "hisness" of the experimenter's operations.

By "hisness" I refer again to the crucial part played in the experiment by the experimenter's interpersonal operations—his nods and smiles, glances and gestures, sneers and smirks. Israel and Goldstein have written that "operational definitions are merely a device for insuring full understanding and communication of all the conditions surrounding observation, particularly the conditions connected with the observational procedure itself" (1944, p. 177). The way the observer (experimenter) behaves kinesically and paralinguistically is surely part of the observational procedure itself.

---

[8] They also require, as Benjamin (1955) and Feigl (1956) have pointed out, something to be operated upon. Feigl, the Viennese philosopher of science who introduced Bridgman to the Harvard psychologists who popularized operationism, has recently completely repudiated the operationism which he helped to foster and which was to put a revolutionary end to the possibility of revolution in psychology. The operationists, he writes, confused evidence with evidenced. It is important to realize that my critique of operationism is quite different from that of the philosophers. It is not directed at the question as to whether there is a unitary standard criterion operation by which to define a term such as "ego" or "temperature." Hence it is not obviated by the shift from an operational to a construct-validity methodology. As we shall see, the question still remains as to what constitutes an adequate statement of the experimental conditions under which the construct is introduced and which need to be replicated if the nomological network is to be extended.

It is thus apparent that operationalization of procedure has not been carried far enough to guarantee the achievement of the aims of controlled observations, replication, and intersubjective validity:

1. The unformalized interpersonal operations of the date-collector, which are often not controlled, operate as excess baggage in the data-collection situation.

2. Not being formalized, these operations, of which the data-collector is often not aware, are usually not reported. To the extent that they do in fact make a difference of a relevant nature in the subjects' responses, the research will not be replicable.

3. Operations which are not formalized are not made publicly accessible. If they are response relevant but not publicly accessible, then the research will not provide facts that can be intersubjectively checked up on.

IV

How does psychology's adoption of a construct-validity point of view affect this discussion (Cronbach and Meehl, 1956)? The empirical revolution which was to put an end, you will recall, to the possibility of revolution (a prophecy directly antithetical to true empiricism) has proved less than perfect. Operationism is no longer the only respectable methodological approach among even those who consider themselves behaviorists. A subtle transformation in psychologists' philosophy of science has been taking place these past ten years, and it is imperative to see whether this transformation satisfies the basic objections raised in the present critical appraisal of psychological research.

The construct-validity perspective emerged from work on the validation of psychological tests. According to the authors of the main paper on the subject, construct validation "is involved whenever a test is to be interpreted as a measure of some attribute or quality which is not 'operationally defined' " (Cronbach and Meehl, 1956, p. 175). When would such a situation, impossible from a strict operational point of view, arise? They answer that "construct validity must be investigated whenever no criterion or universe of content is accepted as entirely adequate to define the quality to be measured" (p. 176). Such a situation frequently occurs: "Typically . . . the psychologist is unwilling to use the directly operational approach because he is interested in building a theory about a generalized construct. A theorist trying to relate behavior to 'hunger' almost certainly invests that term with meanings other than the operation 'elapsed-time-since-feeding' . . ." (p. 179). In fact, as Koch has demonstrated by his distinction between systematic and empirical independent variables (1959), the operationists of the Hullian era were engaged in just such a procedure, albeit *sub rosa.*

In other words, according to the construct-validation procedure, a single criterion definition, an ostensive definition, is no longer necessary for every term in the psychological vocabulary. We no longer need that mythical gold bar somewhere in Paris to be the criterion by which a construct such as "ego" is to be uniquely defined. Instead we have to construct a "nomological network" which defines the construct at many points and so, rather than defining it by an observable, relates it to observables. The elaboration of the nomological network as a means of defining constructs is psychology's response to the liberalization of the meaning criteria originally promulgated by the physicalists (Koch, 1964, pp. 21–30).

A few introductory words must be said about construct validation. In the first place, as Cronbach has pointed out elsewhere (1957), it represents a rapprochement between experimental and correlational methods. This in itself represents an advance over the operational attitude which tended to set up an invidious distinction between the experiment and the test. It also indicates that although in their pioneering article Cronbach and Meehl write about construct validity in psychological tests, the implications of their work are not limited solely to the domain of testing. Construct validity is in fact a point of view which is susceptible to broad application in psychology.

The greater scope than the title Construct Validity in Psychological Tests suggests is related to the general conservativeness of that article. Construct validity is presented there as a means to supplement rather than supplant operational definition. In fact, however, the two have proved somewhat incompatible. The single criterion versus the nomological network approaches is linked to two different clusters of attitudes about the nature of psychological science. And it seems to be the construct-validity approach which is gaining in usage nowadays, although seldom is the net cast with the finesse Cronbach and Meehl suggested in their article.

So much for preliminaries. Does construct validation represent a position which satisfies the basic concerns raised here? Let us look closely at how Cronbach and Meehl describe the demonstration of construct validity.

Suppose measure X correlates .50 with Y, the amount of palmar sweating induced when we tell a student that he has failed a Psychology 1 exam. Predictive validity of X for Y is adequately described by the coefficient, and a statement of the experimental and sampling conditions. If someone were to ask, "Isn't there perhaps another way to interpret this correlation?" or "What other kinds of evidence can you bring to support your interpretation?" we would hardly understand what he was asking because no interpretation has been made. These questions become relevant when the correlation is advanced as evidence that "test X measures anxiety proneness." Alternative interpretations are possible; e.g., perhaps the test measures "academic aspiration," in which case we will expect different results if we induce palmar sweating by economic threat. It is then reasonable to inquire about other kinds of evidence.

Add these facts from further studies: Test X correlates .45 with fraternity brothers' ratings on "tenseness." Text X correlates .55 with amount of intellectual inefficiency induced by painful electric shock, and .68 with the Taylor Anxiety Scale. Mean X score decreases among four diagnosed groups in this order: anxiety state, reactive depression, "normal," and psychopathic personality. And palmar sweat under threat of failure in Psychology 1 correlates .60 with threat of failure in mathematics. Negative results eliminate competing explanations of the X score; thus, findings of negligible correlations between X and social class, vocational aim, and value-orientation make it fairly safe to reject the suggestion that X measures "academic aspiration." We can have substantial confidence that X does measure anxiety proneness if the current theory of anxiety can embrace the variates which yield positive correlations, and does not predict correlations where we found none. (Cronbach and Meehl, 1956, pp. 177–78.)

This passage immediately raises questions. Who administered test X in each of these uses of it? Did the setting change? What would happen to the results if at any juncture test X was given by Mr. A rather than Miss B? Would the correlations, and therefore the boundaries of the network, be different? Who gave all those other tests? Who is the "we" of "when we tell a student that he has failed a Psychology 1 exam?" Does it make a difference whether "we" are his teachers in Psychology 1, his classmates, his counselors, or strangers? Would mean X score decrease in the same order of diagnosis regardless of who did the diagnosing and who administered the test and the amount of communication between them?

The point should be obvious. Cronbach and Meehl are still talking as if so long as the name of the test stays the same, the name of the tester is irrelevant. Their article retains that frame of reference from which the tester is excluded. To them, studies of examiner differences indicate "upper limits to test validity" (p. 185). This is the negative approach with its unattainable ideal of cleanliness—the tester-free test. Examiner differences are seen as deviations from the goal of anonymity rather than part and parcel of psychological research, good and bad.

In other words, the construct-validity procedure as outlined in the article would need amendment to free it from the myth of the absent examiner. Trans-examiner construct validation as well as the more usual kinds would have to be demonstrated in order for the nomological network to advance. That is, situational and interpersonal factors of the testing situation have to be built into the directions for elaborating the net, thus, of course, complicating the procedure. The procedure as outlined at present still assumes that tests can be plucked from one testing situation and plopped down in another one without this making a difference.

Construct validity, then, still focuses the camera on just the test and the subject. The tester is a kind of blur. The extent of his presence defines how clearly the picture has been taken. Construct validity does not bring the tester back into the picture. However, it does represent an advance over operationism in that there is no fundamental reason why it could not be adapted to include "the neglected one." Constructs could include in their definitions ("laws") statements about the interpersonal conditions under which various results are obtained as the nomological network advances.

This is not the only problem raised by the construct-validity approach. In particular, there is the danger that it can be so stretched as to allow a wholesale and indiscriminate return to an inner-state psychology.[9] What I have tried to show is simply that, as presently conceived, it still shares with operationism an inadequate approach to the role of the examiner or experimenter but that it could be amended to take this into consideration.

V

To sum up: I have suggested that there is a good deal of consternation on the part of psychologically oriented philosophers of science and philosophically attuned psychologists of science right now over the fact that the basic assumptions of an extrinsic philosophy of science which is, in some areas, "twenty years or more out of date" (Koch, 1959, p. 787) no longer seem conducive to the growth of psychology. The question is where to turn for new models, new indications of the directions in which psychology should go. Construct validation is not enough. I have suggested that those engaged in this re-evaluation of the very bases of psychology should look closely at the basic methods of obtaining psychological knowledge—research. They would do well to pay attention to the contradiction between the ideal data-collection situations envisaged in the various philosophies of science, with which we have been burdened at least since Watson, and the data-collection

[9] A final introductory point: to the extent that operational definition was an attempt at ostensive definition, it corresponds in many ways to the early Wittgenstein of the *Tractatus*. Wittgenstein's later repudiation of his earlier position (1958) has interesting parallels to the present transition in psychology from an operational to a construct-validity approach. However, there is little evidence of his having had a direct influence on Cronbach and Meehl, although it is clear that there was indirect influence. Unfortunately in certain ways the philosophy of psychology outlined by Wittgenstein in his *Philosophical Investigations* (1958) is quite superior to the construct-validity approach. Further research into Wittgenstein's influence on American psychology (or lack of same) is called for.

situations of real psychological research. To vary slightly an earlier formulation: psychological experiments are supposed to be standardized, controlled, replicable, objective. These experimental sessions were in a significant sense unstandardized, uncontrolled, heterogeneous, different one from another. Psychological experimenters are supposed to be interchangeable, anonymous, "programmed," objective. These experimenters improvised, interpolated, and ad-libbed and were nonconforming, different, and variable in their behavior.

It is, in the final analysis, ironic that the operationists, who were bent on operationalizing all psychological constructs, retained *normative* and *idealistic* definitions of the psychological experiment. In most experimental texts, both beginning and advanced, the "is" in "A psychological experiment is . . ." is most exactly translated as "ought to be." Psychologists have accepted a normative definition of the "clean" psychological experiment, based on the authority of the definition of the physical experiment, rather than an operational definition based on what is observed to go on in the psychological experiment.

Now, after looking instead of legislating, we are beginning to have some evidence as to what does go on in a psychological experiment as opposed to what is supposed to go on. The difference is anything but indescribable. It is systematically and intricately related to the fact that the psychological experiment is a social interaction. Until more attention is paid to the consequences of this fact, the traditional definition of the psychological experiment will remain a pious hope masquerading as an established fact.

What is wrong with the contemporary philoso-
phy of psychological experimentation? Simply this: it does not treat the
experiment as a transient dyadic relationship which needs to be formulated
as a single system. When one uses dyadic interactions as a test of the contemporary formulation of the experiment, its inadequacy becomes clear.

But the dyadic interaction is the subject matter of social psychology.
And the psychological experiment has been traditionally identified with individual psychology.

Thus we come to our next topic.

II

The years between the importation of the operational definition (c. 1930)
and the emergence of the "New Look" approach to perception (c. 1950)
represent the heyday within academic psychology of a very special era, some
of whose major characteristics have been indicated in the preceding chapter. A related characteristic was the focal position within general psychology

held by individual psychology and the marginal position held by social psychology.

Psychology's prize projects during the 1930's and 1940's were highly systematic, axiomatic, formal and mathematical learning theories which seemed to permit the derivation of specific hypotheses which could in turn be put to seemingly rigorous experimental test. The results of this activity were full-blown psychologies of learning (which were in reality psychologies of the learner, for learning was studied as a monadic rather than a dyadic event) which formed the nuclei of programmatic general psychologies. The needs, drives, habits, and motives of *the individual*—these were the crucial constructs of general psychological theories. Operationally defined for purposes of experimentation as intervening variables mediating stimulus and response, these constructs all too easily and frequently performed double duty in theoretical formulations in which psychologists cashed in on their surplus meaning as intrapsychic states and processes. In this way, methodological behaviorism ("Connectionism") was able to remain intrapersonal in its focus rather than becoming interpersonal.

The situation in academic psychology had interesting parallels in clinical psychology. Learning theory was not unique in its emphasis on the individual as the unit of analysis. *Perhaps* it was more sophisticated than its clinical antagonists concerning the question whether its inner-state constructs really existed. More importantly, however, the Yale group, especially Dollard and Miller (1950), were able to translate psychoanalytic theory into learning theory because there was an essential underlying similarity between them—both began from the individual perspective.

Consider classical psychoanalysis. The setting is so arranged as to place the analyst out of the visual field of the analysand. This is supposed to allow him to be truly a nonperson. The extent of his presence is supposed to be summed up in the words "transference" and "countertransference." By remaining a nonperson, the analyst becomes related in the analysand's unconscious to some other person(s) not present in the analytic setting who have been influential in the formation of the analysand's problem. The cure consists of the analysand's working through the transference and accepting, after great resistance, the interpretations which lead to insight. All of this is conceptualized as an intrapsychic process. Add to it the prohibition against social contact with the analyst outside the office, the moratorium during which the analysand may make no major life changes, the disinclination of the analyst to see the analysand's significant others (family, friends, etc.) either with him or without him, and the rather cavalier attitude in psychoanalysis toward what is called "reality"—and one is left with a therapeutic scheme in which the encapsulated individual struggles with internal conflicting forces in order to achieve mental health. If, as Bakan suggests, behaviorism is based upon "the postulate of epistemological loneliness" (1956, p. 656) psychoanalysis goes it one better, for not only can no one else know one's mind but neither can one know it all oneself. Paradoxically, then, through the intervention of a nonperson whom the analysand struggles to make into a person, that loneliness is diminished and clarity achieved.

Now, transference has been revisited and shown to be a response to a peculiar social situation (Jackson and Haley, 1963). The entire process of psychotherapy has begun to look different as interpersonal aspects of it are attended to. Families are being seen together. Their role in the establishment, maintenance, and resolution of *the family problem* is being recognized and conceptualized. In fact, the difference between calling someone "the patient" and calling him "the identified patient" is the difference between an individual-focused and an interpersonal-focused point of view.[1]

Psychotherapy has moved in this direction haltingly but steadily. Psychological testing is moving in this direction. The "three broad emphases in American psychology" which Carl Rogers and Abraham Maslow (among others) have more or less delineated—behaviorism, psychoanalysis, and existentialism—still share a common base which, given the three-cornered hostility often involved, each group might be somewhat embarrassed to acknowledge—namely, an emphasis on the individual as the unit of observation, analysis, and ontology, and a resulting inadequate recognition of social psychology.

Where was social psychology when the psychological systems based upon learning theory were in their prime? It was off in the wings, far from the center of attention. Its bewildering hodgepodge of unresearchable abstract theories and untheoretical concrete research appeared to sum up everything that had been holding psychology back from achieving respectability. Social psychology—which was customarily identified with the direct study of the "real" world—did not measure up to the accepted scientific criteria. It was relegated to the last chapter in those psychological textbooks which took off from learning theory. It was shunned as "somewhat raw, disquietingly unorthodox, basically unscientific, and with a slight flavor of ill-repute about it" (Krech, 1951, p. 657).

Again, as in the case of the Age's strong requirement that psychology become scientific, the inferior position given to social psychology was not new. The idea that social psychology is a weak sister dependent upon individual psychology for its basic principles can be traced right back to the

---

[1] See Haley (1964b) for a systematic comparison of therapies from an interpersonal-communication perspective. For an introduction to one kind of family diagnosis and family therapy see Satir (1964). In retrospect, it might be suggested that a history of psychological schools and systems (introspection, behaviorism, gestalt, psychoanalysis, client-centered therapy, psychodiagnostics, etc.) cutting across what are often treated as dissimilar realms might be written from the point of view of the individual as conceptual unit.

origins of experimental psychology. We have to trace it back that far before we can go a bit forward, correctly.

III

Wundt was responsible for the fateful and misleading division of his new psychology into individual (physiological) and social (folk) psychology. The former had as its professed subject matter the individual mind and as its method experimentation (introspection). The latter had as its professed subject matter the mental products of the group mind and as its method uncontrolled observation. Wundt considered these to be the fundamental divisions of psychology (1902, pp. 26–28). Moreover, he considered social psychology to be dependent upon individual psychology for its basic principles: "Wundt proceeded on the theory that the fundamental processes of the individual mind are psychologically basic to the processes of the 'collective mind' and that individual psychology is therefore basic to the study of the collective mental life of society" (Karpf, 1932, p. 56).

This conception of the relation of individual to social psychology reflected rather faithfully the view of nineteenth-century liberal thought concerning the relation of the individual to society. As a habit of mind, liberalism inspired emphasis on the individual as the fundamental unit of analysis and value. The state was seen as the resultant of a contractual relation entered into by pre-existent individuals. It was not much of a jump to conceive of the origin of society in the same way, or to think of social interaction as merely the resultant expression of the personalities of the individuals who came together to make it up.

The entire thrust of the new physiological psychology was fiercely individualistic. The method of introspection was necessarily so, since only one's own mind was available to oneself. Having inherited the problems of sensation and perception and the methods for studying them from physics and physiology, psychology proceeded to place exclusive emphasis upon their psychophysiological aspects without recognizing the social factors involved. Ebbinghaus's creation of the nonsense syllable seemed to give individual psychology an entrée to the higher mental processes, while circumventing the problem of the social psychology of memory. Philosophical concentration on the problem of the relation of the mind to the body reduced the study of society to the problem of whether other minds existed.

Nowhere can the deforming influence exerted by the prevailing modes of thought upon the definition and distribution of the subject matters of individual and social psychology be better seen than in the opposition of the rational individual in isolation to the irrational influence of the group. The former was defined as the subject matter of individual, the latter of social psychology. As a result of this intellectual gerrymandering, the legitimate territory of social psychology included, not the study of personal equations and reaction times, but the study of mobs, crowds, panics, and riots. Only Simmel would have cared that the Maskeleyne-Kinnebrook affair involved a superordinate-subordinate relation—as does the psychological experiment in general.[2]

The new world gave rise to a new individual psychology and a new social psychology, both of which were born at Chicago. Mentalism gave way to behaviorism. The group mind gave way to social interaction. But the unfortunate division between individual and social psychology was perpetuated. Individual behaviorism retained introspection's unit of analysis. And it declared psychology to be a natural rather than a social science. Watson's customary use of the white rat as a proper laboratory analogue to man obviated issues of language, thought, culture, and society. Perception—whose social nature was to be the great discovery which ended the era—was replaced by learning as the central topic of psychology.

The social psychology developed by G. H. Mead was as contrary to the prevailing temper of rugged individualism as Watson's individual psychology was congenial to it. Whereas the transition from feudalism to liberalism represented a movement "from a world in which individual well-being is regarded as the outcome of action socially controlled to one in which social well-being is regarded as the outcome of action individually controlled" (Laski, 1962, p. 21), Mead proposed to "explain the conduct of the individual in terms of the organized conduct of the social group rather than to account for the organized conduct of the social group in terms of the conduct of the separate individuals belonging to it" (1934, p. 134).

When the psychology department at the University of Chicago separated from the philosophy department in 1904, Watson went into psychology and Mead stayed in philosophy. This split was symptomatic of the subsequent paths to be taken by individual and social behaviorism. Watson's behaviorism passed via operationism into the methodological behaviorism which became the dominant *Weltanschauung* in psychology depart-

---

[2] Following a not uncommon practice of superordinates in dealing with discrepancies between their own work and that of subordinates, Maskeleyne assumed he was using "a right method of observing" and Kinnebrook a wrong method. Thus, an interpersonal discrepancy was treated as a subordinate's personal deficiency. But cf. Duncombe: "Only after Bessel's theory of prior entry was established did it become clear that the 0.8 difference between Maskeleyne and Kinnebrook might have been caused in part by Maskeleyne's tendency to observe transits too early. This seems to be borne out by the discovery that Maskeleyne observed transits .27, .18, and .14 earlier than three of his other assistants. H. P. Hollis has even gone so far as to suggest that Maskeleyne's perception of sound was impeded by old age and that he, rather than Kinnebrook, was responsible for the 0.8 relative equation. In this connection it may be significant that Newcombe found Maskeleyne's catalogue to be systematically .128 too small in right ascension." (Duncombe, 1945, p. 5.)

ments. Social behaviorism of the Meadian variety was tucked away in sociology departments and exerted practically no influence on the developing notions within psychology of the relations between individual, social, and general psychology.

These notions were as follows: The relation of general to social psychology is that of whole to very minor part. Social psychology is but one province on the outskirts of general psychology. Moreover, it is a contested outpost, having been at various times under the domain of psychology and sociology. As such it has not been able to set its own house in order. As Robert Faris put it, "social psychology has mainly borderline trends because social psychology is itself a borderline area" (1937, p. 167).

The bulk of the domain of general psychology, so the notion continues, is made up of individual psychology. (Sometimes the two are even equated.) The influence of this notion can be seen in those psychological texts in which all the chapters save the last deal with, e.g., the memory, perception, intelligence, personality, and motivation of the individual. The last chapter, then, is called "Social Psychology," and social psychology is treated as if it were but one more subdivision, one more subject matter, one more topic above and beyond those topics covered by individual psychology.

The relation of individual to social psychology, finally, is seen as that of producer to consumer. Individual psychology provides the basic theoretical principles which social psychology then applies to behavior in social settings. Just as social structure is seen in this perspective as superstructure, so social psychology is seen as a derivative or applied discipline utilizing, extending, and extrapolating the hard-core facts of human behavior which are discovered in the experiment by individual psychology.

IV

One of the potentially most far-reaching implications of the emergence of the study of the social psychology of the psychological experiment is that this prevalent view of the relation of individual to social psychology is fundamentally mistaken.

Just how fundamentally mistaken it may be will become clear if we view the development of this new approach in historical perspective. For it represents the second attack within academic psychology on the hegemony of individual psychology. By reviewing two reformulations of the relation of individual to social psychology which were produced by the first onslaught, we will begin to appreciate the profound significance of this redistricting of the psychological terrain.

In 1949 Gardner Murphy was already arguing that the accepted version of the relation between individual and social psychology "is based more upon a habit of thinking of what social psychology used to be than upon a realistic confrontation of the present scene" (1949, p. 414 fn.). That present scene had just witnessed the emergence of the "New Look" approach to the social factors involved in perception. It was becoming clear that memory, perception, and cognition could no longer be adequately studied as "asocial" events.

In light of this work, David Krech reopened the question of the boundary lines within psychology by asking whether "the principles which the general psychologist [i.e., the individual psychologist] discovers or invents in his laboratory are also the principles which the social psychologist will find applicable to his own data? In other words, are there two psychologies—general and social—or only one?" (Krech, 1951, p. 663.)

Krech answers his own question by entitling the next section of his paper, "General psychology is social psychology." He deplores the error whereby the general psychologist has acted as if "the only unit he need consider is the individual." He cites the book he wrote with Crutchfield to show that this is never the unit which the psychologist actually studies:

> . . . the general psychologist . . . is literally forced to study the behavior of man as a social being. Whether we are studying the behavior of a man in a laboratory, in the clinic, or in a crowd . . . we are studying the behavior of a man as influenced by his perception of the social world . . . The effects of a man's group membership, of his experience with other men, of his past and present interpersonal relationships reach into each of his psychological activities no matter how simple or apparently remote . . . no psychologist, whatever his interests, does or can study the behavior of an asocial man. (Krech, 1951, p. 665.)

Krech goes on to state that the "New Look" work on perception is concerned with the "intrinsic nature of perception" rather than with the effects of one independent set of events (social values, attitudes, etc.) on another independent set of events ("pure perception"). He continues:

> This position, of course, presents a serious challenge to the experimental psychologist. For the experimental psychologist has always assumed, usually implicitly, that, in studying perception, for instance, he was studying a process independent of the social background, affiliations, prejudices, and values of the perceiver. It didn't matter to him whether his subject was a student at Berlin University or Swarthmore College; whether his subject came from the poorer lower class or the wealthier middle class. Among the variables which the perception psychologist or the learning psychologist included in his theoretical model of the perceiver and the learner there was no room for social values and mores.

In so far as he recognized the influence of these factors, they were ascribed to interfering and uncontrolled influences—"imperfections" in his subject.

But, Krech warns,

we cannot explain away those "imperfections" as nuisances which "mess up" a good experiment. We must realize that the social values and mores of men are just as significant a set of variables as any others, and that therefore many of the general psychologist's principles and laws must necessarily be in error—for he has omitted a whole family of important variables in his theoretical formulations. (Krech, 1951, pp. 665–66.)

In this paper Krech was attacking the vertical framework in which social psychology was viewed as a separate subject matter dependent upon the individual psychology of perception, learning, memory, etc. for its basic principles. He recognized that social and individual psychology are not separate subject matters but separate approaches to the same subject matter. He also made clear which he considered more adequate.

What does the recognition that the psychological experiment is a social interaction do to Krech's argument? Krech is concerned with showing that the laws discovered by the general psychologist have to be social-psychological laws. But he considers the laws that are discovered without considering the contribution of the discoverer to his discovery. He considers the results of experimentation to be social-psychological without explicitly noting that the experiment is itself a subject for social-psychological investigation. He discusses the social factors in perception without considering the fact that the experimenter is himself a perceiver. He alludes to the effects of the subject's present interpersonal relations without explicitly recognizing that one of these is his interpersonal relation with the experimenter. He never explicitly frees himself from the notion that the experimenter is a nonperson.

Perhaps all this will become clearer if we consider a second statement of—and less sophisticated objection to—the prevailing notion of the relation between individual and social psychology. Solomon Asch (1959) writes that social psychology grew up in order to augment an experimental-individual psychology which "restricted its observations to the relations between an individual and an environment that strictly excluded other persons." The prestige of that experimental psychology rendered social psychology "an applied discipline . . . [involving] little more than the application of some of the laws of 'nonsocial' psychology to more complex data." This was because it was believed that "all principles of psychological functioning will be discovered in the nonsocial setting." This belief follows from the further assumption that "the basic data of psychology are those that concern the most elementary phenomena and that more extended phenomena are complications of these." So "let general psychology [i.e., individual psychology] discover the principles and let social psychology extrapolate them."

But Asch objects to this program:

> Social psychology is not an applied discipline. Its task is to contribute to a theory of the psychological functions. This cannot be accomplished only by studying individuals in exclusively individual settings; it requires also the direct investigation of happenings between persons, or the extension of observation beyond the limits that experimental psychology [has] traditionally imposed. (Asch, 1959, p. 366.)

Asch's sentiment is better than his analysis. For he is unnecessarily generous to the individual psychologist when he concedes the existence of "nonsocial," "exclusively individual settings." For the fact is that the environment to which experimental psychology has restricted its observations (the laboratory) was never an environment that "strictly excluded other persons." Experimenters talked as if it did, but only by treating the experimenter as a nonperson, a treatment which now appears to have been illegitimate.

The experiment, then, was never in fact a "nonsocial setting." Thus, one need not extend observations beyond the experiment in order to study "happenings between persons." All one need do is recognize the huge blind spot in the traditional philosophy of psychological experimentation. *Whereas the ideal psychological experiment is an asocial situation, the real psychological experiment is a social situation.* Or, as W. W. Lambert puts it:

> Relative to experimental psychology . . . social psychology is the study of the dyad . . . But . . . although experimenters use a single-person model in their own thinking . . . an additional person is necessary. . . . In all monadic experiments there is an experimenter who has a sex, a language, and a personality. . . . This view leads us to suggest that . . . traditional psychology proper is at least a dyadic activity which uses a monadic model. . . .
>
> In the long run it [social psychology] may affect traditional psychology by engulfing it in an explicit rendering of the implicit dyadic general case. (Lambert, 1963, pp. 205-7.)

V

The social psychologist, then, is no mere gadgeteer applying out there in the "real" world the empirical generalizations developed in the antiseptic environment of the laboratory by an "individual" psychology. His insights are needed right there at the very gathering of those empirical generalizations. For the data of the so-called individual psychology are always obtained in a social situation. An adequate psychology of learning, memory, perception, etc. will be a social psychology. Its achievement must await our increasing understanding of the social situation from which our knowledge of learning, memory, perception, etc. arise.

In fact, to see this we need never have even gone beyond operationism. For the real contribution of operationism was its insight into the crucial role played in the gathering of knowledge by the interaction of observer and observed. When both observer and observed are human, as is often the case in psychological experiments, we have two-person interaction, the study of which is one of the specialties of social psychology.

To conclude: here is one of the fundamental implications of founding our conception of psychology upon the real rather than the ideal psychological experiment. Psychology's hitherto most "applied" discipline becomes, in many ways, its most basic. For, in the constant talk about extrapolating from the experiment to the "real" or the "social" world, we must never forget that the experiment is itself a part of that real and that social world. When this is recalled, the social psychologist's status in psychology becomes potentially quite different from what it has been. It may be akin to that of the epistemologist in philosophy, for the social psychologist should study the processes by which psychological knowledge is obtained.

9 Methodological Suggestions

The final three chapters of this work are addressed to analytically separable but actually overlapping audiences. Chapter 7 was addressed primarily to empirically oriented philosophers of science and psychological theorists and system builders. Its main objective was to suggest that, in developing desperately needed new philosophies of science and theories and systems of psychology, they look carefully at what happens in a psychological experiment. Chapter 8 was addressed primarily to social psychologists and psychologists interested in surveying the borders of psychology's territory. Its main objective was to suggest that social psychologists tackle the new specialty called "the social psychology of the psychological experiment" with vigor and that both groups appreciate its fundamental importance for the reapportionment of the districts of psychology. The reader will note that taken together these two chapters suggest the potential value of considerable social interaction and communication among all these groups in the interest of further clarification of the bases of psychological knowledge and hence the advancement of psychology. Historians of psychology should also find material of interest in the chapters. It is in some cases an overworked notion, but it does seem to hold at times that insight into the historical etiology of our maladies can be of help in freeing us of them.

It should be made explicit that the same individual often holds membership in more than one of these groups *and* the group to which this final chapter is primarily addressed: the working psychological researcher. I want first to present some specific recommendations to the researcher who wants to take practical steps in order either to minimize or to study experimenter effect, experimenter bias, and/or variability in experimental procedure. Then I will raise for further examination certain considerations arising out of this work concerning the place of experimentation in psychology.

II

Rosenthal (1966) has listed some specific measures for bridging the gap between the pretensions and practices of empirical psychological research. Some of these have also been indicated in one of our papers (Friedman *et al.*, 1966) and in Rosenthal's earlier writings. Unless otherwise indicated, the specific recommendations for the reform of research procedures that follow owe their pedigree to him, and more extensive discussions can be found in the final sections of his book.

One way to minimize bias is to use a double-blind procedure. Carried to its extreme this becomes a "total-blind" procedure in which no one knows which subjects are in which treatment condition. When it is impossible or impractical to use such a procedure, then various methods for minimizing bias can be used. Data-collection can be automated. Experimenter constancy can be assured by the use of a tape recording or film as the instruction giver. One should be aware, however, that this still requires someone to guide the subject to the mechanical experimenter. Another approach is to restrict the cues available to the subject, by, for example, placing a screen between experimenter and subject. Some combination of these techniques can also be employed. For example, the guide can be blind as to the treatment condition to which he leads the subject who meets the machine. These are steps toward minimizing bias. They will not necessarily remove it altogether.

Sampling experimenters from a population in which biases are normally distributed will also serve to minimize bias. It will also allow an assessment of experimenter effect. I would further suggest that one way to minimize experimenter effect while sampling experimenters would be by alerting them to the importance of maintaining as near standard as possible their interpersonal operations, giving them monitored practice at so doing, and then, before any "real" subjects have been run, perhaps weeding out faulty interactors.

More important than the minimization of experimenter effect, however, is its assessment. It is here that replication comes in. Rosenthal's work points out the centrality of replication for the establishment of a trans-experimenter generality of results. Rosenthal discusses this in considerable detail and proposes how to go about developing a "replication index."

He also recognizes one crucial problem. Replications should be regularly and routinely carried out by relatively noncorrelated investigators. However, given current journal policies, which are related to current statistical vogues, only a biased sample of replications ever makes its way into the literature. This touches upon a central paradox: the discrepancy in status accorded replications by the rules of science and by the behavior of scientists. Rosenthal has noted that, although "the crucial role of replication is well established in science generally," in psychology, at least, "as an enterprise replication (it has been said) lacks status" (1966, ch. 18). The professed goal of accumulating carefully checked knowledge is thus somewhat in conflict with what actually goes on. Although there is neither a journal of "Successful Replications" nor one of "Negative Results," [1] what usually happens is that failures of replication, especially when they are deemed especially significant, get published, and whether other studies are ever replicated is sometimes anyone's guess. Those interested in the sociology of research might also ponder just how long it would take to read, let alone replicate, every piece of that biased subset of psychological research which manages to get published each month.

Hence replication as an ideal is somewhat at odds with social reality. But so much for specific recommendations. Here are two research models whose aim is primarily to study rather than to minimize experimenter-related factors in psychological research.

The first model consists of three steps, the first two of which could also be instituted independently.

1. *Data-collectors, be they experimenters or examiners, should be representatively sampled just as assiduously as subjects are.* This is not a new idea. Brunswik made a similar suggestion (for examiners, at least) quite some time ago. His reasoning, as previously remarked, was based upon considerations of statistical inference and ecological validity. That reasoning is now bolstered by the accumulating evidence, which shows that in those cases in which more than one experimenter or examiner is employed, the data-gatherers do often obtain divergent data. It is also bolstered by the fact that we can now give at least one good reason why they do obtain different data; namely, they conduct the experiment differently. Thus, statistical interaction between experimenters and subjects in experimental results now makes sense in terms of the social interaction in the experimental sessions between experimenters and subjects. There is no way when only one experimenter is used to dissociate the results he obtains from his own personal

---

[1] I believe Brendan Maher once half-jokingly mentioned this idea.

and interpersonal equations. Empirical generalizations formulated on the basis of data obtained by a single experimenter may hold for only that experimenter or for only that type of experimenter. If the correlationist still wants to try to make statements of the form, "People who are high on anxiety give more shading responses on the Rorschach than people who are low on anxiety," he needs to sample examiners in order to see whether his results are "examiner-fair." If the experimentalist still wants to try to make statements of the form, "Verbal conditioning increases shading responses on the Rorschach," he needs to sample experimenters in order to see whether his results are "experimenter-fair." It is more likely that both correlationists and experimentalists will by this procedure be in a better position to say for what kinds of data-collectors their generalizations hold true. That is, their generalizations will become interpersonal in nature rather than intrapersonal and so represent a significant departure from current efforts to discover regularities in individual behavior.

2. *Researchers should have samples of their data-collecting sessions filmed.* The rationale for this suggestion is the public-accessibility clause of science. The change-over from an introspective to a behavioral methodology was intended to secure psychological research from the vulnerable position of the unscientific analyst whom Ernst Nagel unintentionally caricatures in the following passage:

> Only passing mention need be made of the circumstance that although in the interview the analyst is supposedly a "passive" auditor of the "free association" narration of the subject, in point of fact the analyst does direct the course of the narrative. This by itself does not impair the evidential worth of the outcome, for even in the most meticulously conducted lab experiment the experimenter intervenes to obtain the data he is after. There is nevertheless the difficulty that in the nature of the case the full extent of the analyst's intervention is not a matter that is open to public scrutiny, so that by and large one has only his own testimony as to what transpires in the consulting room. It is perhaps unnecessary to say that this is not a question about the personal integrity of psychoanalytic practitioners. The point is the fundamental one that no matter how firmly we may resolve to make explicit our biases, no human being is aware of all of them, and that objectivity in science is achieved through the criticism of publicly accessible material by a community of independent inquirers. (Nagel, 1959, p. 49.)

Nagel is at once too uncharitable to the clinician and too generous to the experimenter. The full extent of the clinician's intervention is increasingly becoming a matter open to public scrutiny. Witness, for example, the tape recordings and sound films of Rogers, the work of the Kaiser Foundation, and the elegant research of Pittenger, Hockett, and Danehy. But, beyond the experimenter's own testimony, what evidence do we usually have as to what transpires in the experimental room? Only passing mention need be made of the circumstance that public scrutiny of an experiment in progress is at least as exceptional as public scrutiny of a psychiatric interview in progress. It is perhaps unnecessary to say that this is not a question about the personal integrity of psychological experimenters. But, just as the case report does not meet the criterion of publicly accessible material since it is merely a *post hoc* reconstruction by one of the interested parties, so the journal report does not.

Part of the answer, then, lies with the use of films.[2] If experiments (or a sample of interactions from them) are filmed, people can get to see just what does happen in a psychological experiment. Filming can be useful both to the specific experimenter involved and to the scientific public at large. In leisurely analysis researchers will be able to view and re-view their own activities and so become sensitized to their own habitual and usually unwitting interpersonal operations. Other interested parties will be able to check up on the researchers via this publicly accessible material. And, when combined with the third procedure to be suggested, filming will help produce "control."

3. *The regular use of* post hoc *methods of control (e.g., analysis of covariance, partial correlation) can help assess and correct for the contribution of the data-collector to the results.*

Taken together, the three suggestions present this picture: The study is conducted with a representative sample of data-gatherers. A sample of the data-collecting sessions are filmed. The films are then analyzed to discover any activities which were in fact not controlled. When they are discovered, their contribution to the results can in fact be controlled by the use of either partial correlations or analysis of covariance, depending upon the nature of the research design.

Thus, in a merger of correlational and experimental designs, *post hoc* methods of control can be used to supplement *a priori* methods of control. For example, say that one has found in a conditioning study a correlation of .40 between subject anxiety and conditionability. On analyzing films taken of the conditioning session, one discovers that the people running the study varied in the number of glances they exchanged with their subjects. This was not part of the design, for in correlational studies there should be no differential treatment of subjects. One can then find out the respective cor-

---

[2] Films are in general a means of monitoring and so studying variability in experimental procedure. Alternatively Rosenthal proposes and discusses the pros and cons of observation by subjects, by experts, by representative observers, and by observers with special talents. The literature on participant observation becomes especially relevant in the choice of strategy here.

relations between exchanged glances and subject anxiety and exchanged glances and conditionability and so partial out the contribution of mutual glancing to the result—or find out whether it is in fact a more powerful predictor of conditionability than is subject anxiety.

I consider a procedure such as this three-pronged design more practical in the long run than the simple announcement of what unintentional variations in a specific laboratory study seem to be the relevant ones. For there is no guarantee that they will remain the significant contextual variables from test to test or from experiment to experiment. It should also be clear that the use of this procedure will not create complete control. For one thing, the number of unanticipated variables caught by the movie camera will be huge. Correction for all of them will be quite impossible. For another thing, movie cameras do not catch variations in certain modalities. Hence, these procedures are offered as asymptotic approaches to control.

These procedures have a dual value. They allow the researcher to minimize by the appropriate statistical methods the contribution of unanticipated variations to his results. And they also allow him to study these variations in their own right.

Filming is also a fine technique for the naturalistic study of other aspects of the experiment as a social occasion. Hence, such procedures should encourage both the gathering of more valid information in substantive areas and simultaneously the gathering of the desperately needed information about the laboratory situation.

Rosenthal (1966) has suggested an alternative procedure which will likewise accomplish this dual purpose. He calls the procedure "the expectancy control group" approach.

In Table 9 the usual experimental setup is described in cells one and four. The experimenter creates two groups, the treatment group and the control group. To the treatment group he applies the treatment and expects behavior change. From the control group he withholds the treatment and expects no behavior change. Thus, the experimenter's expectancy and the treatment are covaried. And so, to the extent that the experimenter's

Table 9.   Experimental Setup

| | | TREATMENT | |
		APPLIED	WITHHELD
EXPERIMENTER EXPECTANCY	CHANGE	1 (usual treatment condition)	(2)
	NO CHANGE	(3)	4 (usual control condition)

expectancy can influence experimental results, this setup increases the likelihood of rejecting the null hypothesis when it is in fact true.

Rosenthal suggests the employment of two expectancy control groups. In Table 9 they are described by cells two and three. In one group the treatment is withheld but the experimenter is led to expect behavior change. In the other group the treatment is applied but the experimenter is led to expect no behavior change.

To see how this experimental design might be employed, consider a verbal-conditioning study in which increased I-we emission is the target. Experimenters in cell two can be led to expect increased I-we emission by telling them that they have a group of subjects who have been preselected for naturally accelerating I-we emission. Experimenters in cell three can be led to expect no increase by telling them that verbal conditioning of I-we emission usually does not work given the kinds of subjects they have, a fact which they are then invited to replicate.

Or, consider a drug study. Experimenters in cell two are misled to believe that their subjects have received the drug treatment. Experimenters in cell three are misled to believe that their subjects have not received the drug treatment. Thus one can study the placebo effect where the expectancy is not that of the subject who has taken the drug but that of the experimenter who has given it.

The use of expectancy-control groups opens up fascinating possibilities for the study of the experimental situation. It allows the investigator, via a two-way analysis of variance (treatment × expectancy), to tell just how much the expectancy contributes to the results. If more than one experimenter is assigned to each of the four groups and a nested design used (Winter, 1962), then experimenter effect can also be studied. And finally, if the filming procedure is added to this kind of design, the mediation process can be studied group by group.

III

These practical suggestions have been addressed primarily to practicing researchers. *The most basic is the need to representatively sample data-collectors.* Doing so will tend to randomize biases, thus increasing the validity of results. It will also allow the study of the trans-experimenter generality of results.

And here we come to a paradox. On the one hand, probably 80 per cent of psychological research does not meet this minimal requirement for the establishment of the validity and generality of correlational or experimental results. On the other hand, experimentation *qua* experimentation holds a privileged place at the top of the hierarchy of psychological methods.

This paradox leads to our final consideration.

It is an open secret that there is a widespread bias to the effect that experimentation is in principle *the* method for psychology and, for that matter, for all of the social sciences to embrace. In its most stereotypical form the opposition is set up between armchair theorists and experimenters. Armchair theorists, so the notion goes, project their own biases upon the world. Since they use only "uncontrolled" observation, there is no guarantee that the results of their unsystematic investigations will have any validity whatsoever. They discover only what they want, need, or expect to find. Their efforts may result in poetry, mythology, or history, but the one thing they cannot result in is science.

The experimenter, on the other hand, relies upon the crucible of experimentation to separate fact from fancy. *Theories* of motivation, *theories* of personality, *theories* of learning remain *merely* theories until they have kept, via the rigors of experimentation, their rendezvous with validity. The experiment is seen as providing the ruthlessly sanitary context in which, like the germs cleansed from the hands of the surgeon after immersion, the personal contaminations associated with the biases of woolly-minded speculators and tender-minded theorists are sterilized out by experimental test.

A family of related beliefs and practices is involved in this homage to experimentation. One is the high premium placed in psychology on work within the context of validation as opposed to the context of discovery (a false dichotomy to start with). Search can be left to the theorist; his ideas must be tested by research. Another is the notion that the only true control is experimental control. Any other observation process is stigmatized under the general heading "uncontrolled." A third is the notion that operationism and experimentation are the only means of ultimately clarifying ideas, of stripping them of their subjectivity, of rendering public property what were initially private autisms. And finally, according to the intervening-variable paradigm which regulates much contemporary psychological theorizing, the experiment becomes both the crucial generator and the crucial tester of theory.

Claims such as these are responsible for the elevation of the experimental method to its favored place among psychological methods. Let us see how well each factor fares when the evidence from the present work is brought to bear on these claims.

We will treat the last separately from the other three. Ever since the intervening-variable paradigm appeared on the psychological scene in Tolman's work in the 1930's, it has functioned as psychology's chief strategy for theory construction. Theories have to have independent, intervening, and dependent variables, which in experimental terms correspond to the S-O-R symbolization. The intervening-variable paradigm has had associated with it a "strategy" for constructing intervening variable functions . . . The strategy was to select or design a series of defining experiments, the variables of which would be placed in correspondence with (that is, "represent" or "realize") the theoretical variables whose relationships were under determination. (Koch, 1959, p. 734.)

Intervening-variable doctrine thus provided a rule for the theoretical process, a technology for the construction of theory, a technology based ultimately upon the single-variable-defining experiment. Looking back, Tolman writes:

My proposal was that one should set up standard defining experiments in each of which the obtained response or responses could be conceived as depending primarily upon, as being a direct pointer reading for, the variations of one particular intervening variable as this latter is dependent upon the controlled and prescribed manipulations of one or two independent variables.

"But now," he continues, "I really have considerable doubts not only about the practical feasibility of such experiments . . . but also about the validity of the results which would be obtained." (Tolman, 1959, p. 147.)

Koch remarks apropos of this about-face that "now the notion of a 'defining experiment' is itself a metaphor for Tolman . . . the defining experiment is, in other words, a thought experiment in the classical sense of this device of the philosophy of science" (1959, p. 737).

Koch and Tolman have come to this conclusion on theoretical grounds. It is now clear that to an intervening variable there will correspond a variety of pointer readings which will have to be reconciled in some way. But the same conclusion can be reached by simply scrutinizing the implied image of experimental control. The single-variable-defining experiment notion assumed that the experimenter himself was not a source of variability. As soon as the interpersonal nature of the psychological experiment is acknowledged, it becomes clear that the defining experiment—like the ideal psychological experiment envisaged in the texts—is hardly likely to be performed in practice.

This fact is more important than it may seem. In what reads like an autopsy for the intervening variable, Koch concludes that "the critique of 'defining experiment' strategy is a sharp challenge to traditional intervening variable doctrine. It deprives that doctrine of its central recipe for the construction of theory." Koch goes on to recognize that in the construction of theory "the emphasis must shift from empirical towards imaginative rational strategies" (p. 742), a circumstance which calls into question the prestige of experimentation as a generator of theory.

How about its prestige as a tester of theory? The other three factors previously enumerated all involve the hitherto almost unquestioned equation of experimentation with validity. Other methods are seen as being vulnerable to bias. But the experimenter is supposedly able to control the effects of possibly misleading factors. He is supposedly able to get rid of the halo of surplus meaning surrounding his ideas and concepts. He is supposedly able to state with just how much confidence his results can be accepted as valid.

But now Rosenthal has found that experimenters can and at times do bias their results. This incredibly simple and yet incredibly sophisticated rediscovery re-establishes the continuity between experimentation and other methods of investigation. It also suggests a final methodological suggestion. Experimental results have no built-in guarantee of validity. This means that some of the disdain with which psychological researchers customarily treat data obtained by sociologists and anthropologists working in the field is inappropriate. It might be profitably replaced by the study and application of their considerable literature on participant-observation methodology. For, whereas the ideal psychological experimenter is an immaculate perceiver of an objective reality, the real psychological experimenter is, to a far greater extent than has been suspected, very much like his counterparts in the other social studies. He too is a *participant*-observer.

Appendix

Format for Rating Glances, Smiles, Time, and Exchanged Glances

Film # _____ Rater's Name _____

	NAME	FACE SHEET	INSTRUCTIONS	RATINGS
S_1				
S_2				
S_3				
S_4				

Sample of One Reading of Instructions

Film #_____ Subject Name _____ Rater _____

I am going to read to you some instructions. I am not permitted to say anything which is not in the instructions and I cannot answer any questions about this experiment.

We are in the process of developing a test of empathy. This test is designed to show you how well a person is able to put himself into someone else's place. I will show you a series of photographs. For each one I want you to judge whether the person pictured has been experiencing success or failure. To help you make more exact judgments you are to use this rating scale. This one here, Phyllis. As you can see the scale runs from − 10 to + 10. A rating of − 10 means that you judge the person to have experienced extreme failure. + 10 means extreme success. A rating of − 1 means that you judge the person to have experienced mild failure while + 1 means mild success. You are to rate each photo as accurately as you can. Just tell me the rating you assign to each of the photos. All ready? Photo number one.

Format for Noting Experimenter and Subject Clothing

Film # _____

MALE	Exptr	S₁	S₂	S₃	S₄
tie					
suit jacket					
sport jacket					
zipper jacket					
overcoat					
short sleeves					
long sleeves					
long sleeves roled up					
dress shirt					
collar buttoned					
collar open					
sweater					
glasses					
sport shirt					
name					

FEMALE	Exptr	S₁	S₂	S₃	S₄
suit					
skirt					
blouse					
shirt					
collar hi					
collar lo					
shorts					
slacks or pp					
overcoat					
sweatshirt					
uniform					
sweater					
glasses					
name					

References

Abel, Theodora M. Responses of Negro and white morons to the Thematic Apperception Test. *Amer. J. ment. Defic.*, 1945, **49**, 463–68.

Ainsworth, Mary D. Problems of validation. In Klopfer, Ainsworth, Klopfer, and Holt, *Developments in the Rorschach technique*. Vol. 1. *Theory and technique*. Yonkers-on-Hudson, New York: World Book Co., 1954. Pp. 405–501.

Alden, Priscilla, and A. L. Benton. Relationship of sex of examiner to incidence of Rorschach responses with sexual content. *J. proj. Tech.*, 1951, **15**, 231–34.

Allport, G. W. Attitudes. In C. Murchison (Ed.), *A handbook of social psychology*. Worcester: Clark Univer. Press, 1935. Pp. 798–844.

Appelbaum, S. A., and R. S. Siegal. Half-hidden influences on psychological testing and practice. *J. proj. Tech. Pers. Asses.*, 1965, **29**, 128–34.

Asch, S. E. A perspective on social psychology. In S. Koch (Ed.), *Psychology: A study of a science*. Vol. 3. *Formulations of the person and the social context*. New York: McGraw-Hill, 1959. Pp. 363–84.

Baken, D. Learning and the scientific enterprise. *Psychol. Rev.*, 1953, **60**, 45–49.

Bakan, D. Clinical psychology and logic. *Amer. Psychologist*, 1956, **2**, 655–62.

Baldwin, J. M. Reply to Titchener. *Psychol. Rev.*, 1895, **2**, 259–73.

Baughman, E. Rorschach scores as a function of examiner difference. *J. proj. Tech.*, 1951, **15**, 243–49.

Benjamin, A. C. *Operationism*. Springfield: Charles C Thomas, 1955.

Berger, D. Examiner influence on the Rorschach. *J. clin. Psychol.*, 1954, **10**, 245–48.

Bernstein, L. The examiner as inhibiting factor in clinical testing. *J. consult. Psychol.*, 1956, **20**, 287–90.

Binder, A., D. McConnell, and Nancy A. Sjoholm. Verbal conditioning as a function of experimenter characteristics. *J. abnorm. soc. Psychol.*, 1957, **55**, 309–14.

Birdwhistell, R. L. *Introduction to kinesics*. Louisville: Univer. of Louisville Press, 1952.

Birdwhistell, R. L. Paralanguage: 25 years after Sapir. Paper presented at the Pittsburgh Bicentennial, 1959.

Birdwhistell, R. L. Kinesic analysis in the investigation of the emotions. Paper presented at the American Association for the Advancement of Science, December 29, 1960.

Birney, R. C. The achievement motive and task performance: A replication. *J. abnorm. soc. Psychol.*, 1958, **56**, 133–35.

Boring, E. G. The psychology of controversy. *Psychol. Rev.*, 1929, **36**, 97–122.

Boring, E. G. A history of introspection. *Psychol. Bull.*, 1953, **50**, 169–90.

Boring, E. G. A *history of experimental psychology*. (2nd ed.) New York: Appleton-Century-Crofts, 1957.

Bridgman, P. W. *The logic of modern physics*. New York: Macmillan, 1927.

Bridgman, P. W. Some general principles of operational analysis. *Psychol. Rev.*, 1945, **52**, 246–49.

Brunswik, E. *Perception and the representative design of psychological experiments*. Berkeley and Los Angeles: Univer. of California Press, 1956.

Bugelski, B. R. A *first course in experimental psychology*. New York: Henry Holt, 1951.

Campbell, D. T. Systematic errors to be expected of the social scientist on the basis of a general psychology of cognitive bias. Paper read at Symposium on the Problem of Experimenter Bias, APA, Cincinnati, Ohio, September 1959.

Canady, H. G. The effect of "rapport" on the IQ: A new approach to the problem of racial psychology. *J. Negro Educ.*, 1936, **5**, 208–19.

Chappell, V. C. (Ed.). *The philosophy of mind*. Englewood Cliffs: Prentice-Hall, 1962.

Clark, R. A. Projective measurement of experimentally induced levels of sexual motivation. *J. exp. Psychol.*, 1952, **44**, 391–99.

Cohen, E. Is there examiner influence on the W-B? *Proc. Oklahoma Acad. Sci.*, 1950, **31**, 150–53.

Cottrell, L. S., and Ruth Gallagher. Important developments in American social psychology. *Sociometry*, 1941, **4**, 107–39 and 302–24.

Criswell, Joan H. The psychologist as perceiver. In R. Tagiuri and L. Petrullo (Eds.), *Person perception and interpersonal behavior*. Stanford: Stanford Univer. Press, 1958. Pp. 95–110.

Cronbach, L. J. The two disciplines of scientific psychology. *Amer. Psychologist*, 1957, 12, 671–84.

Cronbach, L. J., and P. E. Meehl. Construct validity in psychological tests. In H. Feigl and M. Scriven (Eds.), *Minnesota studies in the philosophy of science*. Vol. 1. Minneapolis: Univer. of Minnesota Press, 1956. Pp. 174–204.

Curtis, H. S., and Elizabeth B. Wolf. Influence of sex of examiner on the prediction of sex responses on the Rorschach. *Amer. Psychologist*, 1951, 6, 345–46.

Dennis, W. The experimental methods of psychology. In C. Murchison (Ed.), *Psychologies of 1925*. Worcester: Clark Univer. Press, 1926. Pp. 331–53.

Dollard, J., and N. E. Miller. *Personality and psychotherapy*. New York: McGraw-Hill, 1950.

Dreger, R. M., and K. S. Miller. Comparative psychological studies of Negroes and whites in the United States. *Psychol. Bull.*, 1960, 57, 361–402.

Duncombe, R. L. The personal equation in astronomy. *Popular Astron.*, 1945, 53, 2–13, 63–76, 110–21.

Edwards, A. L. *Experimental design in psychological research*. New York: Rinehart, 1950.

Einstein, A. On the methods of theoretical physics. In A. Einstein, *The world as I see it*. New York: Covici, Friede, 1933. Pp. 30–40.

Ekman, P., and W. V. Friesen. Status and personality of the experimenter as a determinant of verbal conditioning. *Amer. Psychologist*, 1960, 15, 430.

Erikson, E. *Young man Luther*. New York: W. W. Norton, 1958.

Estes, W. K. The statistical approach to learning theory. In S. Koch (Ed.), *Psychology: A study of a science*. Vol. 2. *General systematic formulations, learning, and special processes*. New York: McGraw-Hill, 1959. Pp. 380–492.

Faris, E. *The nature of human nature*. New York: McGraw-Hill, 1937.

Feigl, H. Operationism and scientific method. *Psychol. Rev.*, 1945, 52, 250–59.

Feigl, H. Some major issues and developments in the philosophy of science of logical empiricism. In H. Feigl and M. Scriven (Eds.), *Minnesota studies in the philosophy of science*. Vol. 1. Minneapolis: Univer. of Minnesota Press, 1956. Pp. 3–38.

Ferguson, D. C., and A. H. Buss. Operant conditioning of hostile verbs in relation to experimenter and subject characteristics. *J. consult. Psychol.*, 1960, 24, 324–27.

Festinger, L. Laboratory experiments. In L. Festinger and D. Katz (Eds.), *Research methods in the behavioral sciences*. New York: Dryden Press, 1953. Pp. 136–73.

Filer, R. N. The clinician's personality and his case reports. *Amer. Psychologist*, 1952, 7, 336.

Fisher, R. A. *The design of experiments*. Edinburgh: Oliver and Boyd, 1942.

Frank, J. D. *Persuasion and healing*. Baltimore: Johns Hopkins Press, 1961.

Frank, L. K. Projective methods for the study of personality. *J. Psychol.*, 1939, 8, 389–413.

Friedman, N. The psychological experiment as a social interaction. Doctoral Dissertation, Harvard Univer., 1965.

Friedman, N., R. Rosenthal, and D. Kurland. The psychological experimenter as an unintended determinant of experimental results. *J. proj. tech. pers. Asses.*, 1965, 29, 479–490.

Gibby, R. G. Examiner influence on the Rorschach inquiry. *J. consult. Psychol.*, 1952, 16, 449–55.

Gibby, R. G., D. R. Miller, and E. L. Walker. The examiner's influence on the Rorschach protocol. *J. consult. Psychol.*, 1953, 17, 425–28.

Goffman, E. On face-work. *Psychiat.*, 1955, 18, 213–31.

Goffman, E. Alienation from interaction. *Hum. Relat.*, 1957, 10, 46–61.

Goffman, E. *The presentation of self in everyday life*. New York: Doubleday, 1959.

Goffman, E. *Encounters*. Indianapolis: Bobbs-Merrill, 1961.

Goffman, E. *Behavior in public places*. New York: The Free Press, 1963. (a)

Goffman, E. *Stigma*. Englewood Cliffs: Prentice-Hall, 1963. (b)

Griffith, R. Rorschach water percepts: A study in conflicting results. *Amer. Psychologist*, 1961, 16, 307–11.

Gross, L. R. Verbal and non-verbal reinforcement in the Rorschach. *J. consult. Psychol.*, 1959, 23, 60–68.

Guilford, J. P. *Fundamental statistics in psychology and education*. New York: McGraw-Hill, 1942.

Haase, W. The role of socio-economic class in examiner bias. In F. Riessman, J. Cohen, and A. Pearl (Eds.), *Mental health of the poor*. New York: The Free Press, 1964. Pp. 241–47.

Haley, J. Family experiments: A new type of experimentation. *Fam. Proc.*, 1962, 1, 265–93.

Haley, J. Communication in learning and psychotherapy. Paper read at the meeting of the Wisconsin Psychiatric Society, 1964. (a)

Haley, J. *Strategies of psychotherapy*. New York: Grune and Stratton, 1964. (b)

Haley, J. Personal communication, 1965.

Hammond, K. R. Representative versus systematic design in clinical psychology. *Psychol. Bull.*, 1954, 51, 150–59.

Henry, Edith M., and J. B. Rotter. Situational influences on Rorschach responses. *J. consult. Psychol.*, 1956, 20, 457–62.

Hyman, H. H. *Interviewing in social research*. Chicago: Univer. of Chicago Press, 1954.

Israel, H. E. Two difficulties in operational thinking. *Psychol. Rev.*, 1945, 52, 260–61.

Israel, H. E., and B. Goldstein. Operationism in psychology. *Psychol. Rev.*, 1944, 51, 177–88.

Jackson, D., and J. Haley. Transference revisited. *J. nerv. and ment. Dis.*, 1963, 4, 363–71.

Joel, W. The interpersonal equation in projective methods. *J. proj. Tech.*, 1949, 13, 479–82.

Karpf, Fay. *American social psychology.* New York: McGraw-Hill, 1932.

Katz, I. Review of evidence relating to effects of desegregation on the intellectual performance of Negroes. *Amer. Psychologist*, 1964, 19, 381–97.

Katz, I., J. Robinson, E. Epps, and Patricia Waly. Race of experimenter and instructions in the expression of hostility by Negro boys. *J. soc. Issues*, 1964, 20, 54–60.

Keller, F. S. *The definition of psychology.* New York: Appleton-Century-Crofts, 1937.

Kennedy, J. L. A methodological review of extra-sensory perception. *Psychol. Bull.*, 1939, 36, 59–103.

Koch, S. Epilogue. In S. Koch (Ed.), *Psychology: A study of a science.* Vol. 3. *Formulations of the person and the social context.* New York: McGraw-Hill, 1959. Pp. 729–89.

Koch, S. Psychology and emerging conceptions of knowledge as unitary. In T. W. Wann (Ed.), *Behaviorism and Phenomenology.* Chicago: Univer. of Chicago Press, 1964. Pp. 1–42.

Krech, D. Psychological theory and social psychology. In H. Helson (Ed.), *Theoretical foundations of psychology.* New York: Van Nostrand, 1951. Pp. 658–98.

Lambert, W. W. Social psychology in relation to general psychology and other behavioral sciences. In S. Koch (Ed.), *Psychology: A study of a science.* Vol. 6. *Investigations of man as socius.* New York: McGraw-Hill, 1963. Pp. 173–244.

Laski, H. J. *The rise of European liberalism.* New York: Barnes and Noble, 1962.

Levy, L. H., and T. B. Orr. The social psychology of Rorschach validity research. *J. abnorm. soc. Psychol.*, 1959, 58, 79–83.

Littell, W. M. Research with the WISC. *Psychol. Bull.*, 1960, 57, 132–56.

Lord, Edith. Experimentally induced variations in Rorschach performance. *Psychol. Monogr.*, 1950, 64, No. 10.

McClelland, D. C. Methods of measuring human motivation. In J. W. Atkinson (Ed.), *Motives in fantasy, action, and society.* New York: Van Nostrand, 1958. Pp. 7–43.

McFarlane, Jean Walker. Problems of validation inherent in projective methods. *Amer. J. Orthopsychiat.*, 1942, 12, 405–10.

McNemar, Q. Opinion-attitude methodology. *Psychol. Bull.*, 1946, 43, 289–374.

McQuigan, F. J. The experimenter: A neglected stimulus object. *Psychol. Bull.*, 1963, 61, 421–28.

Magnussen, M. G. Verbal and non-verbal reinforcers in the Rorschach situation. *J. clin. Psychol.*, 1960, 16, 167–69.

Mahl, G. F., and G. Schulze. Psychological research in the extralinguistic area. Paper prepared for the Interdisciplinary Work Conference on Paralanguage and Kinesics, May 17–19, 1962.

Malcolm, D. Wittgenstein's *Philosophical Investigations.* In V. C. Chappell

(Ed.), *The philosophy of mind*. Englewood Cliffs: Prentice-Hall, 1962. Pp. 74–100.

Marx, M. The general nature of theory construction. In M. Marx (Ed.), *Psychological theory*. New York: Macmillan, 1951. Pp. 4–19.

Maskelyne, N. *Astronomical observations at Greenwich, 1799*.

Masling, J. The effects of warm and cool interaction on the interpretation of a projective protocol. *J. proj. Tech.*, 1957, 21, 377–83.

Masling, J. Effects of warm and cold interaction on the administration and scoring of an intelligence test. *J. consult. Psychol.*, 1959, 23, 336–41.

Masling, J. The influence of situational and interpersonal variables in projective testing. *Psychol. Bull.*, 1960, 57, 65–85.

Matarazzo, J. D., G. Saslow, and E. N. Pareis. Verbal conditioning of two response classes: Some methodological considerations. *J. abnorm. soc. Psychol.*, 1960, 61, 190–206.

Mead, G. H. *Mind, self and society*. Chicago: Univer. of Chicago Press, 1934.

Milam, J. R. Examiner influence on the TAT. *J. proj. Tech.*, 1954, 18, 221–26.

Mintz, Elizabeth Emmons. Personal problems and diagnostic errors of clinical psychologists. *J. proj. Tech.*, 1957, 21, 173–78.

Morgan, C. *Introduction to psychology*. New York: McGraw-Hill, 1956.

Mullan, H., and I. Sangiuliano. *The therapist's contribution to the treatment process; His person, transactions, and treatment methods*. Springfield: Charles C Thomas, 1964.

Murphy, G. *Historical introduction to modern psychology*. (Rev. ed.) New York: Harcourt Brace, 1949.

Nagel, E. Methodological issues in psychoanalytic theory. In S. Hook (Ed.), *Psychoanalysis, scientific method, and philosophy*. New York: Grove Press, 1959. Pp. 38–57.

Oldfield, R. C. *The psychology of the interview*. London: Methuen, 1943.

Orne, M. T. The nature of hypnosis: Artifact and essence. *J. abnorm. soc. Psychol.*, 1959, 58, 277–99.

Orne, M. T. On the social psychology of the psychological experiment: with particular reference to demand characteristics and their implications. *Amer. Psychologist*, 1962, 17, 776–83.

Orne, M. T., and F. J. Evans. Social control in the psychological experiment: antisocial behavior and hypnosis. *J. pers. soc. Psychol.*, 1965, 1, 189–200.

Orne, M. T., and K. E. Scheibe. The contribution of nondeprivation factors in the production of sensory deprivation effects: The psychology of the "panic button." *J. abnorm. soc. Psychol.*, 1964, 68, 3–12.

Pasamanick, B., and Hilda Knobloch. Early language behavior in Negro children and the testing of intelligence. In F. Riessman, J. Cohen, and A. Pearl (Eds.), *Mental health of the poor*. New York: The Free Press, 1964. Pp. 267–70.

Pearson, K. On the mathematical theory of errors of judgment with special reference to the personal equation. *Phil. Trans. Roy. Soc. London*, 1902, 198, 235–99.

Pettigrew, T. A *profile of the Negro American*. Princeton: Van Nostrand, 1964. (a)

Pettigrew, T. The Negro American personality: why isn't more known? *J. soc. Issues*, 1964, **20**, 4–23. (b)

Pittenger, R. E., C. F. Hockett, and J. J. Danehy. *The first five minutes*. Ithaca: Paul Martineau, 1960.

Polanyi, M. *Personal knowledge*. Chicago: Univer. of Chicago Press, 1958.

Post, Emily. *Etiquette*. New York: Funk and Wagnalls, 1940.

Postman, L., and J. P. Egan. *Experimental psychology—An introduction*. New York: Harper and Bros., 1949.

Preston, M. Methodological considerations. In H. Helson (Ed.), *Theoretical foundations of psychology*. New York: Van Nostrand, 1951. Pp. 1–46.

Rabin, A., W. Nelson, and Margaret Clark. Rorschach content as a function of perceptual experience and sex of examiner. *J. clin. Psychol.*, 1954, **10**, 188–90.

Rankin, R., and D. Campbell. Galvanic skin response to Negro and white experimenters. *J. abnorm. soc. Psychol.*, 1955, **51**, 30–33.

Reece, M. M., and R. N. Whitman. Expressive movements, warmth, and verbal reinforcements. *J. abnorm. soc. Psychol.*, 1962, **64**, 234–36.

Reitman, W. R. Experimenter bias as an interaction phenomenon. Paper read at Symposium on the Problem of Experimenter Bias, APA, Cincinnati, Ohio, September 1959.

Rice, S. A. Contagious bias in the interview: A methodological note. *Amer. J. Sociol.*, 1929, **35**, 420–23.

Riecken, H. W. A program for research on experiments in social psychology. Paper read at Behavioral Sciences meeting, New Mexico, 1958. In Vol. 2. N. Washburn (Ed.), *Decisions, values and groups*. Pergamon Press, 1962.

Rieff, P. *Freud: The mind of the moralist*. New York: Viking, 1959.

Riessman, F. *The culturally deprived child*. New York: Harper and Row, 1962.

Riessman, F., J. Cohen, and A. Pearl. *Mental health of the poor*. New York: Macmillan, 1965.

Rosenberg, M. J. When dissonance fails: On eliminating evaluation apprehension from attitude measurement. *J. pers. soc. Psychol.*, 1965, **1**, 28–42.

Rosenhan, D. On the social psychology of hypnosis research. *Educ. test. Serv. Res. Mem.* Princeton: E.T.S., March 1964.

Rosenthal, R. On the social psychology of the psychological experiment: the experimenter's hypothesis as unintended determinant of experimental results. *Amer. Scientist*, 1963, **51**, 268–83. (a)

Rosenthal, R. Experimenter outcome-orientation and the results of the psychological experiment. *Psychol. Bull.*, (1963). (b).

Rosenthal, R. Experimenter attributes as determinants of subjects' responses. *J. proj. Tech. pers. Asses.*, 1963, **27**, 324–31. (c)

Rosenthal, R. Experimenter modeling effects as determinants of subjects' responses. *J. proj. Tech. pers. Asses.*, 1963, **27**, 467–71. (d)

Rosenthal, R. Experimenter effects in the interpretation of data. Unpublished manuscript, Harvard Univer., 1963. (e)

Rosenthal, R. Personal characteristics increasing outcome-orientation effects. Unpublished manuscript, Harvard Univer., 1964.

Rosenthal, R. Clever Hans: A case study of scientific method. Introduction to

O. Pfungst, *Clever Hans*. New York: Holt, Rinehart, and Winston, 1965.

Rosenthal, R. *Experimenter effects in behavioral research*. New York: Appleton-Century-Crofts, 1966.

Rosenthal, R., and K. Fode. The effect of experimenter bias on the performance of the albino rat. Unpublished manuscript, Univer. of North Dakota, 1960.

Rosenthal, R., and K. Fode. Three experiments in experimenter bias. *Psychol. Rep. Monogr.*, 1963, 12, 491–511.

Rosenthal, R., K. L. Fode, C. J. Friedman, and L. Vikan-Kline. Subjects' perception of their experimenter under conditions of experimenter bias. *Percept. mot. Skills*, 1960, 11, 325–31.

Rosenthal, R., N. Friedman, and D. Kurland. The instruction reading behavior of the experimenter as an unintended determinant of experimental results. *J. exp. Res. Pers.*, 1966, 1, 221–226.

Rosenthal, R., and E. S. Halas. Experimenter effect in the study of invertebrate behavior. *Psychol. Rep.*, 1962, 11, 251–56.

Rosenthal, R., and S. Haley. Room characteristics and research results. Unpublished manuscript, 1964.

Rosenthal, R., and R. Lawson. A longitudinal study of the effects of experimenter bias on the operant learning of laboratory rats. *J. psychiat. Res.*, 1964, 2, 61–72.

Rosenthal, R., and G. Persinger. Let's pretend: subjects' perception of imaginary experimenters. *Percept. mot. Skills*, 1962, 14, 407–9.

Rosenthal, R., G. W. Persinger, R. Mulry, Linda Vikan-Kline, and M. Grothe. Changes in experimental hypotheses as determinants of experimental results. *J. proj. Tech. pers. Asses.*, 1964, 28, 465–469. (a)

Rosenthal, R., G. W. Persinger, R. Mulry, Linda Vikan-Kline, and M. Grothe. Emphasis on experimental procedure, sex of subjects, and the biasing effects of experimental hypotheses. *J. proj. Tech. pers. Asses.*, 1964, 28, 470–473. (b)

Rosenthal, R., G. W. Persinger, Linda Vikan-Kline, and K. Fode. The effect of early data returns on data subsequently obtained by outcome-biased experimenters. *Sociometry*, 1963, 26, 487–98. (c)

Rosenthal, R., G. W. Persinger, Linda Vikan-Kline, and K. Fode. The effect of experimenter outcome-bias and subject set on awareness in verbal conditioning experiments. *J. verb. Learn. verb. Behav.*, 1963, 2, 275–83. (d)

Ryle, G. *The concept of mind*. New York: Barnes and Noble, 1949.

Ryle, G. Systematically misleading expressions. In A. Flew, *Logic and language*. (First series.) Oxford: Blackwell, 1951. Pp. 11–37.

Sacks, Eleanor L. Intelligence scores as a function of experimentally established social relations between child and examiner. *J. abnorm. soc. Psychol.*, 1952, 47, 354–58.

Sanders, R., and S. E. Cleveland. The relationship between certain examiner personality variables and subjects' Rorschach scores. *J. proj. Tech.*, 1953, 7, 34–50.

Sanford, E. C. Personal equation. *Amer. J. Psychol.*, 1888–89, 2, 3–38, 271–98, 403–30.

Sapolsky, A. Effect of interpersonal relationships upon verbal conditioning. *J. abnorm. soc. Psychol.*, 1960, 60, 241–46.

Sarason, I. G. Individual differences, situational variables, and personality research. *J. abnorm. soc. Psychol.*, 1962, 65, 376–80.

Sarason, I. G. The human reinforcer in verbal behavior research. In L. Krasner and L. P. Ullman (Eds.), *Research in behavior modification: New developments and their clinical implications*. New York: Holt, Rinehart, and Winston, 1964.

Satir, Virginia. *Conjoint family therapy*. Palo Alto: Behavioral Sciences Press, 1964.

Schmeidler, Gertrude, and R. A. McConnell. *ESP and personality patterns*. New Haven: Yale Univer. Press, 1958.

Scripture, E. W. *The new psychology*. New York: Scribner's, 1897.

Sidman, M. *Tactics of Scientific Research*. New York: Basic Books, 1962.

Simmel, G. Sociology of the senses: Visual interaction. In R. Park and E. W. Burgess (Eds.), *Introduction to the science of sociology*. Chicago: Univer. of Chicago Press, 1921. Pp. 356–61.

Skinner, B. F. The operational analysis of psychological terms. *Psychol. Rev.*, 1945, 52, 270–77.

Skinner, B. F. Experimental psychology. In W. Dennis (Ed.), *Current trends in psychology*. Pittsburgh: Univer. of Pittsburgh Press, 1947. Pp. 16–50.

Skinner, B. F. A case history in scientific method. In S. Koch (Ed.), *Psychology: A study of a science. Vol. 2. General systematic formulations, learning, and special processes*. New York: McGraw-Hill, 1959. Pp. 359–80.

Skinner, B. F. The flight from the laboratory. In M. Marx (Ed.), *Theories in contemporary psychology*. New York: Macmillan, 1963. Pp. 323–41.

SPSSI Work Group. Guidelines for testing minority group children. *J. soc. Issues*, Suppl. to 1964, 20, 127–45.

Stein, M. The poetic metaphors of sociology. In M. Stein and A. Vidich (Eds.), *Sociology on trial*. Englewood Cliffs: Prentice-Hall, 1963. Pp. 173–81.

Stevens, S. S. The operational basis of psychology. *Amer. J. Psychol.*, 1935, 47, 323–30.

Stevens, S. S. *Handbook of experimental psychology*. New York: Wiley, 1951.

Stevenson, H. W. Social reinforcement with children as a function of CA, sex of E, and sex of S. *J. abnorm. soc. Psychol.*, 1961, 63, 147–54.

Strauss, A. *Mirrors and masks*. Glencoe, Ill.: The Free Press, 1959.

Sullivan, H. S. *The psychiatric interview*. New York: Norton, 1954.

Szasz, T. *The myth of mental illness*. New York: Hoeber-Harper, 1961.

Tart, C. The hypnotic dream. *Psychol. Bull.*, 1965, 1, 73–95.

Terman, L. M., and Leona E. Tyler. Psychological sex differences. In L. Carmichael (Ed.), *Manual of child psychology*. New York: Wiley, 1946. Pp. 1064–1114.

Thomas, W. I. The behavior pattern and the situation. In E. Volkart (Ed.), *Social behavior and personality: Contributions of W. I. Thomas to theory and research*. New York: SSRC, 1951. Pp. 59–71.

Thomas, W. I. The primary group and the definition of the situation. In E. Volkart (Ed.), *Social behavior and personality: Contributions of W. I. Thomas to theory and research.* New York: SSRC, 1951.

Thurstone, L. L. The stimulus-response fallacy in psychology. *Psychol. Rev.,* 1923, 30, 354–69.

Titchener, E. B. *Experimental psychology.* New York: Macmillan, 1901.

Titchener, E. B. *A textbook of psychology.* New York: Macmillan, 1926.

Tolman, E. C. Operational behaviorism and current trends in psychology. In *Proc. 25th Anniv. Celebr. Inaug. Grad. Stud.* Los Angeles: Univer. Southern California Press, 1936.

Tolman, E. C. Principles of purposive behavior. In S. Koch (Ed.), *Psychology. A study of a science.* Vol. 2. *General systematic formulations, learning, and special processes.* New York: McGraw-Hill, 1959. Pp. 92–158.

Trent, R. D. The color of the investigator as a variable in experimental research with Negro subjects. *J. soc. Psychol.,* 1954, 40, 281–87.

Troffer, Suzanne A., and C. T. Tart. Experimenter bias in hypnotist performance. *Science,* 1964, 145, 1330–31.

Turner, G. C., and J. C. Coleman. Examiner influence on thematic apperception test responses. *J. proj. Tech.,* 1962, 26, 478–86.

Vanderbilt, Amy. *Complete book of etiquette.* Garden City: Doubleday, 1952.

Waters, R. H., and L. A. Pennington. Operationism in psychology. *Psychol. Rev.,* 1938, 45, 414–23.

Watson, J. B. Psychology as the behaviorist views it. *Psychol. Rev.,* 1913, 20, 158–77.

Watson, J. B. *Psychology from the standpoint of a behaviorist.* Philadelphia: Lippincott, 1919.

Watson, J. B. John Broadus Watson. In C. Murchison (Ed.), *A history of psychology in autobiography.* Vol. 3. Worcester: Clark Univer. Press, 1936. Pp. 271–81.

Watson, J. B., and W. McDougall. *The battle of behaviorism.* London: Kegan Paul, Trench, Trubner and Co., 1928.

Wickes, T. A., Jr. Examiner influence in a testing situation. *J. consult. Psychol.,* 1956, 20, 23–26.

Winer, B. J. *Statistical principles in experimental design.* New York: McGraw-Hill, 1962.

Wisdom, J. The concept of mind. In E. V. Chappell (Ed.), *The philosophy of mind.* Englewood Cliffs: Prentice-Hall, 1962. Pp. 49–59.

Wittgenstein, L. *Philosophical investigations.* Oxford: Basil Blackwell, 1958.

Wohl, J. Traditional and contemporary views of psychological testing. *J. proj. Tech.,* 1963, 27, 359–65.

Woodworth, R. S. *Contemporary schools of psychology.* New York: Roland Press, 1931.

Woodworth, R. S. *Experimental psychology.* New York: Henry Holt, 1938.

Woodworth, R. S., and H. Schlosberg. *Experimental psychology.* (2nd ed.) New York: Rinehart and Winston, 1954.

Wundt, W. *Outlines of psychology.* (2nd rev. Eng. ed.) New York: Gustav E. Stechert, 1902.

Young, R. K. Digit span as a function of the personality of the experimenter. *Amer. Psychologist*, 1959, **14**, 375. (Abstract)

Zax, M., and G. Stricker. Effect of a structured inquiry on Rorschach scores. *J. consult. Psychol.*, 1960, **24**, 328–32.

Index